THE WHIPPET

J P Moran-Healy

Contents

Front cover: (L to r) Am Ch Merci Isle Burncoat Babylon
                  and his sire Am Ch Merci Isle Meridian - 1995
                  and 1993 American Whippet Club National
                  Specialty winners
                  Photo: Samuels Studio, Maynard, MA 01754

Title page: Am Ch Bo-Betts Divine Dessert and Am Ch
                  Misty Moor's Divine Pleasure

Contents page: Ch Pencloe Dutch Gold

Back cover: (L to r) Int Ch Rothbury Bonecrusher and Nor
                  Ch Memoars Lobelia of Librium

Acknowledgements

To my wife Tina for all her help and without whose input this book would never have come to fruition.

I also wholeheartedly thank Rachael Wilkie at Kingdom Books for this once in a lifetime opportunity and for her friendly encouragement and support. I am indebted to the Whippeteers around the world, namely Margaret Martin, Thomas Münch, Miss L E Gut, Magnus Hagstedt, Espen Engh, Sampo Miettinen, Mary Beth Arthur, Linda Buchholz, Frank Pieterse, Nicole L J Harrison, Bryan Kelly and Jo Robertson for taking time out of their busy lives to write such excellent contributions about the breed in their various corners of the world. Thank you also to Colonel Ted Walsh and Joyce Keable for their informative and enthusiastic chapters on coursing and racing respectively. Thanks to Mary Lowe for being supportive and who, although busy with her own writing, took time to give a window into the Nimrodel Whippets. Grateful thanks to all the people who have lent me their treasured photographs and to Steve Halifax and Harry Whimpanny for their expert photography and advice. I am only too sorry that all the photographs couldn't be included. Thanks to Anne Moss for the photographic record of her litter, kindly sent to me long before this book was ever dreamed of. Also, grateful thanks to Viv Rainsbury for her excellent drawings used in the Breed Standard and to the Breed Council for giving permission to use them in their entirety.

Last but not least, thanks to my friends in the Whippet world for their encouragement while I have been writing this book.

Foreword

J P Moran-Healy has been involved with the breed for more than 30 years under the Hillsdown affix. In this period he has been a successful exhibitor and breeder, qualifying to judge the breed at Championship show level a number of years ago. Phil had the honour of judging Whippets at Crufts in 1995. He has also judged at Championship shows in a number of countries abroad including the world's largest Sighthound show held in Skokloster, Sweden.

Hillsdown has been involved in either breeding or showing eight show champions, seven of which were home-bred. Phil was a founder member, and is currently Chairman, of the South Yorkshire Whippet Club, being actively involved in the 'teach ins' and similar other events organised by the club.

Introduction

The World of Dogs

The Whippet
(A dog for all reasons)

> *"In shapes and forms of dogges; of which there are but two sorts, that are useful for a man's profit, which are the mastiffe and the little whippet, or the house dog; all the rest are for pleasure and recreation."*

Taken from 'All the Workes of John Taylor', the water poet 1630.

Ch Pencloe Dutch Gold, Best In Show, Crufts 1992.
I think Morag Bolton-Lockhart's huge smile and the knowing look on Dutch's face
suggests differently from the above quote.
The humble Whippet has certainly travelled a long way.

The first Whippet World Congress, held in Vermont.
Photo: courtesy of A-N Productions/Tom and Linda Nutting

When I was first approached to write this book my brief was that it was to be of interest for existing Whippet owners and a helpful guide for new and would-be owners. Over the last few years there have been a number of excellent and informative books written about the breed, each one giving general information and then usually focusing on one aspect that the author is particularly interested in. To my mind the most fascinating topic has to be breeding to type and consistency which no-one involved in the breed has yet written about this. In this book I hope to take you from the first Whippets down the generations to what we have today. I have followed my own lines and then, in contrast, Mary Lowe has written the Nimrodel kennel history, as we have both travelled quite different routes over the last thirty years or so. I have tried to make the book an easy read for new owners but at the same time fill in the gaps for the not-so-new owners who have Whippets but for whom the dogs way back in the pedigrees are just names.

The Whippet is now quite popular all around the world and for this reason I have included a review from the countries where they are most popular. When I have been lucky enough to have been invited to judge abroad I have seen many lovely exhibits produced from careful and intelligent breeding. Since not everyone interested in the breed will be fortunate enough to see them in the flesh I'm sure the pictures and information will be of great interest.

In 1996 the first International Whippet Congress was held in Burlington, Vermont. I was very fortunate and honoured to be able to take part in a small way. The event was a great success and it was a wonderful opportunity for visitors from all around the world to get together and share information and opinions. The photograph shows top winners in all disciplines that the breed competes in. The whole congress was excellently organised and America has surely set a precedent for other future hosts, it will certainly be a difficult act to follow.

People are never indifferent to Whippets and from my experience once someone has owned a Whippet, be it pedigree or cross, they will always choose to have another. In fact the old and very interesting Hutchinson's Dog Encyclopaedia Volume 3 says of the breed:

"To many people, ignorant of the true nature of the Whippet, it may appear a spineless fragile creature incapable of much effort, but most people, when first introduced to the breed, have fallen victim to the dog's phenomenal intelligence and devotion. Perfect in line, hardy, full of vitality and grace, and game in sport, the Whippet is a life-long companion and friend, unswerving in loyalty and devotion. Stories of the devotion and courage of the Whippet are endless, and the slogan of many owners 'Once a Whippet owner, always a Whippet owner' proves the hold these fragile creatures can gain on one's affections. They are docile to a degree, acquiring in early puppyhood the qualities necessary for showing or leading purposes. A kennel of young healthy Whippet puppies is a joy to the eye. They are almost human in their desire for human companionship and attention, assimilating early the tractability and routine so desirable and so difficult to attain in some breeds. This docility does not in any way infer loss of spirit, for the Whippet is an ideal guard, and playfully inclined. But beware anyone who touches the master or mistress in a rough manner, or enters the house after the family have retired, but with its own folk it is the essence of companionship. It is truly a dog well fitted to grace the portals of castle, mansion or cottage."

On the other side of the argument, when someone dislikes the distinctive make and shape of the breed then no amount of persuasion will convert them. These misguided people are often convinced that Whippets are bony and undernourished. In argument to this I usually reply that if you were to remove the coat from most dogs and put the actual body on show, as with a Whippet, you'd be hard put to find a better built body than that of a healthy Whippet.

What a family snapshot. The author with (l to r): Denorsi Tinkermoon, White Bud of Glenbervie, Hillsdown Pandora, Calm and Grand.

For almost all of my life I have been involved with owning, breeding, showing and then judging Whippets. It all started when, as a young teenager, I went along to the Sheffield Show, a celebration of the city and all its achievements. I was there mainly to look at the pigeons, rabbits and other small livestock being exhibited. Whilst making my way around, I saw a man with two striking dogs and so, with the boldness of youth, went up and asked about them. I enquired how much it would be to buy one and, in true Yorkshire dialect, was told "Too much for thee lad". This man was the last person to breed a Whippet champion in Sheffield until my own followed 20 years later. He was Sam Skelton and his affix was Samena. I didn't actually buy a Whippet at this time but as soon as I was 15 and left school I bought my first dog. His name was Margo's Boy and his sire was Teighways Teddy Boy. I arranged to meet the man I bought him from by the side of the road leading to the motorway. He pulled up in his car at the arranged spot. I handed over my hard earned money, put my treasured charge onto the brand new lead and proudly took home my very first Whippet.

In a world of coincidences, our first married home overlooked the exact spot where I had met Sam Skelton, and my first champions were born just yards away from where I had stood in awe all those years earlier. The very dated picture (page 8)

Denorsi Tinkermoon

was taken in 1972 not a hundred yards away from where we had spoken. The dogs I have with me in the picture proved to be valuable assets to the breed. Denorsi Tinkermoon, who I consider to be the start of the Hillsdown Whippets, was the mother of 3 champions and a direct line to the magnificent Champion Pencloe Dutch Gold (who has the honour of being the only Whippet to win Best In Show at Crufts and has proved to be an outstanding sire). The smaller white bitch, White Bud of Glenbervie, although not of show standard, had some lovely features and she produced my first champion, Nutcracker of Nevedith. Hillsdown Pandora was the dam of Van Olreim Vanessa who is the foundation bitch of most of the successful Barnesmore stock in Northern Ireland. The blue dog, with the statuesque name of Calm and Grand, was of Selbrook breeding on his dam's side. She was a lovely blue bitch named Selbrook Breeze. Breeze had already produced a Champion bitch, Selbrook Bracelet, before coming to Mr George O'Malley in Sheffield. I bought Calm and Grand when he was two years old for my wife before we married and we had lots of fun at local shows with him; he won several Blue classes at Championship shows. Whilst he didn't make a significant stamp on Hillsdown lines, his loving nature did ensure that Whippets would always have a place in our lives.

I have always thought of Whippets as being an all round multi-purpose dog. They have the natural instinct for coursing and have been many a young boy's closest friend out in the fields. They are suited to racing, and have a lovely natural grace that lends itself to showing. They can be either a 'man's dog' and walk proudly on a lead or be the most affectionate loving pet in the home. As toddlers, our children often moved around the house with the help of Denorsi Tinkermoon, who was always gentle and patient.

Whatever your reason for choosing a Whippet, be it showing, racing or purely companionship then I am sure you will never be without one again. I know I couldn't be.

Chapter One

The Origins Of The Whippet

Tapestry of David and Bathsheba, detail of piece
no.8 in linen, silk and gold.
National Museum of the Renaissance, Brussels.

The true origin of the Whippet is something that can never be settled to any satisfactory conclusion. There are many interesting theories abounding as to how the breed evolved but the fact remains that the Greyhound/Whippet/Italian Greyhound type of modern times has been around the world for centuries. There are examples of these strong elegant hounds wherever man has depended on hunting for survival and the natural terrain has determined different aspects of the "type". You will see many ancient works of art from Europe, Greece, Egypt and the Romans featuring their hounds and many bear more than a passing resemblance to the Greyhound/Whippet of modern times.

In a general overview of the differing types of hounds indigenous to the British Isles, my own particular feelings are that it is very plausible that the smooth coated Greyhound type could very possibly have been introduced to the British Isles by the Romans. If one looks at the Scottish

Deerhound or the Irish Wolfhound it can be seen how they have physically adapted to the harsher climates and rougher terrain by developing a strong powerful frame and a thicker harsh coat. Survival elsewhere in England and Wales, in the more moderate climates, didn't demand either so much physical power or the necessary coarse coat for protection against the elements. Consequently the smooth coated hounds in these parts probably remained closer to the original type and more within the make and shape of what we have come to know as the Greyhound/Whippet. One of the theories I support is that these hounds were crossed with terriers. Many years ago different breeds would have been crossed for practical purposes. An interesting extract from the first published Manchester Terrier Standard in 1893 read:

Young falcon hunter.
Master of the Judgement of
Paris by Bargello.
Museum of the Petit Palais,
Avignon.

> *"A terrier calculated to take his own part in the rat pit,*
> *not of the Whippet type".*

I feel by virtue of the fact that this reference to the "Whippet type" was considered important enough to be included in the standard that there must have been quite a definite similarity in some of the dogs of that era. It is therefore not out of the question that the terrier people had, at some time, introduced the different qualities found in the Whippet to their own terrier dogs and my own opinion is that terrier lines were introduced into Whippets for the same reasons. This would have the dual effect of bringing down the size and also introduce an element of gameness into the hound.

During the early 1960s when I first watched non-pedigree Whippet racing in the North of England, it was quite obvious that some of the 'Whippets' were to some degree part Greyhound and others quite definitely had a terrier influence in

Early Manchester Terrier.

Frank Blackwell Mayer: Leisure and Labor. 1879.

L to r: Balzac Barcelona, Serak's Corinne and Corpus Chloe illustrate the adaptability of this breed.

Spot the Whippet. Blue brindle is surprisingly excellent camouflage in the field.

their make and shape. So I think it is logical to believe this would also have been done in the 1800s when looks were immaterial. It was advantageous to bring the size down of the taller, stronger hound because the smaller dog was much cheaper to feed and its size also made it easier to keep in the home. In the nineteenth century this type of dog was very popular with the miners in the North of England and Wales. These hardy little dogs were kept for racing in 150 to 250 yard races. Physical beauty or elegance had absolutely nothing to do with what were the most highly regarded and valuable dogs. Speed, strength and racing intelligence were their only requirements. However, what did become clear to these early breeders was that, from a speed point of view, the balanced lines of the Greyhound/Whippet type was the best structure both in size and weight.

For many years now the Whippet has been actively taking part in a number of disciplines: racing, coursing, showing, agility and obedience. The popularity of the first three demands a full chapter on each to explain the rudiments. The chapters on coursing and racing bring out the hidden skills that the breed has: the intelligence not only to run at speed but also to plan the next move two steps ahead. Agility and obedience are more often secondary disciplines for our breed and not as universally popular, perhaps because of the dedicated training involved. There seems to be more interest in these two hobbies abroad, particularly in Scandinavia and America. However, the enthusiasts in England who take part are very keen and do enjoy success with their Whippets. The very nature of a Whippet does not make it a prime candidate for obedience competition but often they do quite well, proving what an adaptable breed they are.

Chapter Two

The Breed Standard

(Reproduced by kind permission of The Kennel Club and The Whippet Breed Council.)

All breeds of dogs acknowledged by The Kennel Club are required to fall within the requirements of their standard for that dog's particular breed. The standards that have been agreed on are changed very rarely; on occasion they are updated if necessary. The breed standard for Whippets as stated by The Kennel Club is as follows:

General appearance
Balanced combination of muscular power and strength, with elegance and grace of outline. Built for speed and work. All forms of exaggeration should be avoided.

Characteristics
An ideal companion. Highly adaptable in domestic and sporting surroundings.

Temperament
Gentle, affectionate and even disposition.

Head and skull
Long and lean, flat on top tapering to muzzle with slight stop. Rather wide between the eyes. Jaws powerful and clean cut. Nose black (in blues a bluish colour is permitted; in livers a nose of the same colour permitted; in whites or particolours a butterfly nose is permissible).

Neck
Long, muscular, elegantly arched.

Eyes
Oval, bright, expression very alert.

Ears
Rose shaped, small, fine in texture.

Mouth
Jaws strong with a perfect, regular and complete scissor bite, i.e. the upper teeth closely overlapping the lower teeth and set square to the jaws.

Forequarters
Shoulders oblique and muscular, blades carried up to top of spine, where they are clearly defined. Forelegs straight and upright. Front not too wide. Pasterns strong with slight spring. Elbows set well under the body.

Body
Chest very deep with plenty of heart room, brisket deep, well defined. Broad back, firm, somewhat long, showing a definite arch over the loin, but not humped. Loin giving the impression of strength and power. Ribs well-sprung, muscled on back.

Hindquarters
Strong, broad across thighs, stifles well bent, hocks well let down. Well developed second thighs. Dog able to stand over a lot of ground and show great driving power.

Tail
No feathering. Long, tapering, when in action carried in a delicate curve upward, but not over back.

Feet
Very neat, well split up between toes, knuckles well arched, pads thick and strong.

Gait/Movement
Free, hindlegs coming well under body for propulsion. Forelegs thrown well forward low over the ground, true coming and going. General movement not to look stilted, high stepping, short or mincing.

Coat
Fine, short, close in texture.

Colour
Any colour or mixture of colours.

Size
Height: Dogs: 47-51 cms (18.5-20 ins)
             Bitches: 44-47 cms (17.5-18.5 ins)

Faults
Any departure from the foregoing points should be considered a fault and the seriousness with which the fault should be regarded should be in direct proportion to its degree.

Note
Male animals should have two apparently normal testicles fully descended into the scrotum.

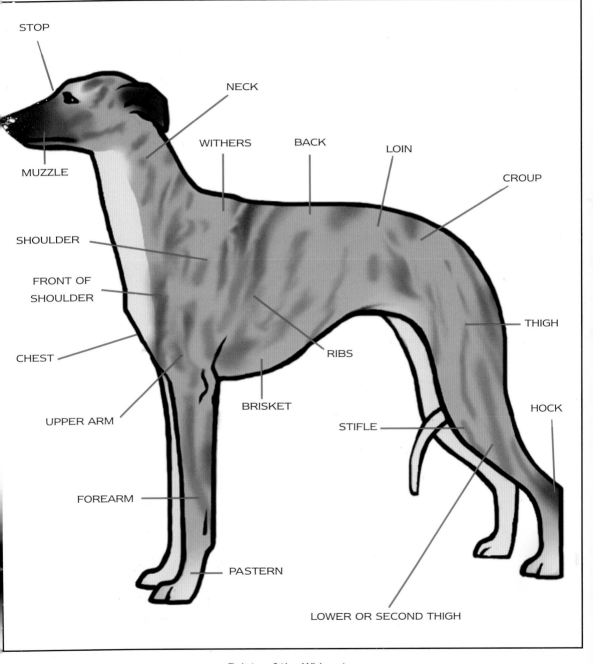

Points of the Whippet.

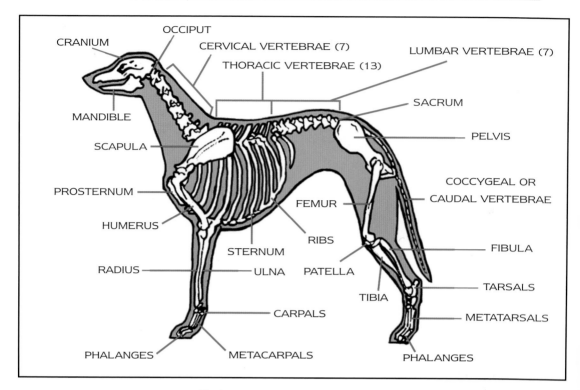

Skeletal structure of the Whippet.

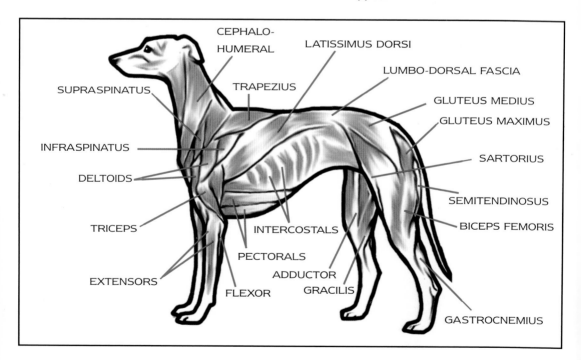

Main muscles in the Whippet.

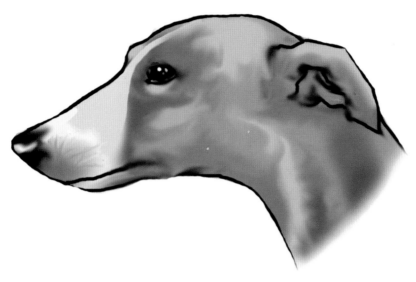

Good example of head and skull.

Head faults.
Left and middle: rounded, 'apple' skull. Right: 'Terrier' head.

Head faults.
L to r: insufficient stop; weak muzzle; weak underjaw.

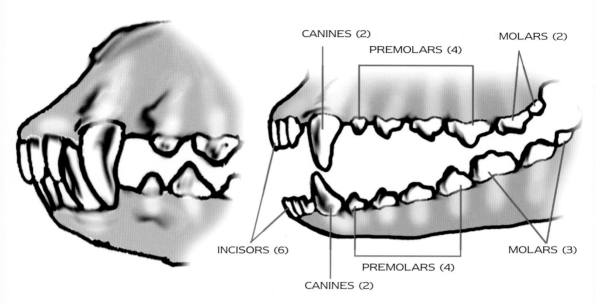

Left: good mouth. Jaws strong with a perfect scissor bite.
Right: dentition.

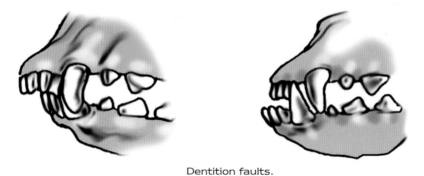

Dentition faults.
Left: overshot 'parrot' mouth. Right: undershot.

Dentition faults.
Left: level or even bite. Right: teeth not set square to the jaw.

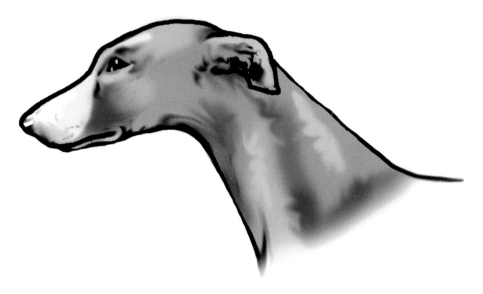

Excellent neck: long, muscular and elegantly arched.

Neck fault: too short and thick.

Neck fault: throaty.

Neck fault: ewe neck.

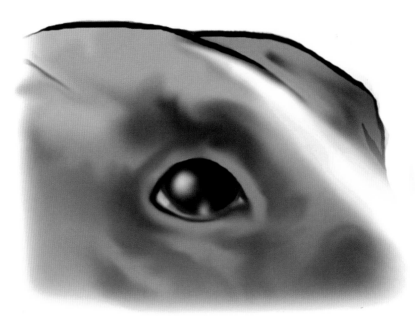

The eye should be oval, bright and very alert.

Eye fault: round and prominent.

Eye fault: harsh and staring.

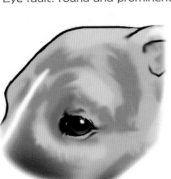

Eye fault: too small.

Eye fault: 'almond' eye.

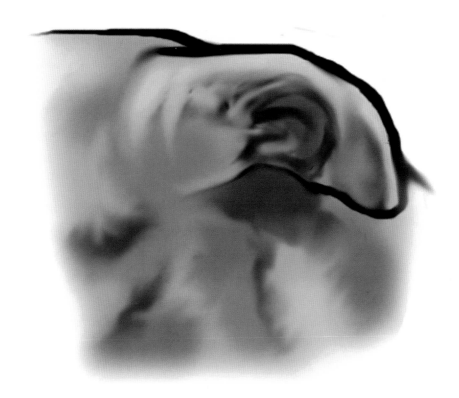

Excellent ears: rose-shaped, small and fine in texture.

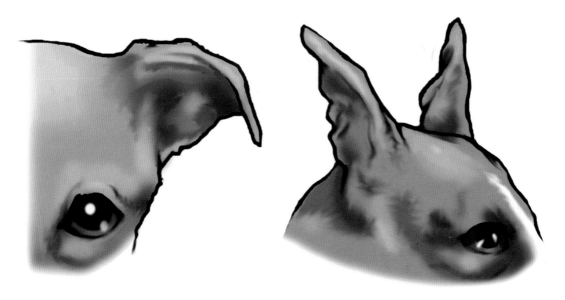

Left: ears may be carried semi-erect when the dog is alert.
Right: ear fault. Flying, prick ears.

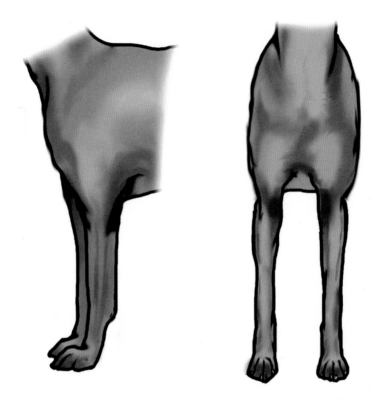

Good forequarters. Shoulders oblique and muscular, forelegs straight and upright, front not too wide, elbows set well under the body.

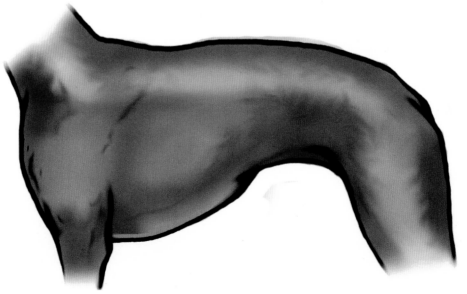

Chest very deep with plenty of heart room. Brisket deep and well-defined.

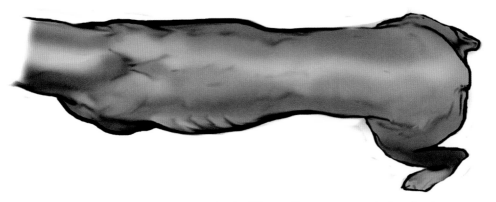

Broad, firm, somewhat long back. Ribs well-sprung, muscled on back.

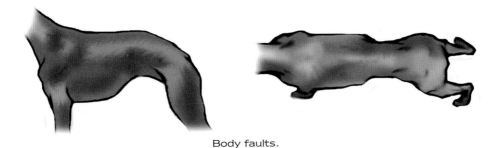

Body faults.
Left: loin too short. Right: flat ribs ('slab sided').

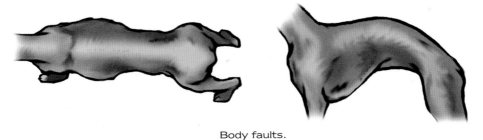

Body faults.
Left: 'barrel' ribs. Right: roached or wheel back.

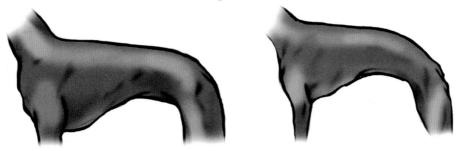

Topline faults.
Left: flat topline. Right: topline falling away too sharply.

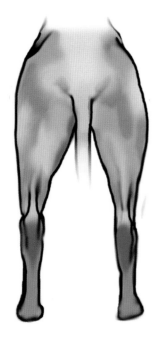

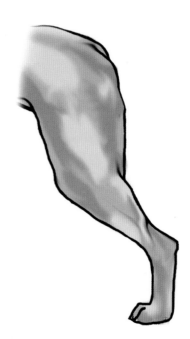

Good hindquarters. Strong, broad across thighs. Stifles well bent, hocks well let down, well-developed second thighs.

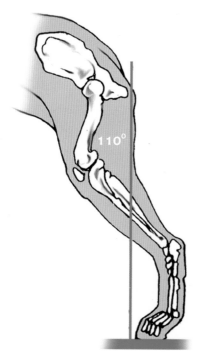

Ideal hind angulation showing skeletal structure.

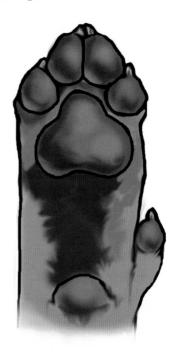

Underside of foot showing dewclaw (usually removed).

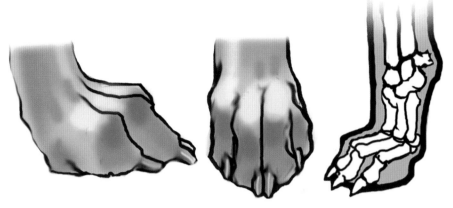

Good feet. Very neat, well split up between toes.

Knuckles well arched, pads thick and strong.

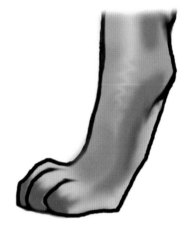

Foot fault: cat foot.

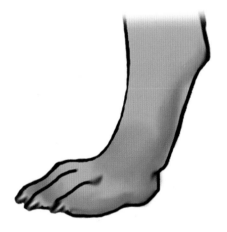

Foot fault: hare foot.

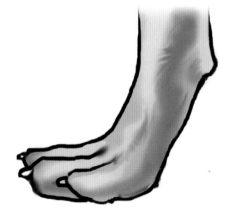

Foot fault: flat foot, weak pastern.

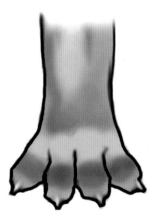

Foot fault: splayed, open foot.

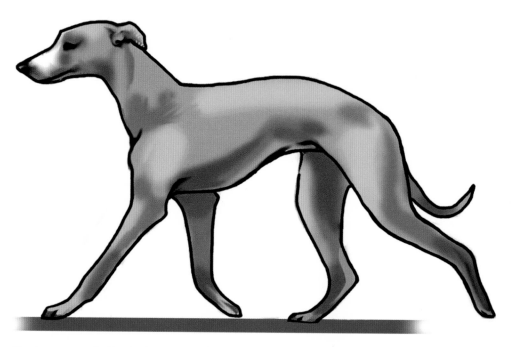

Ideal movement. General movement not to look stilted, high stepping, short or mincing.

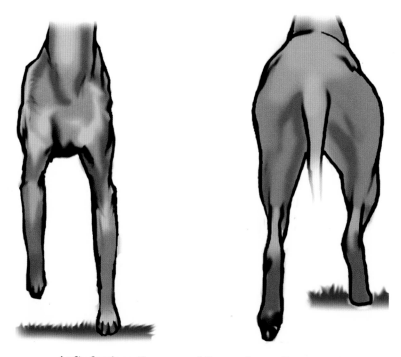

Left: forelegs thrown well forward over the ground.
Right: hindlegs coming well under body for propulsion.

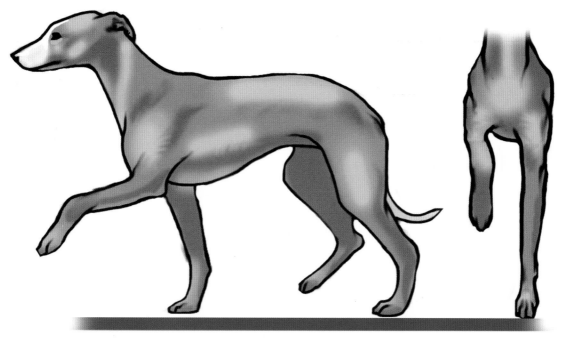

Movement fault: high stepping, 'hackney' action.

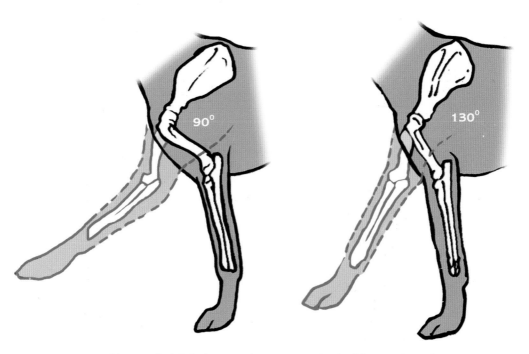

Above: skeletal placement governs extent of forward reach.

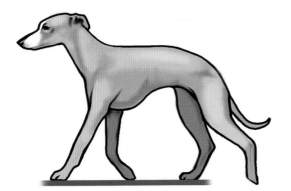

Movement fault: lacking drive.

Movement fault: pacing.

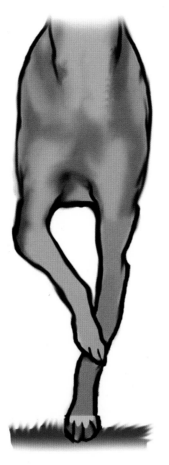

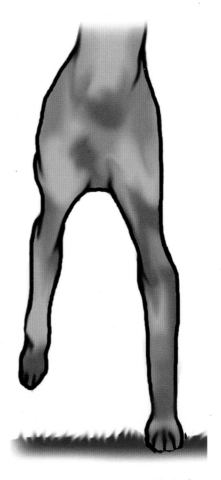

Movement fault: 'plaiting' in front.

Movement fault: going wide in front.

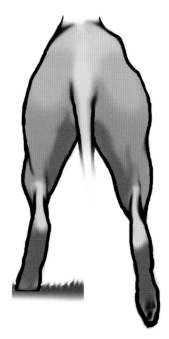

Movement fault: going close behind.

Movement fault: going wide behind.

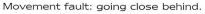

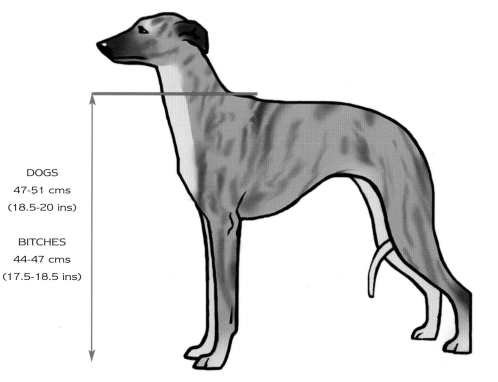

DOGS
47-51 cms
(18.5-20 ins)

BITCHES
44-47 cms
(17.5-18.5 ins)

Height measurement for dogs and bitches.

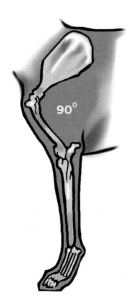

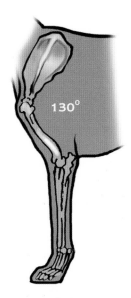

Front angulation showing correct skeletal structure.

Incorrect angulation: too upright in shoulder.

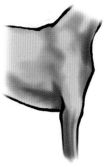

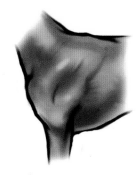

Fault: upright or short upper arm.

Fault: no depth of chest.

Fault: loaded, 'bossy' shoulders.

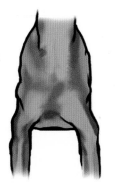

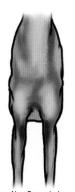

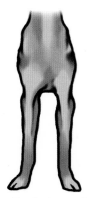

Fault: front too wide and out at elbow.

Fault: front too narrow.

Fault: toeing in.

Fault: toes at "10 to 2".

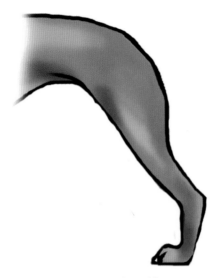

Fault: straight stifle.

Fault: exaggerated angulation.

Fault: sickle hocks.

Fault: cow hocks.

Fault: wide behind.

Fault: narrow behind.

Ideal tail: no feathering, long, tapering; when in action carried in a delicate curve upward but not over the back.

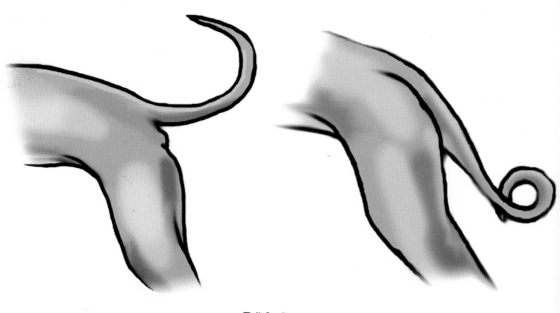

Tail faults.
Left: gay tail. Right: ringed tail.

Chapter Three

Guide To Owning
And Rearing A Puppy

Starting off an eight week old puppy on the table.

Well you've arrived at the big moment. You have chosen to own a Whippet, decided which breeder's type you prefer and you're eager to get your pup. Ideally you should be able to see the whole of the litter (although not necessarily have the pick) but if you see them all together, hopefully with the dam and you know of the sire, then you can have a good picture of what to expect your puppy to be like. The breeder will probably have a picture of the sire if you're not able to see him in the flesh.

Most breeders will let you have a look at the litter when they are about 6 weeks old. At this age the pups are quite active and limited handling shouldn't be a problem. By now the puppies are more resistant to infections and are becoming more outgoing. The dam, although protective, is not usually quite so keen and therefore won't be too put out by your interest in the puppies. She will probably not even be in with the pups when you visit but you should be able to see her. A puppy shouldn't really leave the litter before 8 weeks old.

Very often, most breeders who show or race have puppies already promised; this may be based on a particular colour preference, sex or size. If you are buying your pup purely as a family pet then you may be offered a particular one from the litter. This doesn't necessarily mean that you are getting the leftovers. If the litter has been bred from show

Not all promising puppies fulfil their potential. This exquisite bitch puppy (bred from two Champions) failed to have the correct movement, which goes to prove that nothing is a certainty.

stock then, whilst your puppy is just as adorable as his litter brothers and sisters at that time, he may not be quite up to scratch from a show potential point of view.

Making a decision about an 8 week old puppy is a very difficult thing to do. The Whippet goes through many stages whilst developing and the ugly duckling can often turn out to be a swan and the elegant striking one can be left behind in the glamour stakes. I have had experience of both these events over the years. My dog, Champion Hillsdown Sorcerer, although a nice healthy puppy, was nothing particularly promising and was sold as a puppy to a pet household. His owner's circumstances changed and I took him back at 14 months old, put some work into getting him into shape for the show ring and he made a handsome champion, gaining his title in just one year. He won the CC at his final show, Crufts, just sixteen months after his debut in the show ring. The only piece of advice I can offer with absolute certainty is that a short back and a short tail never get longer. If you are having a dog puppy then check to see he has two testicles descended. If your puppy is purely to be a family pet then he will still be a delightful lovable companion regardless of whether he has two, one or no descended testicles so don't let this put you off. Don't think that at three months old you have the finished product and that nothing else will change. I'm never sure of what the puppy will be like until around nine months. For other points to check please see Chapter 2 which outlines the standard required by the breed as defined by The Kennel Club.

Young Whippets don't really resemble the lovely elegant hound that's the finished product. At eight weeks old the puppies should be well rounded and with no bones showing; they should be lively and playful and not unduly timid. In a litter there will always be the braver more outgoing ones and the quieter more cautious ones. A litter that has been well fed and reared will have good bone, plenty of substance and thoroughly enjoy life. At 8 weeks the puppies will be fully weaned and established in a regular eating pattern, the breeder should also have wormed the pups twice. Make sure you get full details on what and when the puppy has been fed and try to keep to the same pattern when you get the puppy home. Introduce changes gradually over a period of time.

Leaving the litter is a big step and so familiar food will be a comfort. Don't allow the puppy to drop too much weight as it is essential to their development and can be really difficult to build back up.

On the day you go to bring your puppy home it's advisable for two people to go; then the puppy can sit on a lap for probably the first and certainly longest, most frightening journey of his short life. Arm yourself with an old towel, newspaper and plenty of kitchen roll as it's almost a certainty that you will be christened from both ends before you reach home. If its not possible for the puppy to travel on someone's lap then you really need to put him in a small travel cage of some sort. A cat box is ideal and plenty big enough for a puppy. Once again put in something soft and warm like an old towel, piece of blanket or even an old pullover, ideally something that if spoiled can be thrown away. The breeder should give you a signed pedigree, the Kennel Club registration papers and a list of the puppy's dietary requirements. You may also be given a small supply of the main meal that your puppy has been having to get you over the first couple of days. It is often the case that the Kennel Club registration will need to be forwarded on to you as this can sometimes take a while to be processed. The breeder will usually forward them as soon as they are received but follow this up if they do not arrive within a reasonable time.

Settling In

Once you arrive home take every precaution when getting the puppy from the car; even very young pups can shoot away given half the chance. When you get indoors don't let everyone make a fuss of the little chap; it will be quite a daunting experience after the car journey so keep the room calm and just let him find his feet and become acquainted with his new surroundings and noises.

It's a waste of money to buy a bed straight away as your puppy will grow out of it so quickly. A cardboard box with some warm bedding in (old cot blankets, duvets and shapeless pullovers) is ideal. The box can be replaced easily when outgrown or damaged and the bedding washed. Have a sheet of newspaper with his water bowl quite near his bed and, at meal times, his feeding bowl. I find it easier to have them separate rather than the joint ones. Small bowls are adequate at first for a young puppy, he'll soon get to know that this is where he is to eat and drink from, rather than hanging around the table at family meal times. Don't encourage him to wait for titbits from your meal, it's not a good habit to get into and should be discouraged from the start. If you were to give him a leftover treat then make sure you put it into his feed bowl. Have a couple of soft toys for him that he can claim as his own. Put the box in a warm corner away from draughts and let the puppy know that the area is his by putting him in the box. If he drags out the bedding then put it back in each time and it will eventually make sense to the young puppy. If you have small children then it's important that they understand the puppy is a baby, needs plenty of rest and isn't a toy. When the puppy is resting in his bed don't let your child disturb him. He has to know that the place is his as a refuge to feed, sleep or just relax. It is his own little sanctuary.

Discipline and Rules

Every household has its own rules and starting off with a carefully thought out plan for your puppy can save tears and trouble all around in the future. The rules you decide on are up to you and whatever suits your own situation. Whippets are intelligent and will usually do anything to please. Good behaviour should always be praised and naughty behaviour punished quickly at the time it happens. A short rap on the rump (*never* the head) with a rolled up newspaper whilst showing your displeasure by scolding is usually enough for a youngster and, as they get older, a verbal reprimand in a low tone is usually sufficient to bring the offender to order.

With good rules learned from an early age, everyone can be comfortable and happy together.

Free standing soft bed, ideal for the pup that has finished teething!

Whippets are natural moral blackmailers and so adorable and affectionate that it is easy to spoil your puppy. Remember that you are responsible for shaping his future behaviour and social acceptability, so you must be firm. Make sure that the first word he understands is "No". Whenever the puppy is out of line a short "No" said in the right tone will warn him he's not making himself popular with you. It's very sad and quite unfair to see an older dog confused by being punished for doing something that was considered a cute party trick just a few months earlier. Don't encourage the puppy to jump or climb up onto and off the furniture. Not only is it dangerous for the long slender legs but do you really want a grown up Whippet covered in mud after exercising on a wet day jumping onto your favourite chair? Any Whippet regardless of age, sex, colour or purpose in life will commandeer the best seat in the house if you let him, so start him off while still young knowing where and when he can relax.

Many households with dogs find indoor cages very useful. A puppy must not be kept fastened in for any length of time but they are an ideal way to restrict the puppy's movements for short periods of time and overnight whilst training. If the cage is left open for the puppy to wander in and out at will then the times when you have to close the door won't be a problem. I would only advise closing the puppy in when you are leaving the room for a short time and overnight until the

Above: another fur-lined bed being put to good use by the author's dogs.

puppy is trustworthy. Whippets aren't particularly destructive but a puppy can reduce a room to chaos if left alone. If you leave your new Italian shoes out whilst you're not in the room, believe me your puppy will think it a great wheeze to chew on them rather than any of his toys. Once the pup is used to the cage and happy with the door closed, you will be able to put him in it when travelling. It's safer for all concerned if his movements are restricted in the car and the dog will be perfectly happy. If you are staying away from home then there's no problem - just take the cage along and your dog will usually be perfectly at ease in his familiar cage, regardless of the room and company.

Bedding

As your puppy grows and becomes trained, his bed will need to grow with him. There are quite a few options and this again is whatever suits the home. Bean bags are ideal but make sure you get one big enough for your dog to be comfortable. They can be quite deceptive so it's as well to have an idea of the weight of your dog when you go to purchase one. The covers on these are almost always easily removed for washing. There

are also soft, free standing beds that can be washed and will fit quite nicely into a corner. If your dog has the run of the house then it can be useful to have a couple around the house in different rooms. Another option is a hard plastic bed which will need to have some sort of bedding in. These are very easy to clean and the bedding can be a blanket, a duvet or special machine washable dog bedding. Whatever you choose, remember it must be washed regularly.

House Training

Whippets are peace loving, clean dogs by nature and consequently not too difficult to house train. You will need patience but Whippets usually react well to praise and so the more time and effort you put in at the beginning, the sooner and better your results will be for a clean and puddle-free floor early on in your relationship.

From day one have a large piece of newspaper down on the floor near to the door. You will have a good idea when the puppy needs to 'go' from his actions so make

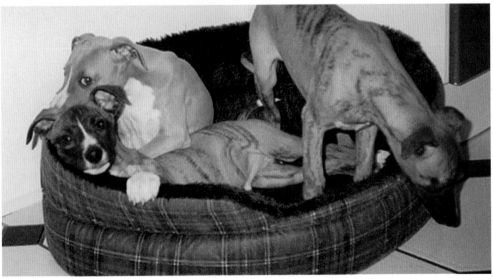

Learning to share sleeping quarters.

it easy by putting him on to the newspaper. The most usual times are just after waking, after a hectic play and always a short time after feeding. There will be accidents at first but don't go overboard, just a firm "No" and then put the pup onto the newspaper. On the other hand, when your pup has performed to command then no praise can be enough. This makes the puppy look forward to the attention and it doesn't take long for him to figure out that he has just done something good and therefore will be eager to please you in the same way again.

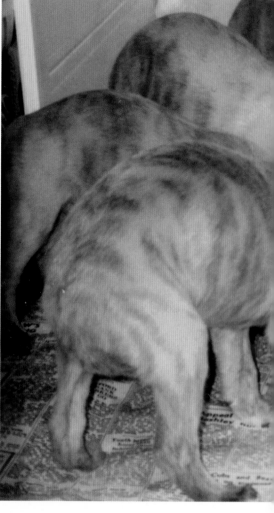

To progress from using the newspaper is easier when they are able to go out and be lead trained, since the older they get the more predictable toilet time is. Over a period of a few weeks gradually make the newspaper smaller and introduce popping the puppy outside onto a designated area in the garden. When your pup makes signs that he is about to defecate (sniffing the ground, circling and starting to crouch), then some people find it useful to introduce a command for the dog to associate the action with. It can be whatever you like but always use the same word when out with your dog. Being able to have some control over this action makes for an easier life all round and prevents unnecessary fouling. Don't be forgetful or inconsiderate towards your adult Whippet - remember, they are dependent on you. If you have to leave them indoors for any length of time then make sure that you take them out at the last possible moment and make it the first thing you do on returning. Sometimes owners can expect too much from their dogs and then are critical if the dog has an 'accident' indoors. An adult Whippet will very rarely seek to displease, hates being told off and punished and, for this reason, will hang on as long as possible before 'going' indoors so don't push him to the limit.

If you decide to have your Whippet live or sleep outdoors then a different set of guidelines apply. Most of my dogs live and sleep outside. However, I would never have a young pup kennelled alone. A Whippet loves company and a pair of youngsters will play constantly, which brings its own rewards. As part of a pair your pups will thrive much better as they will be happy, eat better and be more alert. My thoughts on this are that if your life is committed to having one dog with you then you may as well have two.

Aged 4 weeks. In another month or so these pups will be off to their new homes.

However, do be sure to spend time individually with each dog, to build a bond between you, and also socialise them separately. In this way you are ensuring that each dog is confident and not overly reliant on the other.

The kennel should be free from draughts and water proof. Inside the kennel you will need a warm dry bed, raised off the floor. There is a wide range of acceptable bedding and really it's down to what suits your situation and keeps your dogs warm and clean. Many people have some form of heating and lighting in the kennels but, if you do, it is essential that you ensure that this is perfectly safe and out of reach of the kennel's inquisitive and agile tenants. From my experience if it shouldn't be touched then my dogs will go out of their way to give it a go. I would still advise you to house train your outdoor dogs as, when they do come indoors with you, it should be a pleasurable time - not a continual tense watching, waiting and then mop-up time.

Lead Training

One of the most rewarding aspects of getting to know your Whippet is lead training. Some take to it straight away whilst others dig their toes in and positively refuse to move. It only takes patience and reassurance to get them going and they all come to realise very quickly that the arrival of the lead is the beginning of fun, going out and having your full attention. Everyone has their own methods but I always use a fine slip lead, the sort that most people use for showing. This way, if the puppy is pulling against you then his head can't slip out and the lead will be quite uncomfortable. They soon learn that not pulling away from you is far more comfortable and makes breathing much easier. If you decide to use a collar and lead instead then it's essential that the collar is the correct size and not big enough for the puppy to pull his head out. Believe me, a puppy who is not keen on being trained will get his head out of the tightest collar and be off quicker than you can stop him. The very nature of a Whippet means he'll run as fast as he can anywhere to escape and, if there is a road nearby, fate decrees that is where your pup will head. If your pup turns into a bucking bronco on your first attempts at getting the lead on him, then just put it on and let him walk around freely in the house or garden a few times. Introduce holding on to the lead just for short periods whilst he's walking around. It really isn't too difficult with patience and is well worth the effort.

Feeding

At 8 weeks old your puppy will probably be having four meals a day. A typical diet is milk and/or cereal for breakfast, meat or fish and biscuit at midday, meat or fish and biscuit early evening and then a supper of milk and/or cereal at bedtime. There are many varieties of puppy food available on the market nowadays, each having its own virtues. Basically what it comes down to is the method on which your dog thrives best and is acceptable to you. All commercial dog foods are well balanced and so, in general, supplements shouldn't be given. If you use one of the complete meals then be certain to follow the instructions and always make sure your dog has access to fresh, clean water.

At 12 weeks of age your pup will probably be ready to come down to 3 more substantial meals, possibly cutting out the one at midday and bringing the early evening one forward. I would normally feed three meals until about 6 months old but the puppy is the best guide and rigid rules don't apply. If some food is being left but the puppy is still keeping a good weight then reduce the amount of food given; however, if everything is being eaten and the puppy is not doing particularly well then you need to increase either the size of the portion or the number of meals. Some puppies can take a big meal at one go whilst others prefer to have smaller meals more often.

Once they are 6 months old I find it best to keep them on two meals each day, a light breakfast and a good feed of meat or fish in the evening. Once they are adult and turn twelve months I just feed once each day. Don't make your dog a fussy eater, a finicky puppy is quite rare. Adult dogs who are very choosy about their food have quite often been spoiled by well-meaning owners who think that by feeding the youngster meat intended for the family they are serving them well whilst, in fact, the reverse is true.

Exercise

When you have both mastered the lead training technique and you're out and about then be socially responsible and don't let your dog foul the streets and public places. Ideally you should train your dog to 'go' in your garden where you can remove the excreta by flushing away or burying but if your dog has to 'go' whilst out, away from home territory, then carry a small supply of plastic bags to pick up any deposits from the pavement or park. This can then be disposed of in a more acceptable way. Many local councils fine owners for dogs fouling public places and quite rightly. Some dog owners are their own worst enemies, allowing their pets to foul parks and playing areas; little wonder some people are so anti-dog when their youngster has innocently trodden in a mess or, even worse, fallen in some. Excreta can carry Toxicara larvae which can be picked up by humans. There are around 100 cases of Toxicariasis recorded each year. Symptoms can be quite serious, causing damage to eyesight, asthma, stomach upsets and listlessness. Not something that would endear a sufferer to you and your dog. It's also important not to let your dog go bounding around and jumping up at strangers; remember not everyone has the same views and affection for your prized companion as you do.

Don't overdo the exercise with a young Whippet. By all means let them play and fool around but don't have them running for any distance, and certainly not for any length of time, until they are almost adult. Too much hard walking is also not a good thing. A short walk is far better for the puppy and helps build the muscles in a more natural gentle way. Always keep your Whippet on a lead near traffic. They are so unpredictable and even the most faithful obedient Whippet will shoot away in any direction if suddenly frightened or startled. If you don't restrict your dog in a cage when travelling it's essential to train him from a very early age not to leap out of the car as soon as the door opens, the dangers from this are obvious. It's far better to have a command of "Stay" well learned from the start.

Inoculations

At 10-12 weeks the puppy should have the first of his course of inoculations. The vet will advise which injections are necessary and when they should be given. The main injections against Distemper, Canine Hepatitis, Leptospirosis and Parvovirus are always necessary. It's almost a certainty that any unprotected dog falling ill with any of these diseases rarely survives and will also suffer a terrible and painful death. The second course is two weeks later and then all that is required is a booster as advised by your vet. Keep the inoculation/vaccination certificate in a safe place, with the pedigree, then you can check when his booster is due. Should you ever wish to board your Whippet in kennels the certificate will normally be required as proof of inoculation. As the vaccination is a small live dose of these diseases you are required not to let your dog walk in public places or mix with other dogs until two weeks after the second dose. During this time just exercise your puppy in the garden. Don't allow visitors to bring along their dogs to your home as their dog could carry the disease on to an unprotected dog elsewhere.

The growing dog may exercise your patience. Providing a safe chewing object like this Nylaring may help to deter undesirable activities such as shredding cushions!

Teething

Around three months of age, most puppies start teething and so a little more patience and understanding is required. Make sure they have something to chew on all the time and, hopefully, your furniture will be left alone. It's probably advisable to buy an anti-chew spray; it can be sprayed on to furniture with no ill effect but is really quite a good deterrent to a puppy. Pet stores and most supermarkets sell a wide range of chewy sticks and shapes and you can also get a large marrow bone from the butcher. The marrow bone has to be boiled really well to prevent the bone splintering. Once hardened it will last for absolutely ages and, whilst not attractive to look at, your puppy will be quite happy to gnaw away at it for some time. As it is when human babies cut new teeth the puppies, too, have sore mouths and the easiest way to get the old tooth out to make way for the new one is to chew on anything hard. Don't be surprised to find the odd tooth around the house; it won't be white and perfect but probably quite dark and chipped as it has more than likely been forced out by the new tooth and so was loose for some time. The discomfort from teething can also cause ears to go a little awry but, if the ears are well set in the first place, any undue flapping around will sort itself out once the teeth have settled down. If this does happen then you may find that your puppy tends to look as if he has lost his attractive head but be patient, it should right itself.

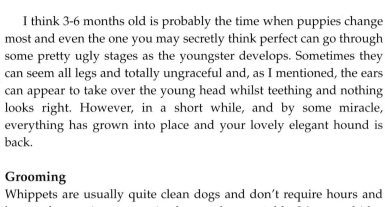

I think 3-6 months old is probably the time when puppies change most and even the one you may secretly think perfect can go through some pretty ugly stages as the youngster develops. Sometimes they can seem all legs and totally ungraceful and, as I mentioned, the ears can appear to take over the young head whilst teething and nothing looks right. However, in a short while, and by some miracle, everything has grown into place and your lovely elegant hound is back.

Grooming

Whippets are usually quite clean dogs and don't require hours and hours of grooming to remain clean and presentable. It's a good idea to get your puppy used to a structured grooming session right from the start; it's a good bonding process and also necessary to keep your

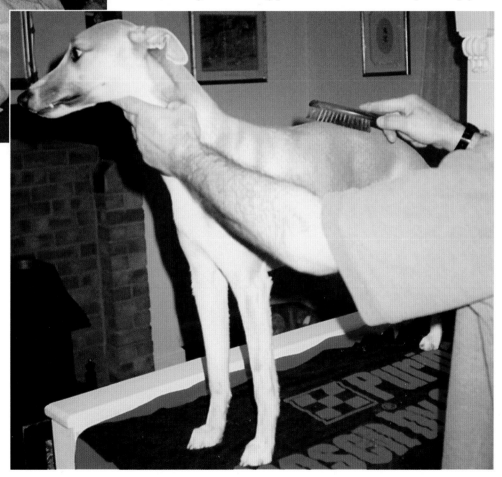

A bristle brush will help keep the coat clean and give it a healthy shine.

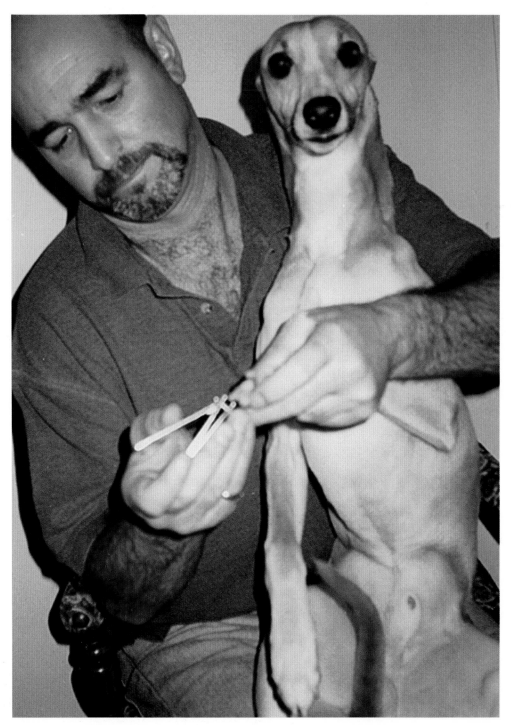

The author using human nail clippers to keep the nails short.

pet and home clean. As you get into it and your dog knows what to expect the whole thing can be completed in quite a short time. The only essential equipment is a good quality brush, human or pet nail clippers (I always use large sized human nail clippers), and a child's soft tooth brush. You can, of course, use more than these items but it's not essential. A short, brisk brush every day and an occasional bath should keep the coat nice and clean. There are a variety of shampoos available from pet stores. Make bathtime as painless a process as possible. If you are using the family bath then move everything away from the sides and have shampoo, jug or showerhead and, most important, a large towel to dry him with all close to hand. The water should be no hotter than blood heat, don't forget dogs have a different ideal temperature to humans. Put an old small towel, or a non-slip bath mat on the bottom of the bath to help create a more secure feeling. Be firm and quick and you will take away the fear; bathtime doesn't have to be a pantomime or nightmare. Gently clean the inside of the ears with a cotton wool bud. Afterwards, give him a brisk rub down to remove any excess water and then I find it useful to put an old sheet down on the floor near to the heater and the dogs will roll around on it until they have dried off.

Most dogs, and particularly a house dog, will need to have regular nail trimming sessions because being constantly indoors on carpet won't wear the nails down sufficiently. Don't allow them to become too long; not only are they unsightly but long nails can be quite painful and also ruin the shape of the foot. Short regular clipping sessions are the easiest way to keep them in shape. Nail clipping, too, is something that many dogs dislike but only because they are unsure and may have had a painful experience when the nails have been neglected and the guilty owner isn't confident or practised enough. Don't try to take too much nail at one go; I find it easier to nibble away with the clippers and then tidy up with a file if necessary. If your dog's nails do become unmanageable and you are unable to clip them then the vet will be able to do this for you but it does seem an unnecessary expense for something that can be controlled quite easily. It's surprising what a detrimental effect poor feet can have on the overall picture of a Whippet.

The teeth should be brushed very regularly. Use a soft tooth brush and salted water or a special dog toothpaste. Human toothpaste isn't suitable because of the strong taste and foaming sensation.

Adulthood

By the time your puppy has reached 12 months he should be happy, healthy and a good companion. You don't have to keep reminding Whippets, once they have learned good behaviour they very rarely fall from grace so you should have many years of enjoyment together.

As the years pass on and your Whippet gets older, slight changes will have to be made. Regular exercise is the best way to keep your dog fit but don't expect a ten year old to be able to run forever or even go for very long walks. Some older dogs can still manage to wear out their owners but don't push yours too much. You may also need to change his diet. Missing teeth can make chewing a hearty meal quite difficult so, if there are quite a few gaps between his teeth, then cut up the meat to make his life easier and also this will ensure that your dog is getting all the goodness as easily as possible. Don't forget, the waterworks may not be quite so reliable and to prevent accidents make sure your dog is able to get out when necessary. Really, old Whippets are just like old grandma and grandpa, they just need the extra thought. For more information on caring for the older dog, please see the chapter on Health and Welfare.

These elderly Whippets (aged 8 and 10 years old) still enjoy a good quality of life.

Chapter Four

Coursing With Whippets

by Colonel Ted Walsh

Coursing is defined as 'a competitive test of the merits of coursing dogs - two dogs only in each course - under formalised conditions regulated by a strict and detailed code of rules'. It is the oldest of all field sports and it evolved from early man's use of dogs to hunt for food. Over many centuries, with the spread of agriculture and the availability of meat and cereals from farming, coursing with Greyhounds became a sport of the nobility and landowners who, from running hares on their own land, began to challenge a neighbour's dog in competition. This led to the start of coursing clubs, the first being the Swaffham Coursing Club in 1776. In 1997 the club is still running some six and more meetings a season. The biggest meeting is the Anglia cup for 64 greyhounds, the only other 64 dog stake after the Waterloo cup which is the 'Blue Riband' of coursing.

In the middle of the 19th century there were some 380 coursing clubs and in 1858 the National Coursing Club was formed to control and regulate coursing. In 1880 the Ground Game Act - the 'Hares and Rabbits Act' - gave occupiers as well as owners of land the right to kill hares as a form of crop protection. This led to such a reduction in hare numbers that Parliament had to pass the Hares Preservation Act which limited the sale of hares to the period of August to February, though there is still no close season for hares. By the turn of the century the number of Greyhound coursing clubs had dropped to about 120. Despite the ensuing fluctuation in hare numbers (caused by changes in land use, farming practises, urban development and repeated attacks by those who would stop country sports), coursing still continues with 23 Greyhound clubs affiliated to the National Coursing Club. Depending on the weather, these clubs run some 80 - 100 meetings a season, from September 15 to March 10.

Throughout history there have been three sizes of 'gazehound', that is dogs which hunt by sight. The large dog for large game; the medium dog (the Greyhound) for medium game; and the small dog (the Whippet as we know it now) for small game. Whippets had been used for rabbitting and chasing hares over a great many years but it was not until 1962 that a small group of Whippet owners got together to form the Whippet Coursing Club, for formal coursing with Whippets. As not all the members were interested in showing their dogs the Club was to be independent and not affiliated to the existing Whippet breed clubs. Nevertheless, some of the early members will be recognised by their kennel names which included Laguna, Porthurst, Ballagan, Hungryhall, Shalfleet, Dragonhill, Linknumstar, Nipalong, Karryanup, Twiggen, Taimo, Padneyhill, Culverstreet, Nimrodel, Martinsell, and Tweseldown. With the help and co-operation of many landowners and farmers, the Club made steady progress until meetings were being run in an area bounded by Newbury and Stow-on-the-Wold in the west and Braintree and Kings Lynn in the east.

In 1970 applications for membership had increased to the point where it was becoming difficult to give each member even one runner per meeting. At this point the Hon. Mrs Richardson (Hungryhall) and Mrs Webb (Padneyhill) started the East of England Coursing Club and in 1971 Mrs Gilpin (Wenonah) and Mrs Webb (Padneyhill) started the East Anglian Whippet Coursing Club. With three clubs in existence and others becoming a possibility, some form of central control and representation was thought necessary and the National Whippet Coursing Club (NWCC) was formed. In 1974 a fourth club was started, the Woolley and District Coursing Club, running meetings in the Huntingdon area. Whilst Greyhound coursing is a professional sport, with the Greyhound Stud Book, the Coursing Calendar, prize money, professional trainers (though fewer now than in recent years) and betting, Whippet coursing is entirely amateur with no prize money to be won and owners run their dogs for the pure joy of seeing them work.

Coursing, whether for Greyhounds or Whippets, is run on a knock-out principle. Stakes are made up of multiples of 8. Hence there may be 8 dogs, 16 dogs, 32 dogs or 64 dogs though almost all NWCC meetings consist of 8 dog stakes. Pairs of dogs run against each other as drawn on the card, 1 and 2, 3 and 4, and so on and the winner of each pair goes through to the second round. In an 8 dog stake this will be 4 dogs, down to 2 dogs in the final. In each course the upper dog on the card runs in a red collar and is buckled in on the slipper's left while the lower dog on the card runs in a white collar on the slipper's right. As in pheasant or grouse shooting, coursing can be walked or driven. Almost all Greyhound coursing is driven whilst almost all Whippet coursing is walked. For both disciplines there are two paid, licensed officials: the slipper, who holds the two dogs to run in a quick-release slip lead ready to slip them after the hare; and the judge, who is mounted on a horse and follows the dogs and hare close enough to see exactly what each dog does, for which he allots points. He does not ride so close as to interfere with the course.

A walked meeting means just that. Members and their dogs walk each field in line looking for hares. If the cover is thick, such as long stubble in the autumn, the line will be close (30-35 yards), but on thin cover such as grass or arable it may be 50-70 yards wide. The slipper walks with two dogs in slips some 20 yards ahead of the centre of the line and the judge will ride on a flank.

When a hare gets up the slipper must be decide whether it is coursable - not lame and not a leveret - and makes certain that both dogs have seen it. He runs forward until the hare is some 40-50 yards ahead and then slips the two dogs. The Whippets streak off after the hare and the judge gallops after them. If the hare was too far away when they were slipped they may not reach it before it disappears into cover, in which case he may signal a 'no-course' and the dogs go back into slips or he may award the course to the dog which

The right flanker, the judge and the slipper.
Photo: Walsh

Almost all Whippet coursing meetings are walked. Members walk in line with their dogs,
the slipper in front of the centre of the line.
Photo: Walsh

Slipping: the judge starts to move forward.

Photo: Walsh

showed more pace. If the slip is made at a reasonable distance the dogs should get to the hare within 100-150 yards when the hare will turn right or left or even straight back without pausing. The Whippets will swing round after the hare and on catching up with it again it will turn again; this goes on until either one of the dogs catches the hare or the hare, through repeated turning and twisting, tires out the dogs and it escapes into cover. The judge has been counting points and will signal the winner by showing a handkerchief

As the hare and dogs reach his position, the judge starts to move with them.
Photo: Walsh

the colour of the winning dog's collar, red or white. Meanwhile the next two dogs to run are ready in slips and, as soon as the previous pair have been picked up by their owners, the line will move forward again for another hare and so on until the card has been finished.

For a driven meeting beaters are required. The number will depend on the ground and the men available but at least 25 beaters are needed if hares are to be driven forward

White collar just ahead. Photo: Walsh

Unlike Greyhound coursing, the hare and Whippet are not all that different in size.
Photo: Walsh

White collar with a one metre lead. This is a driven meeting; two beaters with white
flags can be seen over the hedge.
Photo: Walsh

successfully; 25 beaters should be able to take in about 75 acres at a time but they have to be paid and this is why only about four Whippet meetings a season are driven. A running ground will have been selected and the beaters go out on foot or in a tractor-trailer while the slipper and a few members walk the running ground to clear it of hares, with perhaps a course or two. The slipper will then go to the hedge or wall towards which the hares are to be driven. The spectators line up on one side of the running ground with a few flankers on the other side to keep hares running straight. The beaters move forward slowly and a hare gets up and runs towards the hedge where the slipper is standing out of sight. There will be a shout from the nearest beater of "Coming through, slipper, on your right", the hare comes through the hedge and gallops up the running ground, the slipper judges the distance and slips the Whippets after it and the course proceeds as at a walked meeting. When the beat is 'up' the beaters will go to another side of the running ground and drive that in or everyone may go to another field and start again, depending on the farm and the supply of hares. The meeting will continue until the last course is run and the winners declared.

When the Whippet Club was started it was obvious that the rules should be based on those of the National Coursing Club but adjusted where necessary for Whippets. Greyhounds are registered with the Greyhound Stud Book, Whippets are registered with the Kennel Club. In order to preserve what those who started the Club consider to be the true Whippet, the 'little dog', those running under what became NWCC Rules have to measure 20 inches or under at the shoulder and the length of the slip was laid down as 'not less than 35 yards' as opposed to 80 -120 yards for Greyhounds. Otherwise the rules are very much the same. To understand and enjoy a coursing meeting a basic knowledge of the rules is necessary. The judge decides all courses on the one principle that the dog that scores the greatest number of points during the course is the winner.

Points of the Course:
a. SPEED to the hare: 0.5, 1 or 1.5 according to the degree of superiority shown.

b. The GO-BYE: where a dog starting a length behind passes its opponent and reaches the hare a length ahead, 2 points or, if scored on the outer circle, 3 points.

c. The TURN: where a dog turns the hare at more than a right angle, 1 point.

d. The WRENCH: where a dog turns the hare at less than a right angle, 0.5 point.

e. The KILL: not more than 1 point and a kill may not score any points at all.

What happens is that the judge, watching a course in which red collar reaches the hare several lengths ahead of white collar, will say to himself 'red 1.5'. Red then turns the hare more than a right angle and the judge says 'red 2.5'. The hare having gone back down the field, white collar turns faster than the red and gets to the hare to turn it back up the field.

The judge gallops to keep level, watching to see what each dog does.
Photo: Walsh

The judge gives white one point but for simplicity's sake subtracts it from red's score which is now 1.5. So the course goes on until either one dog catches the hare or it escapes into cover when the judge will wave the red or white handkerchief for the winner. In practice, 15 out of 16 hares get away untouched in Whippet coursing and some 7 out of 9 in Greyhound coursing.

Coursing under Rules with Whippets can be the greatest fun but results should not be taken too seriously. For certain reasons it cannot be the same as with Greyhounds. Greyhound coursing is professional and a lot of time and money is involved. The dogs are bred only for coursing (though some do run at Greyhound racing tracks), litters are expensive to breed and rear and the dogs are, or were, all sent to professional trainers and run in their puppy season when the successful ones are retained and the unsuccessful disposed of. Meetings are driven despite the expenses involved and there is some money to be won as well as trophies.

Coursing with Whippets is an amateur sport. Whippets are almost never bred solely for coursing but, even if they are, puppies can be sold for showing, racing or as pets. If the slip is too long the dogs may not get to the hare at all. The slipper has about 4 seconds to judge the hare compared to 15-20 seconds for the Greyhound slipper; many courses are processions to the horizon. The best dog may not win the stake; a 'swinging hare, a bye into the final' has been seen more than once, but Whippets are exciting little dogs and most of us wouldn't miss it for anything.

"Where the hare goes, we go too!"
Photo: Walsh

Slipping.
Photo: Walsh

Chapter Five

Pedigree Racing

by Joyce Keable

Pedigree Whippet racing takes place at a number of clubs throughout the country. These clubs are affiliated to the Whippet Club Racing Association (WCRA) which is a subsidiary of the Whippet Club. Each club is allowed to hold two Opens per year inviting members from other clubs to participate. Most Open events are run in weight groups and there is usually a separate veteran section. At many venues the winners of the various weight groups compete to be 'Supreme' dog of the day.

The WCRA itself holds four Championship meetings a year (two for veterans). To become a 'Whippet Club Racing Champion' a Whippet must win the final of two weight groups. Points are awarded to the successful Whippets at Opens and Championships and hence the SA 37 Superstar Leagues are compiled (Master Veteran in the case of veterans), with only the twelve most successful scores counting at the end of the year.

In the write up the Kennel Club registered name of the Whippet is given first, followed by its WCRA name (which is the name most familiar on the track).

WCR Ch Firebird lying behind Firebrand on the last bend. Firebird went on to win the event comfortably. Photo: Harvey

Choosing a Racing Whippet from a litter

When choosing a Whippet puppy specifically for the purpose of racing there are many points to consider:

- A close consideration of the breeding must be the first priority. People almost always know which sex they require. Some breeders are well known for producing a strong line in dogs, while others are respected more for their successful bitch line.
- The eventual size at maturity is also an important fact to consider. The prospective owner needs to decide whether he wants an elegant light made Whippet, a middle-weight, or does he favour a heavier built type? There are always breeders who specialise in size.

After having decided on these facts the next decision is how to choose the right puppy from a litter. Most pups leave their mother at eight weeks old and so selection takes place while the pups are still very young. Many Whippeteers have their own 'guaranteed' ways of choosing a successful racing Whippet. The list seems endless and varied, with many theories held. Some people will look for the pup with the longest back, others will look for a good deep brisket, some a wide front and others a long tail. Many select by colour, or for the liveliest in the litter. Others require a pup born in a specific order, for example the second born and some even look for the number of hairs under the chin. There certainly do not seem to be any hard and fast rules when choosing.

I personally believe that having decided which sex and type of Whippet you require, and on visiting the breeding kennels of your chosen lines to view a litter, there is always one in the litter that appeals more than the others. Rely on your own instinct, for only you have that special feeling that says 'this is the one'. After all, ultimately, whether it has speed or not does not really matter, it is the love and relationship between you and your puppy that is all-important.

The Track in 1997

There are many Whippets racing really well at the moment and giving their owners a great deal of fun, unfortunately too numerous to mention here. The ones selected are the best performers so far in the 1997 Leagues.

The most outstanding bitch to grace the pedigree racing scene for many years is Angela Parker's home bred two year old Sunlay's Queen of Diamonds - Whippet Club Racing (WCR) Champion Black Diamond Queen. She is from Tell Um Straight (WCR Ch Striker) and Sunlay's Black Satin (Black Satin). This beautiful 24lb black bitch oozes class with each stride. She is a consistently fast trapper and has good early pace, coupled with the ability of being able to seemingly stay forever. She frequently records the fastest time of the day. WCR Ch Black Diamond Queen has won five WCRA Championships to date, winning every 24lb group possible since her racing career began. This year so far she has won eight Supremes: one on a curve track at Harvel, straights at the Northern WRC, at Linton, at South Cotswold, at East Sussex, at Maidstone and Mid-Kent, at the Welsh

Black Pearl, Black Angel and WCR Ch Black Diamond Queen with some of the trophies they won in 1997.

Grand National and on the bend at the East Anglia Black Velvet Derby, the Andover Summer Open and the Stanborough Bluebell Bend Open. WCR Ch Black Diamond Queen is currently well in the lead in the SA 37 Superstar Bitch League and the Whippet News Top Ten, demonstrating what a brilliant season both she and her owner are enjoying.

To keep WCR Ch Black Diamond Queen fit, her main exercise is rounding up the sheep and lambs when they need to be moved from one field to another. She also enjoys being lunged, along with her mother and sisters. However, her real excitement comes from walks on Horsall Common where there are always lots of rabbits to be seen. Her kennel mates and litter sisters 'Black Pearl' and 'Black Angel' are both consistent finalists, with Black Pearl having won the Supreme at Gloucester bend earlier this year.

Another two year old who can always be relied on to give of her best is Steve Berg's home bred, fast trapping little 18lb fawn bitch Townshend Chivas Regal (Nose to the Ground) from Casaloma Perry's Boy and WCR Ch Ear To The Ground. Up to the time of writing this consistent little bitch has reached the final of every Open she has been entered in, being good on both bend and straight.

She began her Open career by winning the Supreme at the Harvel Maiden Open and then the Andover Junior Open. She continued her winning ways and has subsequently won Supremes at Linton, Independent, Phoenix and two on the bend at Stanborough, plus weight groups at Andover, East Anglia, Welsh Grand National, Harvel and the 18lb group

L to r: Nose To The Ground and her dam, WCR Ch Ear To The Ground.

at the WCRA Championship on the bend at Church Gresley in June. Nose to the Ground finished second in the SA37 Superstar Bitch Competition at the end of 1996, having only competed since July. She is currently lying second to WCR Ch Black Diamond Queen in the SA 37 1997 Bitch Competition.

Her littermates Shelley's Boy and Ballyhasty Kirsch are also dogs to be reckoned with and often reach finals. Her mother WCR Ch Ear to the Ground, bred from Sir Samuel and Pippawood Grass Jewel, is proving a competitive lightweight veteran this season, even though an unfortunate toe injury earlier this year has hampered her success. She has won at the Independent and has managed to reach six other finals so far.

A truly brilliant little bitch over the last few years has been Andrew Brooks home-bred little bitch Pearlway Serena - WCR Ch Serena from Tell Um Straight (WCR Ch Striker) and Pearlway Valentine (Valentine). This 16lb fawn and white parti-colour bitch took the lightweight group by storm in 1995 and became a Racing Champion before her second birthday, really delighting Andrew and Julie. This little bitch has tremendous strength both physically and mentally and on the track shows great speed and stamina.

For WCR Ch Serena, the 1996 season started very well. She won the first Open at East Anglia and then the Harvel Open, going on that day to win her first Supreme. Her winning ways continued and the year unfolded into something her owners could only have dreamt about. Serena was entered in nineteen events throughout the year. She reached the final in seventeen and won eleven of them. She also had three Supreme wins

WCR Ch Serena.

and became a Sporting Champion. The crowning glory was, as a result of her Open final wins, the honour of winning the Whippet News Top Ten trophy awarded to the most successful pedigree Whippet each year. WCR Ch Serena also won the SA 37 Superstar Best Bitch 1996. The dream for her owners had come true.

1997 has been somewhat slower in terms of successful racing. Serena has suffered a near fatal digestive disorder, which appeared to be under control, but periodically makes an unwelcome return. This has put back her training programme and has left her somewhat too weak to compete regularly in many events. However a little sparkle came back a couple of months ago and so far this year she has reached eight finals. Serena is currently in third place in the 1997 Superstar Bitch League.

Brother to this great bitch is Jane Rankin's 20lb black dog Pearlway Blackbird - (Blackbird) who runs with equal enthusiasm to his sister. At this time Blackbird does not trap too well and consequently has to make up a lot of ground. In 1996 Blackbird reached nineteen finals, had five group wins and won two supremes, at the Northern and the Independent WRC. He finished second in the SA 37 Superstar Dog League. This year Blackbird continues to be a consistent finalist and has won Opens at Andover, Linton and East Anglia. He is currently placed fourth in the 1997 Superstar Dog competition.

With young bitches seeming to dominate the lightweight groups, yet another to make a name for herself this season is John Smith's Karyon John's Skylark (WCR Ch Greencroft Skylark) out of Saxon Blade (WCR Ch Hammeron) and Karyon Paddy Flash (WCR Ch

Firepower). At not yet two and a half years old, this little parti-colour bitch, bred by Joyce Keable, has already won three 16lb weight groups at WCRA Championships. Her first on the bends over a distance of 240 yards at Moreton-in-the-Marsh, Gloucestershire; her second, also a bend, at Church Gresley, Derbyshire; and her third on the straight at Abbotts Ann in Hampshire. She has won weight groups at the Maidstone and Mid-Kent Sprint Open, the John Porter Bend at East Anglia and at the Andover Springtime Open. She is a regular finalist at other Open events.

WCR Ch Greencroft Skylark is a very single minded determined little bitch. She is an extremely reliable fast trapper and is able to win many races as a result of her brilliant trapping. Full of speed and stamina, it is always a delight to watch this elegant little bitch compete. Her litter brother Karyon Gallanta Venture of Vensutter and litter sisters Darkling Ember and Firebrand are also consistent finalists and winners at Open events. Skylark is currently fourth in the 1997 SA 37 Superstar Bitch Competition.

A black and white bitch reminiscent not only of her father but also her great, great, great-grandmother (WCR Ch Vangirl) is Fred Burton and Joyce Keable's Karyon Rising Flame (WCR Ch Firebird) from Papedaro Augustus (WCR Ch Tommy) and Karyon Final Ascent (WCR Ch Firebug). This young two year old 17lb bitch loses races because of her inconsistent trapping - frequently giving away four or five yards - and then never seeming to work out which way she should go to pass the other dogs once she is behind. To be fair though, she makes every stride count whenever she is able to maintain her handicap, or to trap out alongside the opposition. In her first year she managed to succeed in the lightweight groups - on the straight, at Leckford Hutt Whippet Rescue Open, at Linton and Andover, and on the bends at East Anglia, the WCRA Bend Championship, 18lb group at Church Gresley and at Maidstone where she went on to win her first Supreme. When actually racing round the bend itself she is often seen at the rear of the race; she then seems to be able to put in a strong fast finish along the back straight and catch her opponents by surprise. With other final placings she achieved fourth place in the 1996 SA 37 Superstar Bitch League. This season so far, there have been wins in the 18lb group at both WCRA Straight Championships, at the Northern WRC Tenth Anniversary and at the East Anglia Black Velvet Open at Newmarket where she held off some strong opposition to take the Supreme. Firebird is placed fifth in this year's Superstar Bitch Competition.

Fairmist Time Flies (WCR Ch Time Flies) from Tell Um Straight (WCR Ch Striker) and Spring Sunset of Fairmist (Veteran Crown -VC Mystique) is one of the most genuine dogs running today. This three year old red fawn comes from a very successful line bred by Laurie Evans. His enthusiastic owners, Nigel and Judy Booker, have campaigned their charges well and are very proud of Fly's success. It began in 1995 when he won his maiden on the bend in Gloucester in June, narrowly beating his litter brother Handy Harry and, at the age of just twelve and a half months, he reached the final of his very first Open at East Anglia WRC. In 1996 his winning ways continued and he was a finalist at twenty Opens including all four WCRA Championships and gaining his title by winning both of the Straight Championships. He won a further six Opens including the straight

WCR Ch Greencroft Skylark with her owner John Smith.

Supreme at Maidstone WRC. He finished, at the end of the season, first in the SA 37 Superstar Dog League and runner-up to WCR Ch Serena in the Whippet News Top Ten Pedigree Whippet Competition. So far during the first half of 1997 he has been in 14 Open finals, including winning the first WCRA Championship but due to injuries was unable to compete at the second Championship. Time Flies has also won a further two Opens. He is currently leading the 1997 SA 37 Superstar Dog League and when last known was second in the Whippet News Top Ten to the fantastic WCR Ch Black Diamond Queen.

Last year Time Flies sired a litter of five puppies to Nick and Laverne Gilbert's Hairy Harris (WCR Ch Kizzynite) which were born in February 1996. This litter has only just started running but, at fifteen months, Daphne Kitchen's Flybynite had won a main Open Final. At sixteen months, she had won the Supreme at Harvel WRC, managing to beat both her sire and the brilliant WCR Ch Black Diamond Queen in the group final. She has subsequently gone on to other wins, including her first WCRA Championship final.

Another litter from Time Flies, born in April 1996 out of Mike and Ginny Eaton's Blowing in the Wind (WCR Ch Winds of Change) have also just started to race and include Geoff Cook's Catch the Wind, already an Open and WCRA Championship winner. A good future looks assured for these youngsters and their sire is much in demand at stud.

Another of Nigel and Judy Booker's charges, namely Celtic Black Fox (WCR Ch Time Finder) out of Tell Um Straight (WCR Ch Striker) and Brummie Bertha bred by Kevin Handy is also a dog to be reckoned with, preferring to run bends rather than straights, but is successful at both. This black 22lb dog began his racing career in 1994 when he won the first Maiden group he was entered in at the Northern Pedigree WRC in May. In 1995 he finished in the final of eight Opens including two WCRA Championships, both of which he won to gain his WCR Ch title. He finished the year seventh in the SA 37 Superstar Dog League.

1996 was a fantastic year for Time Finder - he was a finalist at twenty two Opens, including all four WCRA Championships. He won both of the Bend Championships and a further six Opens including the Supreme at East Anglia WRC's John Porter Bend Open. At the second Championships at Church Gresley, he won the Fastest Time of the Day trophy. He also gained his Sporting Champion title and finished fourth in the SA 37 Superstar Dog League.

Having started 1997 at the age of four and a half, he has so far been in thirteen Open finals including both the WCRA Championships, winning the second Championship at Church Gresley. Time Finder has reached the final of every Open so far this year except on one occasion when he fell over whilst leading a semi-final. He is currently placed third in the SA 37 Superstar Dog League and has just sired his first litter of five puppies to Doug Smith's Karyon Pride of the Mountains (Sheza Fyrefly).

One of the most consistent heavyweights to grace the scene is Sheila Gould's fawn and white parti-colour Captain Scarlet (WCR Ch Flash Bang Wallop) out of Jolly Nippy (WCR Ch VC Cousin Jack) and Leading Lady, bred by Mark Gregory. This super 28lb dog was to be Sheila's introduction to Whippets, calm and quiet at home during the week but, on

WCR Ch Flash Bang Wallop.

Sundays, transformed into a noisy, boisterous dog, chomping at the bit to get to the traps ready for the chase. Success began in 1995 when he won the Maiden group at South Cotswold in May. He then went on to win two WCRA Championships at Church Gresley in June and at Abbotts Ann in August, gaining his title for a really delighted Sheila. Being a consistent weight group winner and finalist found him finishing fourth in the Whippet News Top Ten. Come 1996 Flash Bang Wallop had another good season of racing, reaching the finals of most of his Opens, winning his Sporting Championship and also three more WCRA Championships. He finished fourth in the SA 37 Superstar Dog League. So far in 1997 Flash Bang Wallop continues to be a consistent weight group finalist. He has had wins at Leckford Hutt Whippet Rescue, Northern Pedigree Tenth Anniversary and Maidstone Grand Prix, plus his sixth WCRA Championship win on the bend at Church Gresley. Quite a record! He is currently in fourth position in the SA 37 Superstar Dog League.

WCR Ch VC Firebug in action.
Photo: Harvey

The veteran currently leading both veteran leagues is Fred Burton and Joyce Keable's six year old red brindle bitch Karyon Final Ascent (WCR Ch VC Firebug). This little 17lb bitch often disappoints with her trapping, but has good stamina. After an eighteen month lay off due to a foot injury, she returned to racing in the late autumn of 1996 and won the Autumn Bronze Veteran Supreme at Gloucester WRC. Her exercise consists of just over a mile of road walking daily. For her owners every race meeting she finishes sound is a bonus. This season, 1997, she has so far dominated the lightweight veteran group, winning six Opens and finishing in the final of every veteran event entered to date. She became a Veteran Crown (VC) at the first WCRA Championships at Newmarket and repeated the performance at the only other opportunity this year at Abbotts Ann. In her earlier career she won three WCRA Championships and became a Sporting Champion as well as a consistent finalist in the highly competitive lightweight groups. This year other wins have been achieved at the East Sussex Veteran Derby, the Northern Pedigree Tenth Anniversary, the Andover Springtime and Andover Summer Veteran opens.

Not to be totally outdone, her 15lb red fawn litter sister and kennel mate Karyon Paddy Flash (WCR Ch Firepower) has provided a little sisterly competition by winning the group at Leckford Hutt, beating her at East Anglia Black Velvet Derby, coming second to her at the East Sussex Derby and the Second WCRA Veteran Crown event, whilst being a finalist with her on many other occasions.

Three middle weight veterans who run as consistently well now as they did in their earlier careers are WCR Ch Smartie, WCR Ch VC She's No Lady and VC Divine Spark.

Fairmist Spring Mistral (WCR Ch Smartie) from Tell Um Straight (WCR Ch Striker) and Spring Sunset of Fairmist (VC Mystique), owned and bred by Laurie Evans, has won five WCRA Championships in all. 1997 was her first year as a veteran. She has achieved four Supreme wins so far at Maidstone, Leckford Hutt and two at East Sussex. She has also won a weight group at Andover. This black bitch gives of her all and is always a delight to see in action.

The outstanding senior veteran, owned by Jim and Maureen Dale and bred by Fred Foley, is Lady Be Dangerous (WCR Ch VC She's No Lady) from Charlie's pride (WCR Ch Latchlifter) and Our Girl Zippy (WCR Ch She's A B). This beautiful black and white parti-colour bitch won her first WCRA Championship way back in 1991. She subsequently won three more. In 1996 she was SA 37 Master Veteran and was also the winner of the Whippet News Veteran Top Ten, winning six Supremes and two Veteran Crowns. This year in 1997 she has won weight groups at East Anglia and Maidstone and has acquired her Senior Veteran Crown in August at the first opportunity.

Finally, there is the lovely fawn bitch Tanimara Bee Orchid (VC Divine Spark) owned by the Rt Hon. Richard and Juliet Cabell-Manners. This six year old bitch has always been a force to be reckoned with. She has won one WCRA Championship in 1994 and was always a regular finalist in the highly competitive 22lb group. This year she has won both Veteran Crown events and been Supreme Veteran at the Black Velvet Open and John Porter Open, both held at Newmarket, and continues to always be a consistent finalist. In fact the veteran groups are equally as competitive as the racing of their younger counterparts.

Chapter Six

Showing And Judging

The Kennel Club is the governing body of all matters concerned with dog showing. It was founded in 1873 and all the rules, regulations and virtually everything to do with breeding and exhibiting show dogs are decided upon by one of the many dedicated committees from within The Kennel Club. I don't intend to go into great detail about The Kennel Club as the information is easily available, but it is necessary to have some knowledge of what is required in order to exhibit at a Kennel Club licensed show.

If you buy your puppy direct from the breeder then you should be given The Kennel Club Registration Certificate along with the pedigree. If your puppy is very young then the registration may not yet be available, in which case the breeder should forward the certificate to you as soon as possible so that you may then apply to have the dog transferred into your ownership. This could depend on the efficiency of the breeder getting the initial form completed and sent off to The Kennel Club for recording. I always find the hardest part deciding on names. If a name is deemed not suitable or is already registered to someone else then the application is returned for another choice of name to be made, which can hold up the procedure.

In order to transfer the pup's registration into your name, the reverse of the Registration Certificate should be completed as indicated and sent with the appropriate fee to The Kennel Club. Part of the form requires you to sign a declaration to abide by Kennel Club rules. The Registration Certificate is an important document and should be kept in a safe place, with the pedigree and innoculation records. If for some reason the Registration Certificate is not available, contact The Kennel Club who will investigate and advise you how to apply for a duplicate.

Before you can enter a licensed show the dog must be fully registered and be at least six months old. There are strict guidelines that govern the running of shows; these apply to the number of classes and dogs, the size of the ring and even the area set aside for your dog to 'go to the toilet' (known as the exercise area). The Kennel Club set the rules, regulations and guidelines to ensure that shows are run smoothly and safely for dogs, exhibitors and spectators alike. Falling foul of the rules can result in clubs not being granted a license to hold future shows. Similarly, any exhibitor or breeder who breaks the rules can be banned from taking part in further activities governed by The Kennel Club.

Showing can be a great hobby because you can be involved as much or as little as you choose. Its an ideal way to meet a wide variety of people, all with a common interest. I say

An indoor exercise area at a show.
It is important to keep venues clean and free from fouling.

common interest but you will find many varying opinions and preferences. There are, as in all competitive pastimes, petty jealousies and suchlike but in general the majority of the showing fraternity in Whippets are genuinely interested in promoting the breed and welcome newcomers with open friendship. A top award going to a novice exhibitor will always be greeted with applause and genuine pleasure.

If you are completely new to showing probably the best way to find out how to get involved is to go along to a local Open Show. As the name suggests they are open to all dogs, novice or champion, and a great number are held across the country. It's a good way to get the feel of showing and to see if you want to take it any further. Most Open shows are a good friendly day out and it will be less expensive than "practising" at Championship shows. Only dogs that are entered for the show are allowed in so you will have to leave your own dog at home, tempting though it may be to show him off. As a rule, the catalogue for the show will be on sale at the entrance. Its well worth buying because inside are all the details of the dogs at the show together with the names and addresses of the owners. The classes are all listed and, as you watch, you will be able to identify any dogs that take your interest and maybe speak to the owner, whose name you will find listed in the catalogue.

The best place to start to gain actual handling and showing experience is at club training nights. Many dog clubs have a monthly training night to enable novice handlers and puppies to build up confidence in order to exhibit at a show. The judges, too, are often experienced exhibitors who have decided to move on to judging and so they too need to build up experience and confidence in examining many different dogs. The night is very often a family social night out as the meetings are often held in function rooms of pubs

Moving the dog away from the judge.

Movement in profile.

and clubs. Well behaved children are always welcome and it's an easy atmosphere where you can seek help and advice or even just talk dog. You will come to realise that most people who own Whippets are also blessed with an urge to mix and talk "Whippet" with anyone. All in all the training club nights are usually a sociable learning experience all round and very probably accompanied by the thrill of a raffle!

After a few wins at training class you will more than likely be anticipating having a try at the real thing. You can find out what's happening when and where from either of the two weekly doggy papers, Our Dogs and Dog World - essential reading to anyone interested in the show world. In both publications there is an extensive section given over to advertising forthcoming shows, closing dates for entries

Front view of the dog as she approaches the judge.

to be received by and details of shows taking part during the current week. When you have decided to enter for a show then the very first step is to contact the Secretary of the show for a schedule. The schedule will contain full information about the day, the venue, date and starting time, the judge, the classification, the prizes on offer and an entry form, also the specific Kennel Club rules that apply to the show. Most entry forms are pretty much the same, as the information needed is always the same. You will need to state your dog's registered name, date of birth, breed, sex, breeder, sire, dam and the classes you would like to enter. There will be information to help you decide on which would be the most appropriate classes for you to enter. The classes are graded by the age of the dog and previous successes in the ring of the dog and/or handler. Once completed, the form needs to be sent off with the required fee before the closing date.

If you keep your Whippet in good firm condition and he is generally fit and healthy then not too much work is usually needed other than extra grooming before the show, probably a bath, an extra clean of the teeth and maybe a little trimming. One thing that can be said about a Whippet is that you can't hide anything in the outline, everything is there on view. It may sometimes be necessary to trim down certain areas of the coat, particularly the tail, to give a final sleek look but don't attempt this yourself before learning how first as you could ruin the natural line of the tail with a few wrong snips and it seems to take an age to grow back. Ask an experienced exhibitor for advice. Most will help out a novice - we've all had to learn and most have made those mistakes! The best place to look out for grooming aids is at one of the large general Championship shows. Some of the equipment you can buy is amazing.

Exhibitors going to shows are, perhaps, hooked on the atmosphere in a similar way to entertainers. The saying "smell of the greasepaint and roar of the crowd" is not too dissimilar to the effect a dog show has on the senses. At an outdoor show the smell of the grass mingling with various grooming sprays, the crackling public address system and flapping of the tents are all part of it, dogs barking and friends meeting up and calling to each other at ridiculously early hours is great and all adds to the atmosphere.

Allow your dog to relax whilst the judge is examining other exhibits in the class. He may need to be fully alert for some time when the judge is selecting his final dogs.

When the big day arrives you probably will walk through the entrance of your local sports hall or similar and wonder what is about to happen. At an indoor show the very first thing you will notice is the noise and your dog really has to get used to this at the outset, the training nights will have helped a great deal. Shows are pretty much the same everywhere and so here is what to expect.

The Kennel Club require that shows start promptly at the time stated on the schedule so if you're in a puppy class make sure you're there in plenty of time to settle yourself and, more importantly, your dog. Remember if you are tense then your tension will pass like an electric current down the lead to your dog. As you go in, buy a catalogue for the show and check your ring number. Then, as soon as you have your dog settled in, check to see that your entry has been made correctly. If there have been any errors then report to the Secretary of the show immediately.

At Championship shows, Whippet classes are usually very well supported and so it is often necessary to have two judges - one for the dog and another for the bitch classes. When there are two judges there will also be a qualified referee, just in case the two judges cannot decide on joint awards such as Best of Breed and Best Puppy. A referee is an experienced person who is qualified to judge the breed at Championship show level. If,

Judge about to examine the teeth and bite.

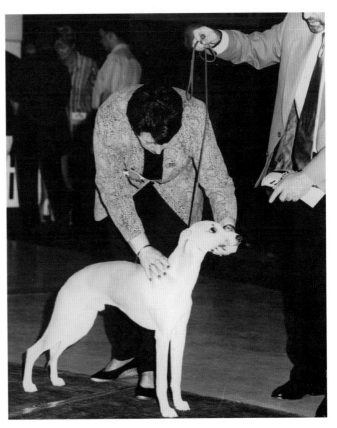
Checking the shoulders.

The judge will now assess the dog's movement.

however, there is only one judge for the breed then, regardless of the standard of show, dog classes are always first. It isn't really very sporting to take a bitch to a show if she is in season because of the obvious effect it can have on dogs, so if this happens then you really ought to leave her at home.

As each class starts the Ring Steward will call the class name and number and then check the ring number of each exhibit entered in the class. You will then be given your ring number, unless you are at a benched show and the number had previously been placed on your allocated bench. Your ring number card must be displayed whenever you are in the ring. When all dogs are in the ring the judge will first wish to see them all set up in line together and then the whole class will be asked to move in line right around the ring a couple or so times. Each exhibitor will then in turn set up their dog for the judge to examine. There will be a table at the top of the ring for you to set up your dog for the judge who will then examine your dog in detail, comparing mentally your dog against the breed standard requirements. Do not speak to the judge, the only conversation you really should have is when the judge asks the age of your dog. You will then be asked to move the dog. This is usually up and down the length of the ring and then in a triangle. Don't cut the walk short; utilise as much area as you can to give your dog a chance to get into his stride. This will enable the judge to view the movement from all sides. Don't make the mistake

The author's dog being gone over at a Championship show. Stalls and the benching areas (inside the tents) can be seen in the background.

Judging completed; judge writing critique of his winning dogs.

of putting yourself between the judge and his view of your dog. It is good sense to practise holding the lead and moving your dog from either hand. The judge is looking to see if your dog moves freely and true but if you are on the wrong side then his view will be blocked by your legs. Learn the correct pace at which your dog gets into a good driving action; don't run him at a gallop but don't plod along either. The judge will work down the line and examine all the dogs entered in the class. Whilst the judge is examining each exhibit he is only interested and concentrating on that particular one, so let your dog relax. Don't keep him stood to attention as it can often be some time before you need to set him up again. It is acceptable to join in conversation with fellow exhibitors in the ring and certainly helps pass the time in a well-supported class. This is also a good time to build up your knowledge by watching experienced handlers and seeing how they present and move their exhibits. When the judge has examined the last dog all the dogs are then set up again and the judge decides who are to be the winners. It may be that you have to walk

your dog again or the judge may come and re-examine your dog's shoulders or some other part. This is probably the the most tense time. The dogs may sometimes be required to stand alert for quite some time, consequently this is certainly not the time to relax just because the judge may be looking at the other side of the ring for a moment. In a large class the judge will probably shortlist a number of exhibits to make more room in the ring and also release any exhibits that are not to be included in the final placings. There are usually five placings in each

Benching: a cage and familiar blanket help this pup to settle on his first visit to a show.

class. That was a quick run down of what to expect from your first class, you will pick up what happens next by being at the show.

The basic principles of showing are the same regardless of breed or level of show. Kennel Club Challenge Certificates (CCs), can only be gained at a Championship show and as a result of being unbeaten in your classes. A Reserve CC winner is also decided on in case the CC winner should be disqualified for some reason at a later time. All first prize winners of the same sex "challenge " to be awarded the CC on the day and then the best dog and best bitch "challenge" for the Best Of Breed, or BOB. The Reserve CC winner could have been placed second to the CC winner in their class and then brought back in the ring to challenge for the Reserve award. At a Breed Club show the Best of Breed is automatically Best in Show (BIS) but in a general show the Best of Breed winner then goes on to represent the breed in the Hound Group, and the winner of the Hound Group then goes on to 'challenge' all the winners of the other Groups for BIS. In order to become a champion a dog must be awarded 3 CCs, by three different judges; one of these must have been awarded after the dog has reached the age of twelve months. There are no limits to how many CCs can be won. The smaller shows work on a similar process of elimination to arrive at the eventual BIS winner.

Crufts is by far the most famous Championship show. It is The Kennel Club's own show and is the only one where you must qualify to enter. This means that you must have previously attained a certain standard at Championship show level in order to compete. The show is now held over 4 days with different Groups on each day. It really is the busiest show with many foreign enthusiasts visiting. A win here is no more valuable than at any other of the Championship shows throughout the year but because of the qualification restrictions, the publicity, and media interest there is an exciting buzz going around the whole place and so it can often seem more important.

The essential thing to remember, and lots of people often forget along the way, is that the whole purpose of competing at a show is for enjoyment and a good way of passing time with like-minded people. Its supposed to be fun! A little tension doesn't hurt in any competition but try not to let nerves take over. Try to relax and be reassuring with the dog. When you're in the ring waiting to be judged speak to the other exhibitors around you in the ring and let the dog relax - Whippet classes are often very well supported and so judging can take some time. If you aren't given a placing and don't understand why then at the end of judging wait and ask the judge for advice on how to improve your handling or maybe what work needs to be done on your dog to improve him. Remember, all judges have had to start somewhere and most will be more than happy to help a keen newcomer. Be polite to the judge; many appointments don't pay a fee, often just expenses and sometimes nothing at all and the judge is there purely for the enjoyment of the day along with everyone else. Don't be a poor loser, remember the result is still down to the judge's opinion. No one dog can win every time under every judge - thats what makes for a good competition.

At almost all of the larger shows there is a benching area where you will find your own allocated bench, identified by your ring number. The benches are long runs of wooden panels sectioned off into an individual area for each dog. The dog should be on the bench for the duration of the show whenever not in the ring or being exercised. There are metal rings to attach a special bench lead to keep your dog fastened there and many people also use a travelling cage on the bench to make the dog more comfortable and feel secure away from home. Most Whippets take to being on the bench as long as they have a nice comfortable rug or blanket and aren't left for too long. With a young dog it's advisable not to stray too far or, better still, arrange with another exhibitor to watch over each others dogs. If you become a regular exhibitor you will very often find yourself benched next to the same people as they are almost always set out in catalogue (and, therefore, alphabetical) order. The bench is also a good base to meet at and leave refreshments, grooming bags, raincoats and wellingtons (essential for an outdoor British summer show) and everything else that you suddenly can't be without for a day.

The smaller local shows are an ideal way to start off. If you've been to local training classes then you probably will see some of the same people at the show. Benching is very expensive and not used at many small shows so it's advisable to take a travelling cage or at least a blanket for your dog to lie comfortably on. There are usually a few side stalls to help raise money for the clubs and it would be a sin not to try the home made cakes that the ladies of the hard working committee have usually spent the day before baking! At the larger shows it's usually advisable to take some refreshments with you, most certainly a flask of something hot in winter and cold drinks in the summer. There are almost always refreshments available but there can be long queues and if all the family have gone along for the outing it can prove to be quite expensive.

Other things you'll need to take with you on the day are: a drinking bowl for your dog and perhaps a little treat of something nice to nibble on for him, grooming equipment, and be prepared for any weather at an outdoor show. Wellingtons, umbrellas and wet weather outfits are always handy to have at British outdoor shows.

There you are, all the basic information you need to get started. You too can join the armies of people going up and down the motorways at incredible hours of the night and day in all weathers just for the fun of it. Believe me, when the show goes really well and you get a good result you don't even notice the journey home or remember that you last saw your bed in the early hours and many miles away.

Judging

In order to fully understand the principles of showing it is important to also have some knowledge about the other aspect involved, judging.

Before anyone is able to judge or referee at a Championship show they must first be approved by The Kennel Club. In order to obtain this approval the potential judge must have gained a great deal of experience in judging the breed at Limit and Open show level. This experience has to be backed up by actual facts and figures of all judging appointments. The Kennel Club will also seek confirmation of the person's suitability to judge from a number of Breed Clubs before passing approval.

I feel very strongly about the responsibility of people involved with Breed Clubs whose opinions are counselled concerning applications to judge. In my view, at Championship show level the opinion of a judge can only be respected if that judge has bred or owned at least one champion. In order to gain the necessary judging experience then the person must have been involved with the breed for a number of years and if, during that time, they have failed to own or breed a champion then I feel they are not capable of deciding what is required to make a champion and, therefore, ultimately not qualified to judge at Championship level.

A judge should be confident in his or her own knowledge to make the decisions on the day and, regardless of the outcome, no-one who has entered in the classes should have any axe to grind. If a judge's opinion is considered worth entering the show for before the day then the opinion on the day should be accepted, with no sour grapes. If in your opinion the judge is not qualified to judge at the top level then save your entry fee for one who is. It brings a sour taste to the ringside when judges are criticised for being inadequate; the blame lies with the people who put them there.

The usual climb to being qualified to judge at top level should really start way down on the bottom rung: judging at club training nights, moving on to small shows, Limit shows, the smaller Open shows, progressing to the large Open shows and so on until enough experience has been gained. Judging isn't just 'knowing a good dog when you see one'; it can be quite hard work, physically and mentally. The

Assessing dog in profile after it has been moved.

judge may be in the show ring for some hours in all kinds of weather - really hot sun can be very draining. The hard work mentally is in keeping alert with every dog and remembering the individual details when it comes down to making those important decisions.

A judge has to feel confident in his or her own knowledge of the breed and the requirements needed to be able to do the job they are there to do. They are there to give an honest, open and fair opinion of each dog on that day. A good judge isn't nervous about going into the ring because they can be confident in their own knowledge of what makes a good specimen of the breed. Keen anticipation with an edge to it is a healthy requirement and not the

Author examining dog on the table.

same feeling at all. When someone sends off an entry to a show, that person is in effect seeking the opinion of the person named to judge the classes in the show and, in having accepted the judging appointment, the judge is agreeing to pass their honest opinion on the dogs that are entered. Its a two way mark of respect for each other and shouldn't be marred by lack of knowledge on either side.

Judging abroad is different and each country has its own rules governing the making up of a champion, but if a foreign judge comes to Britain then he will abide by the system we use and, similarly, when British judges are abroad they will follow the system of the country in which they are judging.

A very friendly show in Germany.
The day started with a glass of bucks fizz and a taste of salmon.

Chapter Seven
History Of The Breed In The Show Ring

Ch Zuber - the first show champion Whippet.

The Whippet was first recognised by The Kennel Club in 1890. This was as a result of a request for official status by Mr H Vickers, a keen fancier of the time. Mr Vickers wanted official classes for the breed at Kennel Club shows. He subsequently was the owner of the first ever Whippet show champion, Zuber. Zuber was home bred. His dam was Herndell and his sire was White Eye. White Eye was the top racing dog at that time and was said to have raced 200 yards in 12 seconds. Ch Zuber has the distinction of being behind all modern Whippet pedigrees. However, the Stud Book recording results from 1879 advises that at Wigan, Ormskirk and the St Helens Agricultural Society show held in July, there was a class for 'Whippets or rabbit coursing'. The winners were: 1st Mr J Payne's Skip; 2nd Mr J Taylor's Janney; and 3rd Mr B Radcliffe's Lady. Nothing is known of their breeding as they are not included in the pedigree section and there is no further mention of the breed until 1891.

The first champion bitch was Ch Manorley Model bred by Mr R Riley. She was a red and white bitch by Spark out of Jenny. Her owners were Messrs F and J Bottomley of the Manorley affix. This affix dominated the show scene up until the First World War. It was around about this time that a young Poppy Martin (Poppy) embarked on an incredible 74 year relationship with the breed. Breeding, exhibiting and judging the breed for many years, this remarkable feat only came to an end with her death in 1984.

The breed did manage to survive throughout the hard times between the two Great Wars and the kennels of note were Mr Albert Lamotte (Shirley), Captain W Lewis Renwick (Watford), Mr W L Beara (Willes), and Mr Stanley Wilkin (Tiptree). The Tiptree breeding was to have a great impact on the breeding of this era; sadly this was after Mr Wilkin's death.

Champion Pilot Officer Prune was the first Whippet to go Best In Show (at Bath Championship Show), in 1947. A year later, at Leicester Championship Show, Lady F M Dankwert's Champion Brekin Spode repeated the feat. She was home bred, owned and shown. Her sire was Sporting Chance and her dam was Champion White Statue of Conevan. Ch Brekin Spode proved herself to be not only a top class show dog but also a great dam and her offspring were to figure in the foundation stock of many successful kennels.

All pedigrees of today's British Whippets trace back to the kennels that emerged in this important post-war period. These kennels all enjoyed success to different degrees and, indeed, some are still active in the breed today. Although lists of names can be tedious for a reader I feel it absolutely necessary to name these kennels so that present day exhibitors and breeders can fully appreciate where today's Whippets have evolved from. It must be said that their influence is still perpetuated in the breed today.

KENNEL OWNERS

Sapperly	Mr and Mrs Evans
Seagift	Mrs D Whitwell
Allways	Mr and Mrs F Jones
Wingedfoot	Mr C H Douglas Todd
Fleeting	Mrs M Garrish
Of Test	Mrs D Lewis
Harque	Mrs A Argyle
Hillgarth	Mrs M F Sheffield
Cockrow	Misses A D and E M Hudson
Teighways	Mr F Barnes
Ladiesfield	Mrs M Wigg
Dragonhill	Mrs C Cleeve
Ballagan	Lady Selway
Tweseldown	Lady Anderson
Poltesco	Miss Ironside
Shalfleet	Mrs Wilton-Clarke
Peppard	Mr and Mrs J Golland
Samarkand	Mr R M James
Banachie	Mrs K Chapman

Mrs Chapman successfully bred and exhibited ten champions, none of which bore her kennel name. Ch Pilot Officer Prune was one of her successes.

Whilst looking back, it is interesting to note that the Barmaud affix started by James E Barker in the early 1920s continued through his son and still enjoys an unbroken continuation to the present time through his grand-daughter Mrs J Northrow and his great grand-daughter Miss E Northrow who has recently campaigned Ch Fullerton Agile Star at Barmaud to her title.

Coming to the fore on the Whippet show scene from the late 1950s and early 1960s

Ch Silver King, by Ch Boy Scrounger.

Ch Zanza Zanita.

Ch Vicar of Yns.

Ch Watford Breeze, by Ch Watford Brilliant.

were an influx of important kennels. Amongst these were Lady Anderson's Tweseldowns. I thought Ch Tweseldown Winchat was an excellent champion. Miss M Ironside had four Poltesco champions, Lady Selway had three Ballagan champions and Mrs D Cleeve (Dragonhill) was also a successful breeder of a number of champions. More in-depth information about these kennels has been included in the chapter about Nimrodel written by Mary Lowe. Most of the following kennels mentioned have bred or owned five or more champions, some maybe less but I felt it necessary to include them because of the great influence they have had on the breed.

Ch Sparkle of Tytterton, also by Ch Watford Brilliant.

		Ch Pilot Officer Prune
Ch Bellavista Barry		
		Brekin Bright Spark
Ch Lily of Laguna		Ch Fieldspring Bartsia of Allways
		Ch Brekin Ballet Shoes

Pedigree of Ch Laguna Ligonier.

The top Whippet sire of all time: Ch Laguna Ligonier.

Notable Kennels

Laguna

No record of Whippets in the show ring this century could fail to mention the Laguna kennels of Mrs D McKay. Laguna breeding is the backbone of countless successful kennels both in Great Britain and overseas. In all there were eleven Laguna champions including the top sire of all time, Ch Laguna Ligonier. There is absolutely no doubt that Mrs McKay and her contemporary breeders are quite rightly held in great esteem by any student of pedigrees and breeding. Not only have the Lagunas proven their prowess in the show ring in the past, they also excel at coursing and racing at the present time - truly dual purpose Whippets. Mrs McKay has kindly loaned me photographs of the two generations behind this great dog. The only one I have been unable to track down is Brekin Bright Spark.

Greenbrae

Mrs B Yerburgh owned the comparatively small and short-lived Greenbrae kennel. This kennel produced Ch Samarkands Greenbrae Tarragon, a top winning and highly

Ch Bellavista Barry, sire of Ch Laguna
Ligonier.

Ch Lily of Laguna, dam of Ch Laguna
Ligonier.

Ch Pilot Officer Prune.

Ch Fieldspring Bartsia of Allways.

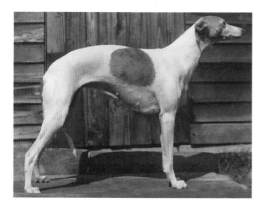

Ch Brekin Ballet Shoes (Ch Balaise Barry x
Ch Brekin Spode).

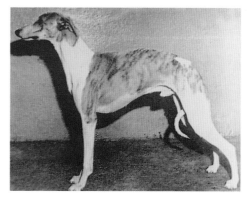

Am Ch Greenbrae Barndance - an
influential sire in America.

influential sire. She also bred Am Ch Greenbrae Barndance who was a sire of great importance in America. A little further north in Canada another dog, Can Ch Coveydown Greenbrae Wayfarer, made his mark on the breed.

Cockrow

The Cockrow kennels were owned by the sisters Misses E M and A D Hudson. Although not a high profile kennel, the Cockrows have been most influential in the breeding and the combining of quality in other kennel lines. Ch Cockrow Tarquogan of Glenbervie sired nine champions, Cockrow Partridge of Crawshaw sired four champions and his son Ch Akeferry Jimmy sired ten champions. Ch Belinda of Hardnott was an influential brood bitch out of Partridge. Cockrow Grouse went to America, gained his title there and also became an influential sire. Other famous Cockrows were Ch Cockrow Pheasant and Cockrow Merle. Merle was the dam of Ch Baydale Cinnamon who, in turn, was the sire of five champions. I have tried to incorporate Cockrow breeding into my own lines wherever possible. Such invaluable breeding by these ladies should be held in high regard.

Iniskelltr

Miss G Usher started out in the breed in the 1950s and her first champion, jointly owned with Mrs L M Daly, was Ch Iniskelltr Lovely Silver. Ch Marlin's Dusty Miller of Iniskelltr sired Mr and Mrs B Kennett's Ch Selinko Another Lady, who was Breed Record Holder in her time with a total of 25 CCs. Miss Usher is still active in the breed and her latest champion is Ch Iniskelltr Make Believe.

Deepridge

Miss Hawthorn had five Deepridge champions, the most famous being the wonderful Ch Deepridge Mintmaster. Not only was he very successful in the ring but he was also an important sire. Another two were Ch Deepridge Minstrel and his lovely sister Ch Deepridge Miniva.

Juneric

Mrs J Minns has been around in the breed since the 1950s. Her first champion was Ch Gypsy Moth of Glenbervie, her second was Ch Nimrodel Wanderer who won twenty two CCs. Her affix Juneric was owned by her late husband. The recent top winner Ch Millwold Gold Dust to Exhurst is owned jointly by Mrs Minns and Mr F Willey.

Peppard

Mr and Mrs Golland had an impressive seven champions. The first was Ch Peppard Pied Piper in the 1950s and the last was was Ch Peppard Royal Victory in the early 1970s.

Allgarth

The Allgarth kennels, owned by Mr and Mrs F Moore, was started in the late 1950s. They made up eight champions, the first being in 1973. In this litter was Ch Allgarth Envoy and

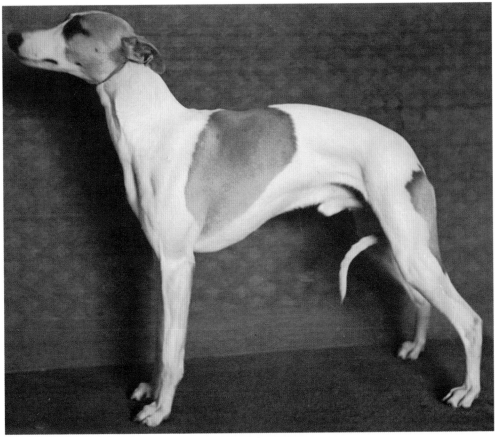

Ch Allgarth Envoy.

Mr F Nicholas' Ch Allgarth Eidelweiss. Envoy was exported to Australia where he made a great impact. Their bitch Ch Deborah of Allgarth was a Hound Group winner. Another litter produced two more champions, the brother and sister Ch Capo Di Monte and Ch Queen of May at Marash. The Allgarth kennel disbanded with Frank's death in 1990.

Harque

Mrs Anne Argyle (Harque) came into force around this time breeding eleven champions, one of which was the lovely Ch Harque the Lark. She was

Ch Harque The Lark.

Ch Selinko Another Lady.

Photo: Whimpanny

awarded nineteen CCs and was Breed Record Holder of her time. She also took BIS at an All Breeds Championship show. Anne was highly respected throughout the show world for her integrity and knowledge and she was a great ambassador for the breed. She was an International Judge of all breeds and at all levels. When Anne had the honour of judging the Best in Show award at Crufts 1992, she awarded Ch Pencloe Dutch Gold the coveted title. I was deeply honoured when Anne chose to use my own Hillsdown Fergal at stud. The mating produced Fergal's first champion, Ch Harque To Milo and, sadly, Anne's last. At the time of her death in early 1994 she had been successfully active in the breed for around 30 years.

Shalfleet

The Shalfleet kennels started in the early fifties and had a highly impressive 30 plus years in the breed. Remarkably, Shalfleet was not only famous for huge success in Whippets but was also equally successful in Greyhounds. These kennels also produced champion Dachshunds and Irish Wolfhounds. Such all-around success must have made Shalfleet the top Hound kennels of this period in Britain. The Shalfleet Whippets were started from

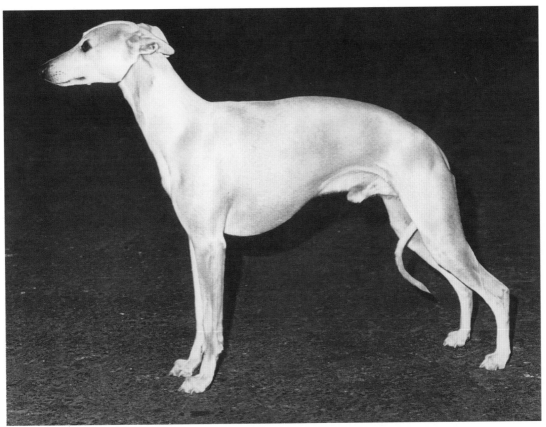

Ch Shalfleet Still So Sharp At Faracre.

Photo: Thomas

Wingedfoot and Allways breeding. One of the top Shalfleets was Ch Sequence of Shalfleet who gained fifteen CCs. When the kennels were disbanded, the Whippet lines were carried forward by Mrs K Thomas (Faracre) with such dogs as Ch Marshall's Milord at Faracre bred by Mrs P Sebley and Ch Shalfleet Still So Sharp at Faracre. Mrs Wilton-Clarke imported two Whippets, the only kennel to do so, and campaigned them to their titles in Britain. Firstly, Samoems Silent Knight of Shalfleet (from Tim Teiller of Holland) and, secondly, Am Can Ch Lorricbrook Runaway at Shalfleet bred by Max Madger of Canada.

Walkabout

Walkabout Whippets are owned by Mrs S A Thompson who has bred or owned five champions. Her first one was Ch Walkabout Waggoners Walk, who was mostly Wingedfoot and Shalfleet breeding. The latest Walkabout champion is Walkabout Woodpecker of Rivedo owned by Mrs J Kennard. Woodpecker is from Nimrodel and Shalfleet lines. Mrs Thompson owned the champion bitch Barmoll Beeswing at Walkabout who went BOB at Crufts in 1993. She was handled by Mrs J Minns.

Barmoll

Mrs McConkey started the Barmoll breeding on mostly Spean and Shalfleet lines and then introduced Walkabout lines. She has bred six champions plus other CC and Res CC winners. At Crufts in 1993 Barmoll had the distinction of winning both dog and bitch CCs, Mrs M Rigby's Ch Barmoll Blackthorn taking the dog and Mrs S Thompson's Ch Barmoll Beeswing at Walkabout taking the bitch honours and BOB.

Ch Barmoll Beeswing at Walkabout.

Flarepath

The Flarepaths are owned by Mr and Mrs (Irene) Woods. There have been eight champions connected to the Flarepath affix and they have been associated with some very well known dogs such as Ch Laguna Ravensdowne Astri, Ch Ravensdowne Bright Star, Ch Flarepath Tambillo Tarquin and Ch Towercrest Flarepath Taurus. The last three mentioned were very important sires. After a time away from the ring they are now back and their latest success is Ch Flarepath Eridon.

Glenbervie

The Glenbervie Whippets were started by Mr A B Nicholson who bred no less than sixteen champions built on the foundations of Cockrow and Hillgarth breeding. Ch Cockrow Tarquogan of Glenbervie proved to be a prolific sire by producing nine champions before his untimely death at the young age of 6. These results came from a comparatively small number of matings and so it can only be wondered what he could have achieved. His progeny has proved to be successful generation after generation. Another outstanding Glenbervie was Ch Gypsy Picture of Glenbervie (owned and shown by Mr R Pye) who won Best of Breed for two consecutive years at Crufts. Another famous Glenbervie son was Int Ch Denorsi Moonduster of Glenbervie. Moonduster was the last Whippet to gain his title while still a puppy. Kennel Club rules have since been changed and in order to be a champion at least one CC has to be awarded over the age of 12 months. He was exported to South Africa and there proved to be a most influential sire. Although Mr Nicholson had fawns and brindles, his kennels most generally produced parti-colours. One thing they all had in common was the Glenbervie stamp and only clever breeding, such as Mr Nicholson managed, could achieve this.

Ch Cockrow Tarquogan of Glenbervie handled by owner A B Nicholson.

Denorsi

It was from the Denorsi kennels, owned by the colourful character Jack Peden, that I bought my foundation stock. There were six Denorsi champions, three were bred by Mr Nicholson and three by Mr Peden. All the Denorsis were Glenbervie bred but the last two champions were sired by a Dondelayo dog. Ch Denorsi Rioch had a Denorsi sire and dam. The two sisters Ch Denorsi Dixie Belle and Ch Denorsi Dancing Belle were by Dondelayo Rufus of Oldwell out of Denorsi Tinkerbelle of Glenbervie.

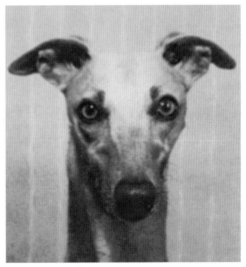

Head study of Ch Samarkand's Greenbrae Tarragon (see page 95).

Ch Dyanne Dondelayo (the author's CC winner and BIS on his first judging appointment). Photo: Pearce

Samarkand and Dondelayo

Although these two kennels of Mr R M James and Mrs A Knight respectively were never joined, it would be hard to speak about the success of one without including the other. Bobby James progressed to being one of the world's most popular judges, judging Best in Show at Crufts before his death. He bred or owned five champions and the one that he is most identified with is Ch Samarkand's Greenbrae Tarragon, Dog CC Record Holder of his time with seventeen CCs. Tarragon was also twice runner-up in the Hound Group at Crufts. Tarragon proved to be a most influential sire through his sons, daughters, grandsons and granddaughters.

Mrs Knight was a clever breeder who managed to achieve an unmistakable kennel type. Her type had a certain quality and style and she bred thirteen champions. In the litter from Ch Cockrow Tarquogan of Glenbervie and Ch Dondelayo Rue was Ch Dondelayo Buckaroo, who became Top Sire of his time and produced ten champions. One litter sister was Ch Dondelayo Ruanne of Charmoll who was the dam of three champions and the other litter sister was Ch Dondelayo Roulette who took the crown of Breed Record Holder from Ch Harque The Lark, having been awarded

Whippet Championship Show 1967.
L to r: Watson's Ch Towercrest Flarepath Taurus, Odell's Ch Shalfleet Starstruck (Bitch CC and BOB), Bucklow's Ch Danegeld Pipers Tune (Dog CC).

Int Ch Silkstone Finesse.
Photo: Pearce

twenty CCs. I remember the tussle that these two lovely champions had in those days. Roulette was mated to Tarragon and produced Ch Dondelayo Duette, who looked wonderful in the big ring at Crufts and was placed Reserve Best in Show.

Due to Bobby James' hectic international judging commitments he placed Tarragon with Anne Knight who used him on her bitches very wisely and it was from here the two kennels seemed to merge.

Silkstone

Roma Wright-Smith's Silkstone kennel has always been small but not only is Roma an intelligent breeder, she also has a certain talent for spotting a good puppy in other breeders' litters. Her first champion was Oakbark Merchant Prince and her second was Beseeka Knight Errant of Silkstone, the latter winning the Hound Group at Crufts prior to being exported to Mr and Mrs Kartsounis in South Africa. In 1980 the Kartsounis took Best In Show with him at the World Show held in Italy. Her homebred bitch Silkstone Astelle also went out to South Africa. The last champion bred by Anne Knight, Firedance of Silkstone, was owned and shown by Roma and she has carried these lines forward in Ch Silkstone Finesse and Ch Silkstone Jewel In The Crown. Jewel In The Crown was Reserve in the Hound Group at Crufts and was exported to Frank and Lee Pieterse in Australia where she was the first Whippet to go Best In Show at the Sydney Royal in 1995. The latest champion to come from the Silkstone kennels is Mrs Amsel's Silkstone Kantara.

Courthill

Ch Dondelayo Duette's sister was Ch Courthill Dondelayo Tiara, who was the first of five champions that Roger Stock (Courthill) has owned to date. Roger has bred on a mixture of Dondelayo and Shalfleet lines. His last two champions, Courthill Crown of Gold and Courthill Classical Jazz of Dollygroves, were both sired by Ch Pencloe Dutch Gold.

Ch Courthill Crown of Gold.

Ch Oakbark Generation Girl.
Photo: Whimpanny

Ch Oakbark Mistic Meg.

Oakbark

The Oakbarks have been going from strength to strength from the 1960s right up to the present time. They began with Mr and Mrs D Meakin and have now been joined by their daughter Julie Greenwood Meakin. The first champion for the Meakins was Oakbark Dondelayo Storming, bred by Mr W Knight. Since that time this kennel has consistently produced winners, Oakbark being the top producing kennel in the breed with an amazing twenty two British champions. They have successfully introduced slightly different lines into their breeding programme which demonstrates a complete understanding of their pedigrees and dogs. This is a rare talent which few breeders achieve in any breed. Their record is testimony of the dedication to the breed held by the Meakin family; one can only admire the regularity with which champions have been produced and also note the success of other kennels founded on or mixed with Oakbark lines both in Britain and abroad. From just two matings of Oakbark bitches with my own Fergal came three champion dogs: Ch Oakbark Master Cobbler, Ch Cobbyco Cavalier and Ch Cobbyco Candyman.

The Meakins acknowledge that they owe so much to having good brood bitches such as Ch Oakbark Generation Girl and they have great hopes that their two young girls Ch Oakbark Mistic Meg and Ch Oakbak Mariel will continue to carry the Oakbarks forward.

Ch Oakbark Mariel
(Ch Oakbark Master Cobbler x Ch Savilepark Saucy Shrimp of Oakbark).

Ch Lowglen Newbold Cavalier
aged 20 months. Photo: Pearce

Lowglen

Lowglen Whippets were owned by Mr Fred Nicholas who had a host of champions, ten in all. Probably the most famous one was Ch Lowglen Newbould Cavalier, who was not only a big winner but also a top sire. The Lowglens were also responsible for exporting the CC winning Lowglen Oakbark Mastermind to Australia who went on to prove himself to be a prolific sire. This kennel's success lasted almost twenty years from the 1960s through to the '80s. The last champion was Lowglen Magic Moments.

Ch Nevedith Justa Jesta (Ch Pencloe Dutch Gold x Ch Nutshell of Nevedith).

Newbould

Mr and Mrs D Howarth had five champions connected with the Newbould kennel including one of the top stud dogs ever, Ch Lowglen Newbould Cavalier. He was the sire of ten English champions. Ch Newbould Muffin Man, by Oakbark Pyramid out of Ch Oakbark Michaela and owned by Mrs H Bradley (Killigrew), also went on to sire champions.

Nevedith

The Nevediths are registered under the name of Miss E Newton but are generally handled by her father Nev Newton. This top kennel has regularly produced champions since the arrival of Ch Akeferry Jimmy on the show scene in the early '70s. Ch Nutshell of Nevedith, bred by Mr and Mrs Barker (Chilka), is the all-time top winner in the breed with an incredible forty four CCs to her credit (thirty seven with BOB awards). This record will surely be intact for some time to come if, indeed, it will ever be beaten in such a strong

Ch Nevedith Justa Jenie, litter sister to Ch Nevedith Justa Jesta.

Ch Peperone Pepper (Ch Charmoll Mactavish x Ch Peperone Plaything).
Photo: Dog World

breed as this. Her other achievements were Top Dog All Breeds in 1989 and then the following year she was runner-up for the same title. In 1990 Nutshell was Reserve BIS at Crufts. Not only was she a great success in the ring but she has also proven to be an excellent brood bitch, producing three British Champions and more overseas. The latest Nevedith champion is Nevedith Rare Rogue.

Peperone
This has been a very successful kennels having bred or owned eight champions. Mr and Mrs McCleod started the Peperone Whippets on Cockrow and Glenbervie lines; their first champion was Ch Peperone Plaything. Ch Peperone Paper Mate, owned by Mr Oliphant,

was a favourite of mine. She was a Ch Charmoll Mactavish daughter. Mr and Mrs McCleod have successfully introduced Hardknott and Oakbark into their lines to produce a string of champions and one such dog is Ch Hardknott Quadrille. Quadrille sired Int Ch Play A While at Peperone who, after being exported to Scandinavia, has proven to be very successful both in the show ring and at stud. Their latest champion is Peperone Paper Model.

Savilepark

The Savilepark kennels owned by Mrs B Robinson has produced six champions. The first of these were litter sisters Savilepark Sweet Harmony and Savilepark Summer Season. The latter was owned by the then Mrs P Nicholas (later Mrs Gilmour) and Mrs F Broadbent. Summer Season took BIS All Breeds handled, on that occasion, by Roger Stock. The latest champion for Mrs Robinson is Savilepark Snowdrift.

Ch Savilepark Snowdrift.

Ch Welstar Royal Mint. Photo: Whimpanny

Welstar

Mrs Linda Jones started her Welstar kennel with a Ch Deepridge Mintmaster x Oakbark Mirielle daughter, Rasaday Amber. Amber is the foundation bitch of seven champions for the kennel, the most famous being Ch Welstar Royal Mint who was Breed Record Holder in the '80s having gained nineteen CCs. Royal Mint was owned and shown by Mrs G Hemstock. The latest star for Linda is Ch Welstar Red Robin.

Baldrey

The Baldrey kennels are owned by Mr and Mrs J White. Their first champion was bought unseen from Mrs Hemstock. She was Ch Broughland Gina of Baldrey, who was sired by Ch Welstar Mint (owned by Mrs Hemstock) and out of Broughland Genevieve. All Baldreys go back to Gina. When mated to Nimrodel Dragoon, Gina produced Ch Baldrey Rainbow's End. In total to date there have been six Baldrey champions, the latest one being Ch Baldrey Christian Dior.

Ch Baldrey My Fair Lady.
Photo: White

Ch Birkonbrae Everlasting Love, owned by Mr D Gilmour (Dumbriton).
Photo: Halifax

Dumbriton

Dumbriton is the kennel of Mr and Mrs Gilmour who also enjoy success in Staffordshire Bull Terriers. The Whippets are usually handled by Patsy who was previously connected with the successful Lowglen kennel. The first Whippet champion for the Gilmours that carried the Dumbriton affix was Dumbriton Wild About Harry who was exported to South Africa. They own and campaigned to their titles the two lovely litter sisters Ch Birkonbrae Forever Love and Ch Birkonbrae Everlasting Love. Everlasting Love won BOB at Crufts in 1995. Their latest champion is Fawnbree Special Brew at Dumbriton.

Other Influential Kennels

The late Mrs Bennet's Hardknott kennel produced four champions, one of which was the beautiful red brindle and white Belinda of Hardknott. When Belinda was mated to Ch Novacroft Madrigal she produced Ch Hardknott Mystery and Am Ch Hardknott Maestro of Bohem. Maestro has sired many champions in America and around the world. The last Hardknott champion was Hardknott Quadrille, owned by Mr and Mrs J McCleod.

The late Mr Charlie Dempster had the small but important kennel of Charmoll, breeding three champion dogs out of two matings from Ch Dondelayo Ruanne of Charmoll to Ch Baydale Cinnamon. In the first litter was Ch Charmoll Clansman who was exported to America, gained his title there and also proved to be a sire of some importance. The repeat mating produced Ch Charmoll Bonnie Prince and Ch Charmoll Mactavish, the latter being Top Stud Dog in Britain at one time.

Ch Tilegreen Tornado, the current Dog CC Record Holder.

The Carmodian Whippets of the late Mr and Mrs G Carmichael also contributed to the modern history of the show ring. They either owned or bred four champions including Ch Carmodian Tawny Knight of Hutaka who was the sire of Ch Tilegreen Tornado, the current Breed Record Holder in dogs. Carmodian breeding is behind Mr R Burton's successful Dunaruna kennel.

Mr and Mrs Marshall were the owners of Ch Jubilant Lady of Tygreen who had an impressive record of twelve CCs, two BIS All Breeds and also won the Hound Group at Crufts in 1979.

Mrs Pip Campbell with her Mithrandir Whippets is constantly successful in the show ring. Ch Mithrandir Panning For Gold had an excellent show career and was a BIS All Breeds winner too.

Mrs P Brown (Curlands) has four champions and Mrs M Rigby, (Poachyn, formerly Poaching), has had three champions. Both these lines have been influential in the pedigrees of some of today's successful Whippets.

The Barnesmore kennel of sisters Margaret Martin and Lucinda Thompson have made up three dual (British and Irish) champions and many Irish Champions. One must admire their spirit for the time spent in travelling across the sea before even getting on to dry land. They then have to drive the length and breadth of the country to campaign their dogs!

Ch Chyton Copy Press.

Ch Ringmore Thief of Time.

Ch Martinsell Wild and Lonely.
Photo: Whimpanny

Over the last two decades great strides have been made with blacks and blues regularly taking CCs. Mesdames Russell and Brown own the black Ch Martinsell Grand Slam and the only blue to become a champion Martinsell Wild and Lonely, who in turn sired the blue and white parti-colour Ch Ringmore Thief of Time, owned by Mrs A Skelley and Miss V Skelley. It is very rare for a show champion to win an Open Coursing Stake but Mrs S Rawlings' Ch Chyton Copy Press and Miss S Baird's Ch Sound Barrier have both achieved this distinction.

No article concerning Whippets in the modern show ring could finish without failing to include the following:

Ch Tilegreen Tornado:	26 CCs and Dog CC Record Holder.
Ch Nutshell of Nevedith:	The Breed Record Holder with 44 CCs.
Ch Pencloe Dutch Gold:	The history making BIS Crufts winner.

The top Whippet sires of the modern show ring:

Ch Laguna Ligonier:	11 champions
Ch Wingedfoot Marksman of Always:	10 champions
Ch Dondelayo Buckaroo:	10 champions
Ch Akeferry Jimmy:	10 champions
Ch Pilot Officer Prune:	9 champions
Ch Cockrow Tarquogan of Glenbervie:	9 champions
Ch Lowglen Newbould Cavalier:	9 champions
Ch Pencloe Dutch Gold:	9 champions
Hillsdown Fergal:	8 champions
Ch Bellavista Barry:	7 champions
Ch Charmoll Mactavish:	7 champions

Ch Nutshell of Nevedith, the current Breed Record Holder.

Ch Pencloe Dutch Gold
Best In Show Crufts 1992 with judge Anne Argyle.

Chapter Eight

Nimrodel

by Mrs I H (Mary) Lowe

My kennel started in 1962 with the purchase, from Mrs Bobby Cooke, of Willow of Allways. Willow was bought as a pet but it was my great good fortune to acquire a bitch puppy by Ch Fieldspring Bartsia of Allways. Although Bartsia sired champions, his great influence on the breed was through his winner-producing daughters and Willow was no exception. Willow herself was a lovely, scopey bitch, quite tall for the time, and a very elegant red fawn. When Mrs Wigg (Ladiesfield) saw her at about two years old, she offered to buy her. Of course I did not contemplate selling my precious companion who slept in my bed and it was not until much later that I came to realise what a compliment Mrs Wigg had paid me through her instant recognition of the quality bitch I had acquired as a pet. Willow produced three champions for me. From her litter by Ch Robmaywin Stargazer of Allways, Dorothy Lewis sent Red Gleam of Test to California where, despite being solid fawn, he gained his title.

The second Whippet I bought, Bilberry of Always, was a blue dog, again from Bobby Cooke. Classically bred - by Black Brocade of Allways (by Playmate) out of a daughter of Ch Evening Star of Allways - Bilberry proved to be a suitable mate for Willow, the mating producing Mal. Ch Nimrodel Stormy Petrel. For her last litter I decided to take Willow to a dog from Cornwall. This stud dog was little known at the time but had sired a bitch I fell totally in love with, Dragonhill Tawny Owl. I saw Tawny Owl at the Hound Association Championship Show where she went Best Puppy in Show. She was everything I thought I wanted in a Whippet, having the most gorgeous red gold coat, a skin like satin, and beautiful flowing lines. I asked Mrs Cleeve if she would sell her to me and she gave me a piece of advice which was perhaps the most important turning point in my career as a breeder. She told me that she would sell her to me but, she said, "You won't do as well with her as I would, and it would do you more good and give you more satisfaction if you bred your own. You have a really good bitch in Willow. Why don't you use Tawny Owl's sire, Poltesco Peewit, and see what you get?".

That advice resulted in a long trip to Cornwall to use Peewit, who had not yet gained his title, and was, of course, unrecognised as the really great sire he would become. That mating produced my first Champion, Nimrodel Willow Daughter and her litter brother, Windhover. Willow Daughter produced NZ Ch Nimrodel Wild Duck and (by Bilberry) the

Ch Fieldspring Bartsia of Allways	Fleeting Hillgarth Sovereign	Flight Lieutenant	Watford Sapper Oficer
			Take Me
		Sapperley Christobel	Tiptree Progress
			Sapperley Queen
	Brekin Willow Pattern	Sapperley Tiptree Pilot	Tiptree Progress
			Tiptree Stella
		Ch Brekin Spode	Sporting Chance
			Ch White Statue of Connevan
Ravensdowne Penelope	Conneil Stately Fox of Knotknum	Ch Allways Wingedfoot Running Fox	Ch Wingedfoot Marksman of Allways
			Perpetual Motion
		Ch Wingedfoot To Whit To Whoo	Ch Wingedfoot Marksman of Allways
			Ch A For Adorable
	Samarkand's Sea Nymph	Samarkand's Victor of Thistlecroft	Laguna Luke of Allways
			Fantasia of Allways
		Sparkling Cascade	Ch Cliftongate Flak
			Shining Dawn of Allways

Pedigree of Willow of Allways.

Ch Poltesco Peewit.

Ch Nimrodel Willow Daughter.

Photo: Cooke

Res CC winning blue bitch Belladonna through whom all my colour lines down to Ch Noir descend. Windhover was to prove, however, even more influential if anything. He sired a litter to Tweseldown Glentopic (by Ch Peppard Topflight) which produced the following litter sisters: Miss Baird's Woodlark, Lady Anderson's Ch Tweseldown Whinchat and my own Withywindle, from whom forty United Kingdom champions descend with others abroad and numbers still rising.

In the meantime I had purchased a charming little gold bitch, Nimrodel Sweet Amber. She was by a very well bred and successful coursing dog, Apbrenin Piquet, out of a top coursing bitch carrying old Sapperley and Seagift lines. My passion for the Dragonhills led me to mate her to Ch Dragonhill Woodpecker, and their daughter was to become (by Peewit) the dam of Ch

Poltesco Phoenix	Tweseldown Merdeka	Dragonhill Socklet	Seagift Salix
			Dragonhill Wisp of Smoke
		Miss Chief	Ch Old Mortality
			Minuet of Allways
	Poltesco Peri	Seagift Sportsmaster	Ch Seagift Speedlite Mustang
			Ch Seagift Joystock Shana
		Nicola of Trehan	Flyalong Pilot
			Tina of Trehan
Poltesco Clemwade Merry Maid	Ch Bellavista Barry	Ch Pilot Offiecr Prune	Happy Landings
			Silver Nymph
		Brekin Bright Spark	Ch Balaise Barrie
			Ch Brekin Spode
	Poltesco Fantasia	Ch Evening Star of Allways	Ch Wingedfoot Marksman of A.
			Ch Fieldspring Betony
		Fancy of Allways	Ch Bellavista Barry
			Laguna Linnet

Pedigree of Ch Poltesco Peewit.

Nimrodel Ruff. Two factors played a part in leading me in the direction I was to go. Firstly, Mrs Cooke gave up her kennel at the time that I acquired Bilberry, thereby depriving me of the options a larger kennel might have offered me. Secondly, through attending some shows, the learning process began whereby I started to appreciate the type and bloodlines which most appealed to me. The Dragonhill, Poltesco, and Tweseldown Whippets all had the qualities I wanted in my own lines and, although my original lines were Allways,

Ch Nimrodel Ruff.

Photo: Pearce

both Bilberry and Amber carried Dragonhill behind them and Willow was of the same type. Dragonhill, Poltesco and Tweseldown lines were predominantly Seagift in origin; their combinations and permutations were already working successfully for their breeders

			Ch Evening Star of Allways
		Ch Robmaywin Stargazer of Allways	
	Int Ch Playmate of Allways		Ch Minstrals Mrs Miniver
			Ch Fieldspring Bartsia of Allways
		Gayflete Watcherbart of Allways	
Apbrenin Piquet			Carol of Allways
			Ch Sapperley Kinsman
		Ch Wingedfoot Marksman of Allways	
	Brekin Terra Cotta		Bolney Starshine of Allways
			Fleeting Hillgarth Sovereign
		Brekin Fiesta of Fleeting	
			Ch Brekin Spode
			Seagift Sunburst
		Linburnt Spinner	
	Quicksilver		Sapperley Lindy Loo
			Zoalon Brumah
		Zoalon Robeo	
Langford Puppet			Zoalon Ladybird
			Ch Wingedfoot Wild Goose
		Wingedfoot Swallow Swift	
	Tiptoes Linden Lea		Speedlite Prunella
			Blue Slate
		Leading Lady of Lawford	
			Hardings Bluie

Pedigree of Nimrodel Sweet Amber.

and therefore I was able to build on and to benefit from, some very sound, typical and predictable bloodlines which had already proved their worth for established breeders far more experienced than myself.

It is hard to say whether one has a master plan as such, but I think most serious breeders would admit to having an ideal which they are always hoping to produce. I am not talking about breeding the 'big winner' because I do not think, for a breeder, that is the paramount consideration. Fashions come and go, and big winners depend on a number of factors other than their breeder's dreams of excellence. Many big winners have in fact proved themselves incapable of perpetuating themselves. I think that every true breeder hopes to achieve a kennel 'type' which satisfies their own criteria and then, as icing on the cake, one hopes for general recognition. There will always be times, in the long life of a breeder, when current top winners do not conform to one's own pattern; not that one's own stock is necessarily superior, but simply that what one is striving for in one's own kennel is not represented in the ring, regardless of the degree of excellence they may display from the ring-side.

In my early days I was extremely interested in coursing my Whippets, so their ability to work was at least as important to me in their success in the show ring. Working Whippets teaches one very quickly what requirements a dog must have to be successful in the field. As all my dogs have always lived in the house, thus restricting numbers, I could never afford to have some for coursing and others for showing. All have to be capable of doing both. One of the unbending rules of the Whippet Coursing Club is that dogs must not exceed 20" at the shoulder so that in itself was a certain limitation. Although I have never won a major stake I have had a great deal of fun and quite a lot of success running my dogs. As with the show stock, I am proud to have bred three Breeze of Ladiesfield winners for others (Ent Wife, Bezique and Djakarta) plus Nimrodel Pegasus. The latter is litter brother to Ch Nimrodel Peerless and was Top Winner with the East Anglian WCC. Both the top coursing Bench Champions, Sound Barrier and Copy Press, carry lines to Windhover and Ruff respectively. It is perfectly possible for the top show lines to produce top coursing stock, as Mrs McKay's Lagunas have so conclusively demonstrated, but it is difficult to achieve the very top with the same dog at the same time.

Another criterion on which I have based my breeding programme is temperament. I quickly decided that the majority of my puppies would find good homes as pets, and nobody wants nervous or neurotic pets. This in turn limits choice to a certain degree as there have been one or two dogs over the years that I would have loved to have used but dared not. Another criterion is 'type'. Whilst I have never in-bred, I have always line-bred with careful out-crosses every so often. Where to go for fresh bloodlines, without losing what one has established, whilst gaining the extra virtues one needs, is a delicate choice. Some out-crosses I have done have been a great success, others a dismal failure. When you get a failure it is no good blaming the direction in which you have gone - it takes two to tango and some lines just don't click. When you get a click, it is instantly recognisable and you can do endless permutations for several generations until the horrid moment comes when you have to take another plunge into uncharted waters.

I do consider that bitches are the strength of a kennel and a good dam line is worth its weight in gold. I have always been prepared to skip a generation (or more), in terms of winning, in order not to lose a line. Wanderer's dam, for instance, was never shown owing to a greenstick fracture as a puppy. However she won a couple of coursing stakes and produced Wanderer (a Breed Record Holder) and his sister Windleberry, happily still with me and through whom most of my current stock descend.

Ch Withaway Nimrodel. Photo: Whimpanny

One of the problems of the lines I chose to develop is that they are basically different from most of the top winning show lines over the last twenty years. Whilst Mrs Cleeve and Margaret Ironside were alive, a core of us shared the same type and the same bloodlines. Some other kennels came in with success and between us we had some very rewarding years. But times change and, as older breeders die or cease to be active, and others move in a different direction, one's options become more limited unless one can bring in fresh bloodlines whilst maintaining type. Basically I have had two foundation bitches, Willow and Amber. I then acquired Withywindle (by Windhover) thus adding the Tweseldown bitch line plus another line to Topaz through her grandsire, Ch Peppard Topflight. Later I bought in three bitches by Ruff: Ch Wipstych Grandiflora, Ch Ringmore Riff Raff, and Ch Withaway Nimrodel (Ballagan bitch lines). These good bitch lines from other kennels have enormously enriched my breeding and bred on for me.

The important matings which have built up my lines started with Ch Poltesco Peewit. Peewit was sired by Poltesco Phoenix who was by Tweseldown Merdeka. Merdeka was by Dragonhill Socklet, the foundation sire behind all Dragonhill, Poltesco, Tweseldown, and Ringmore breeding. Merdeka was full brother to Ch Dragonhill Tweseldown Minstrel and Tweseldown Mimosa, dam of Ch Bliks Ringmore Bardolph, a beautiful dog and a big winner in his day. Phoenix sired two champions, Peewit and his very lovely sister Ch Greenbrae Poltesco Duskie Maid. It is perhaps interesting that Peewit himself was the result of a grand-father/grand-daughter mating to Ch Bellavista Barry, the sire of Ch Laguna Ligonier who was to have such an enormous impact on Whippets world wide. Peewit, whilst not without fault, proved an enormously influential sire, particularly in so much as it has been possible to line-breed heavily to him over many generations without coming to grief. His two great gifts to his descendants have been his temperament and his

Ch Wipstych Grandiflora.
Photo: Whimpanny

movement. He sired four champions: Ch Poltesco Periquita (BOB at Crufts), Ch Dragonhill Tawny Owl, Ch Nimrodel Willow Daughter and, finally, Ch Nimrodel Ruff. Ironically, perhaps, on Mrs Cleeve's death I inherited Ch Tawny Owl - whom I had coveted as a puppy, and Ch Dragonhill Woodpecker - both ended long lives in my possession. Ruff sired six champions including Ch Woolsocks Summer Blaze, sire of Ch Nimrodel Noir, who in turn sired Ch Nimrodel Zenith, my latest champion. This has been a very dominant male line. Ruff also sired Nimrodel Dragoon who although not a champion (he won 3 Res CCs) sired Ch Nimrodel Wanderer and Ch Baldrey's Rainbow's End plus other CC winners. Wanderer in turn sired three champions: Ch Baldrey Limited Edition of Juneric (dam of Ch Juneric Little Madam), Ch Spyanfly Say No More (sire of Ch Bluestreak Beauty of Bath) and Ch Nimrodel Eagle Wings (sire of Ch Walkabout Woodpecker of Rivedo).

At one point in our breeding plan, Margaret Ironside and I decided that there were two dogs we particularly wished to introduce into our bloodlines. These were Ch Danegeld Piper's Tune and Ch Sticklepath Saracen, both fawns of classic type, but carrying very different lines. Piper's Tune was by Ch Peppard Topflight, thus adding another line to Topaz out of Danegeld Andromeda, carrying a powerful bitch line through Ch Porthurst Atlanta. Saracen was by Ligonier out of a Ch Laguna Linkway daughter. For geographical reasons I used Piper's Tune for Ch Dragonhill Tawny Owl's last litter and Margaret used Saracen on Ruff's litter sister, Poltesco Nimrodel Redwing. Tawny Owl did not have a good litter and there was only one bitch, who was rather small and nondescript. I gave her away locally on breeding terms and in due course she came back and was mated to Ruff by whom she had an excellent litter which included Nimrodel Dragoon. Dragoon was a super little show dog right from the beginning and I was offered a good price to send him to Sweden as a puppy but as Piper's Tune died shortly after the mating I felt I could not let the bloodlines go out of the country. In fact the only reason I did let him go was that he was too close to Wiveton in age and it was impossible to campaign them both so he went to June Minns where he had a long and happy life and was Top Sire one year, as Ruff had twice been before him. Dragoon did particularly well on bitches by Royal Mint and through Wanderer, Windleberry and the bitches Jackie White mated to him, he had quite a lot of influence. Redwing produced Poltesco Sea Breeze by Saracen and he in turn was the sire of Ch Poltesco High Seas, a stunningly beautiful dog who sired Ch Nimrodel Peerless. Peerless tragically died quite young but her daughter Nightingale (by Noir) produced Ch No Angel, Nushka and Nuage who won a Res CC.

The next important move for my breeding was to take a Ruff daughter, Nimrodel Wissendine, to Bartonia of Brough, a dog who had scarcely been shown but who had put up some very fast times on the track. He was a beautiful typey dog of great quality and I was interested in him as he was by Miss Usher's Ch Iniskelltr Lovely Silver, a dog I much

Ch Nimrodel Wiveton.
Photo: Whimpanny

Ch Iniskelltr Lovely Silver	Ch Fieldspring Bartsia of Allways	Fleeting Hillgarth Sovereign	Flight Lieutenant
			Sapperley Christobel
		Brekin Willow Pattern	Sapperley Tiptree Pilot
			Ch Brekin Spode
	Moonlight of Allways	Ch Wingedfoot Marksman of Allways	Ch Sapperley Kinsman
			Bolney Starshine of Allways
		Wild Night of Allways	Laguna Luke of Allways
			Bolney Spring Sylvette of Allways
Mistrey of Test	Ch Mar's of Test	Ch Evening Star of Allways	Ch Wingedfoot Marksman of Allways
			Ch Fieldspring Betony
		Wingedfoot Miss Madcap	Ch Wingedfoot Marksman of Allways
			Wingedfoot Lannette
	Test Dream of Allways	Int Ch Playmate of Allways	Ch Robmaywin Stargazer of Allways
			Gayflete Watcherbart of Allways
		Broken Dreams	Ch Fieldspring Bartsia of Allways
			Brekin Bittersweet

Pedigree of Bartonia of Brough.

regretted not having used as he was by Ch Bartsia. This mating was an instant 'click', producing a gorgeous even litter which included my Ch Nimrodel Wiveton and his litter sister Wissie, the grand-dam of Ch Wanderer. Had Bartonia not died young I would have mated all Ruff's daughters to him. Failing that possibility, when Dr Edward Jones brought his lovely Ch Wipstych Courbette (by Bartonia) to Ruff, I bought in a bitch puppy who was to become Ch Wipstych Grandiflora. A Bartonia daughter to Ruff was just as successful as the other way around and for several generations various permutations of this 'click' produced numerous champions. The most famous of these was Ch Welstar Royal Mint who was bred by Linda Jones, owned and campaigned by Gwen Hempstock. Grandiflora produced two champions, Rare Magic and my own Peerless. Another daughter produced Ch Nimrodel Eagle Wings. Mint sired three champion bitches: Brough Lady Devine, Broughland Gina of Baldrey (who is behind all the consistent winners for Michael and Jackie White and June Minns's successful line from Baldrey Limited Edition) and Rare Magic, as well as Nimrodel Wanton, dam of Ch Wanderer. Wanderer is the sire of Ch Spyanfly Say No More who, in turn, sired the 1997 Crufts BOB Ch Bluestreak Beauty of Bath. So these lines are still producing winners in the ring today.

Windleberry, Wanderer's litter sister (who shared the East of England Open Bitch Stake and was runner-up in the Laguna Cup) is the dam of Ch Nimrodel Wild and Free by Ch Martinsell Wild and Lonely (a Wiveton grandson). When mated to Ch Acomb's Tostig (a successful outcross used for his lovely type and double lines to Ch Oakbark Michaela), she produced Nimrodel Warning, sire of two Irish champions, War Dance and Dream Queen. The latter is the dam of Ch Zenith and his Res CC winning sister Heaven Sent.

Of recent years it must seem that I have concentrated on colour breeding but, whilst these beautiful blacks have been very successful in the show ring, their colour is purely coincidence. I have always had a colour line going back to Bilberry of Allways so throughout the years there has always been a black or blue lying amongst the pile of fawns in front of the Aga. Whilst wishing not

Ch Nimrodel Wanderer.

Photo: Whimpanny

Nimrodel Dragoon	Ch Nimrodel Ruff	Ch Poltesco Peewit	Poltesco Phoenix
			Poltesco Clemwade Merry Maid
		Nimrodel Wintersweet	Ch Dragonhill Woodpecker
			Nimrodel Sweet Amber
	Nimrodel Dipper	Ch Danegeld Pipers Tune	Ch Peppard Topfight
			Danegeld Andromeda
		Ch Dragonhill Tawny Owl	Ch Poltesco Peewit
			Dragonhill Golden Plover
Nimrodel Wanton	Ch Welstar Royal Mint	Ch Nimrodel Wiveton	Bartonia of Brough
			Nimrodel Wissendine
		Ch Welstar Minted Model	Ch Skyeboat Silver Knight of Shalfleet
			Rasaday Amber
	Nimrodel Wissie	Bartonia of Brough	Ch Inskelltr Lovely Silver
			Mistrey of Test
		Nimrodel Wissendine	Ch Nimrodel Ruff
			Nimrodel Withywindle

Pedigree of Ch Nimrodel Wanderer.

to lose this line, and to retain the colour from generation to generation, the matings have been planned in exactly the same way as all my other matings, on the basis of type, pedigree, temperament and performance. To anyone interested in colour breeding, I would say never carry out black to black matings more than once. Every other generation should incorporate the best of non-colour breeding where it suits the pedigree. I had never intended to keep a black male but Ch Nimrodel Noir (see page 122), although initially sold as a puppy, was absolutely determined to spend the rest of his life with me. Despite being an indifferent show-man and a very late developer, he did eventually gain his title and he has been an invaluable sire, producing his especially charming temperament and very sound movement. Being by Ch Woolsocks Summer Blaze out of a Ch Poaching Black Jack daughter, and carrying my own bitch line back through six generations to Willow Daughter and Willow, his pedigree carries all my best lines, both show and coursing. He is the sire of Ch Nimrodel Zenith (see page 122) and also two Res CC blues, Jarmana Dusky Dreamer and Nimrodel Heaven Sent. Zenith, though miraculously black, actually has very little colour in his pedigree. Looking at his pedigree, it is a typically line-bred Ruff pedigree such as you might expect to produce a red fawn.

Ch Nimrodel Eagle Wings.

Ch Nimrodel Wild and Free.
Photo: Horn

At present, having carefully incorporated Ch Martinsell Wild and Lonely and Ch Acomb's Tostig, the lines are combining well and I have a number of options to use my own champion dogs such as Eagle Wings, Wild and Free and Zenith. However I am always conscious of the need to add excellence from elsewhere to strengthen the line and to avoid any abnormalities which might arise through too close a breeding programme. I have been endeavouring to bring in more Oakbark, a kennel whose long term consistency I greatly admire, and whose type I consider to be consistent with my own but current plans have met with some set-backs. Nonetheless that is the excitement of breeding - the future is just around the corner. I have also been able to keep close to the past as can be seen from the pedigrees.

I have always considered myself firstly a breeder and secondly, perhaps, a judge. Breeding is what fascinates me and judging is the most exciting thing a breeder can do. It

Ch Nimrodel Noir.
Photo: Walsh

Ch Nimrodel Zenith.

is only thirdly I consider myself an exhibitor. If you breed you must from time to time exhibit in order to be sure you are not operating in a vacuum. Producing puppies for my own pleasure and, I hope for that of others (by no means all exhibitors), is one of the most satisfying aspects of this curious activity of ours. The great divergence of type today in our Whippet rings, not only here but also in other parts of the world, must be very confusing to people coming into the breed or starting out on a judging career. It is hard to pinpoint why there should be such a divergence of opinion today as to what the breed should look like. Perhaps it is simply that we now have far more exhibitors than breeders and it is hard to find consistent breeding of any line when one is looking for an outcross. When I started off, the great kennels (Allways/Laguna/Shalfleet) were well-established and easily recognisable, yet not so diverse from each other that you could not form a typey line up in an Open class. Today it is much more difficult to find what you want as a judge or as a breeder looking for out-cross lines to incorporate. I feel one must try to appreciate the best of one's own - and of other people's - breeding whilst holding on to what one believes in, regardless of desire for success in the ring. The latter, after all, is ephemeral if it cannot be built upon.

Ch Nimrodel Noir	Ch Woolsocks Summer Blaze	Ch Nimrodel Ruff	Ch Poltesco Peewit
			Nimrodel Wintersweet
		Welstar Royal Amber	Ch Welstar Royal Mint
			Rasaday Amber
	Nimrodel Djarkata	Ch Poaching Black Jack	Ch Shalfleet Sailing Free
			Poaching Penny Black
		Nimrodel Blini	Ch Nimrodel Ruff
			Nimrodel Bezique
Ir Ch Nimrodel Dream Queen	Nimrodel Warning	Ch Acomb's Tostig	Tradewind Norseman
			Tradewind Mistletoe
		Nimrodel Windleberry	Nimrodel Dragoon
			Nimrodel Wanton
	Ch Withaway Nimrodel	Ch Nimrodel Ruff	Ch Poltesco Peewit
			Nimrodel Wintersweet
		Ballagan Wishful	Ch Nimrodel Wiveton
			Ballagan Graceful

Pedigree of Ch Nimrodel Zenith.

Chapter Nine

Hillsdown

Whilst I enjoy exhibiting, judging and just having Whippets around, to my mind the most challenging and satisfying facet is breeding. I am fascinated by type and how it is perpetuated by certain breeders. Whilst my own Hillsdowns are probably not instantly recognisable as a certain kennel type in the same way as the Dondelayos and Glenbervies, I do feel that I've achieved a consistency in 'type' of top winners in a range of colours. For me the colour of a Whippet is immaterial, I think the only colour I haven't had is probably a black. However, I can quite understand that someone may particularly prefer a certain colour or colours and if one breeds to produce that colour the results are more likely to produce a recognisable type. My main regret over the years is that I haven't taken enough photographs and the ones that I do have of the first twenty or so years are more or less just snaps, often not very good ones at that. I also regret not always registering the Hillsdown affix on every puppy. At the time it just never seemed important other than on the ones I intended to keep for myself but I'm sure this has probably caused a few headaches to anyone researching pedigrees. In my own defence I'm not alone in this as I have very often let choice bitches go to people on breeding terms and very often the puppies I've had back have been registered under the owner's affix. I've been very lucky in that most of the arrangements have been amicable, and agreeing on which sire to be used has never been a problem but always a happy joint decision.

I decided on Whippets many years ago because of their perfect temperament together with an elegant and yet powerful physical appearance. My first Whippet was bought purely as a pet. He was of Teighways breeding. At that time he was just what I wanted, a companion that could slip unnoticed into a big family and a very hectic household causing no great problems or, more important, opposition from my parents. I decided that I may like to try my hand at showing and bought a lovely blue bitch called Sapphire Solitaire. Her dam was Selbrook Breeze, who was already the dam of Ch Selbrook Bracelet. At that time a quality blue bitch in Sheffield was quite rare and to my horror she was stolen and disappeared without further trace. A couple of years later I bought her litter brother. He, too, was blue and won a few firsts at Championship Shows. My next Whippet was another blue bitch from racing stock, she was out of Ladiesfield Blackcurrant. I mated her to my blue dog; this produced a healthy litter and all went to pet or racing homes.

I had got the bug and began to take more interest in the top winners at shows. I started to study pedigrees and compare different kennels and the breeding behind the ones that had the qualities I most admired. It was also at this point that I came to realise you couldn't just mate two attractive Whippets and start a dynasty. I also realised that a true sign of good breeding is when generation after generation is consistent and this would take much careful planning and studying to achieve. Over the years there have been some successful champions in the show ring but they have never produced any quality stock. Research into their breeding will very often show that whilst there may be some quality Whippets in their lines, not enough thought has been put into the individual qualities and faults of the sire and dam.

I still had my little blue bitch, who had a heart like a lion but, unfortunately, no show potential whatsoever. I had bred my first litter and was thirsty for knowledge. As I studied the exhibits in the late '60s and early '70s one kennel to me was outstanding: the very successful Glenbervie

Denorsi Tinkermoon.

Whippets of Arthur B Nicholson. The Glenbervies successfully brought together the Hillgarth, Cockrow, Samarkand's and Laguna lines. I realised that these were the lines I wanted to go with and so bought my first two, mostly Glenbervie bred, show Whippets from Jack Peden. These were the mischievous Denorsi Tinkermoon and the more sedate, ladylike Denorsi Cream Top. They were both around twelve weeks old. A year later I got another bitch, of around the same age as these two, and her name was White Bud of Glenbervie. I consider these three bitches to be the starting point of the Hillsdown lines. Throughout this chapter I hope to explain the considerations and planning behind the litters I have bred over the years coming right up to present day. I think it makes it easier to follow one bitch through her different litters coming to the end result rather than follow the chronological order. It could become quite confusing to cross over from litter to litter.

Many years ago I read a piece written by Gwyn Owen that was printed in the Northern Counties year book of 1966. He had been a fancier for forty plus years at the time and so was a knowledgeable man within the breed. The part which most impressed me and has stuck with me as a yardstick to the present day is:

"During my long interest I have seen all the best, and we have had a real spate of good ones over the years. I think the best I have ever seen is still alive in the American Ch Courtenay Fleetfoot. I have never judged him, and only once put my hands on him, and that was on the bench. The owner was not very keen even then, but I will admit it was a very bad day, and owner and dog were about fed up. I hope the stock Fleetfoot left behind will continue to produce similar type.

For my best bitch I plump for Ch Lily of Laguna. Both she and "Fleetfoot" had the range so important to complete the picture.

Going further back, the dog Ch Sapperley Heralder and the bitch Ch White Statue of Conevan were both good champions who have passed on so much to the make -up of our present day best. Even so, I have always thought they had enough body and character to have that extra inch in height to give them the range so very much required in the breed."

My understanding of the "range" he writes of is proportionate length and balance. Incidentally, Gwyn Owen gave me my first Limit Class win at Championship show level.

In the early days I collected quite a library of pedigrees and at that time it seemed that successful breeding came back each time to getting the lines right on paper before anything else. Later, I came to understand that any weaknesses of the sire and dam also have to be taken into consideration. With this fact in mind I decided to mate Cream Top to Ch Denorsi Moondust of Glenbervie. He was a repeat mating of International Ch Denorsi Moonduster of Glenbervie (sire of Tinkermoon - see pedigree). Cream Top's sire was Ch Baydale Cinnamon and her dam was Pencloe Chocolate Soda of Denorsi. Regrettably, I don't have a photograph but Cream Top was more suited to the show ring than Tinkermoon. At her first show she took five second places to a dog who was to become legendary: Marion Spavin's Beagle Ch Dialynne Gamble.

This period was a whole new learning experience for me and I decided Moondust was the only logical dog to use if I intended to carry on producing the type of Whippets I so admired. In the litter there was a very sound bitch, Hillsdown Pandora. She was the first Hillsdown to win at Championship show level and went to another kennel on breeding terms. Sadly, this was to be Cream Top's only litter as she was killed in an accident shortly

Ch Baydale Cinnamon	Ch Samarkand's Sun Courtier	Ch Samarkand's Greenbrae Tarragon	Ch Laguna Limelight
			Ch Greenbrae Laguna Lucia
		Samarkand's Sun Cloud	Ch Allways Wingedfoot Running Fox
			Samarkand's Sun Coral
	Cockrow Merle	Int Ch/Ch/Am Ch Tantivvey Diver of Pennyworth	Ch Laguna Ligonier
			Fleeting Fancy Free
		Cockrow Lady Kate	Trevelmond Imp of Allways
			Laguna Little Lady
Pencloe Chocolate Soda of Denorsi	Ch Cockrow Tarquogan of Glenbervie	Ch Samarkand's Greenbrae Tarragon	Ch Laguna Limelight
			Ch Greenbrae Laguna Lucia
		Cockrow Lady Kate	Trevelmond Imp of Allways
			Laguna Little Lady
	Denorsi Tinkerbelle of Glenbervie	Ch Cockrow Tarquogan of Glenbervie	Ch Samarkand's Greenbrae Tarragon
			Cockrow Lady Kate
		Ch Hillgarth Sunstar of Glenbervie	Hillgarth Snow Boy
			Hillgarth Spun Silk

Pedigree of Denorsi Cream Top.

L to r: Ch Tantivvey Diver; Ch Danegeld Piper's Tune; Tweseldown Glenbarry; Ch Samarkand's Greenbrae Tarragon. Judge Mrs Dorit McKay (Laguna).

after her first litter. When the time came to mate her daughter, Pandora, I used my own dog Dondelayo Lysander. From this union came Van Olreim Vanessa. Dondelayo Lysander was out of Ch Samarkand's Greenbrae Tarragon and his dam was Courthill Country Life. I bought Lysander because his lines tied in with all my bitches and he also introduced the similar line breeding and in-breeding of another kennel I admired, that of Anne Knight's Dondelayos. Vanessa was very sound and I enjoyed some success in the show ring, winning Limit class at Championship level and Best In Show at smaller shows. Vanessa then went on to become the cornerstone of the successful Barnesmore kennel after going to join Margaret Martin in Ireland.

I bought White Bud purely for her breeding. She was by Cockrow Woodchuck out of Tarara of Glenbervie and litter sister to Ch Twigairy of Glenbervie. Tarara also produced another champion from a different mating, Denorsi Quickmatch of Glenbervie. It was never my intention to exhibit her; she came to me at twelve months old and never would be up to show standard. However, I was very lucky to have her. She had some outstanding qualities: a fantastic depth of brisket, good angulation and, although all white, her coat was fine and a really sparkling white colour that contrasted strikingly with excellent black pigmentation. I mated her to Ch Akeferry Jimmy and it was from this little lady that I bred my first champion, Ch Nutcracker of Nevedith. He was also the first champion to be sired by Jimmy and was owned by Miss E Newton.

White Bud was small and short coupled. I had seen Jimmy regularly being shown from puppy classes through to an adult round the local shows and felt that his movement, less angular lines and, more importantly, his breeding would add the necessary ingredients to the mating. His breeding came from all the good kennels: Cockrow and

Ch Akeferry Jimmy	Cockrow Partridge of Cranshaw	Int Ch/Ch/Am Ch Tantivvey of Pennyworth	Ch Laguna Ligonier
			Fleeting Fancy Free
		Cockrow Taradiddle	Ch Samarkand's Greenbrae Tarragon
			Cockrow Lady Kate
	Eegee Jane	Ch Samarkand's Greenbrae Tarragon	Ch Laguna Limelight
			Ch Greenbrae Laguna Lucia
		Eegee Anita	Ch Laguna Ligonier
			Harque to Dreamgirl
White Bud of Glenbervie	Cockrow Woodchuck	Ch Cockrow Tarquogan of Glenbervie	Ch Samarkand's Greenbrae Taragon
			Cockrow Lady Kate
		Cockrow Woodpigeon	Int Ch/Ch/Am Ch Tantivvey Diver of P.
			Cockrow Taradiddle
	Tarara of Glenbervie	Ch/Am Ch Courtenay Fleetfoot of Pennyworth	Ch Bellavista Barry
			Myhorlyns Anita
		Princessa of Glenbervie	Myhorlyns Shooting Star
			Hillgarth So Sweet

Pedigree of Ch Nutcracker of Nevedith.

Laguna, Tantivvey Diver and Samarkand's Greenbrae Tarragon. On his dam's side was Laguna Ligonier. Also in the same litter was Nuzzle of Nevedith who was the dam of Reserve CC winner Barmaud Lord Halifax of Savilepark. He later became a South African champion.

My plans were then to concentrate on Tinkermoon. She had to my mind classic breeding: half brother-sister mating, her sire being International Ch Moonduster of Glenbervie and her dam Denorsi Tinkerbelle of Glenbervie. Tinkermoon had some success in the show ring but she was to prove later that her greatest asset was as a brilliant brood bitch, producing three champions. Her dam, Tinkerbelle, was a litter sister to three champions and she produced two champions in her own litters. Earlier matings between Ch Cockrow Tarquogan of Glenbervie and White Gorse of Glenbervie had also produced three champions: Denorsi Moondust of Glenbervie, Denorsi Moonduster of Glenbervie and Another Rose of Glenbervie. This is excellent, consistent breeding and only proves to re-affirm my strong belief that if you stay within the lines then you will keep the quality and consistency.

Around 1973 Tinkermoon was placed third in, what was, at that time, a world record entry for a Whippet breed show. The bitch judge was Arthur B Nicholson and the dog judge Mr Griffiths. At the same show, Charles Dempster of the Charmoll affix was exhibiting a superb looking red brindle and white dog puppy named Charmoll Clansman and he took third prize on the day. I checked out his breeding and decided on the spot that when the time came he was the ideal dog to mate with Tinkermoon. He gained his title rapidly and, to my utter disappointment and before my plans could come to fruition, he was exported to America. Undeterred by this, I contacted Mr Dempster and when he subsequently repeated the mating he kept two dogs. They were Charmoll Mactavish and

Int Ch Denorsi Moonduster of Glenbervie	Ch Cockrow Tarquogan of Glenbervie	Ch Samarkand's Greenbrae Taragon	Ch Laguna Limelight
			Ch Greenbrae Laguna Lucia
		Cockrow Lady Kate	Trevelmond Imp of Allways
			Laguna Little Lady
	White Gorse of Glenbervie	Am Ch Cockrow Grouse	Ch Tantivvey Diver
			Cockrow Taradiddle
		Tarara of Glenbervie	Ch Courtenay Fleetfoot
			Princessa of Glenbervie
Denorsi Tinkerbelle of Glenbervie	Ch Cockrow Tarquogan of Glenbervie	Ch Samarkand's Greenbrae Taragon	Ch Laguna Limelight
			Ch Greenbrae Laguna Lucia
		Cockrow Lady Kate	Trevelmond Imp of Allways
			Laguna Little Lady
	Ch Hillgarth Sunstar of Glenbervie	Hillgarth Snow Boy	Myhorlyns Shooting Star
			Hillgarth So Sweet
		Hillgarth Spun Silk	Ch Seagift Speedlite Mustang
			Hillgarth Silver Suntan

Pedigree of Denorsi Tinkermoon.

Charmoll Bonnie Prince. Mactavish was equally as good as Clansman and, again, both dogs gained their titles easily. Mactavish was tall and elegant with plenty of length and good free flowing movement. He had excellent pigmentation, as did his sire. Physically he was exactly what was needed for Tinkermoon; she was a little short coupled but nevertheless a good mover. On paper it was just as good a match.

Ch/Am Ch Charmoll Clansman - a type the author has consistently strived for in his breeding programme.

Ch Charmoll Mactavish	Ch Baydale Cinnamon	Ch Samarkand's Sun Courtier	Ch Samarkand's Greenbrae Tarragon
			Samarkand's Sun Cloud
		Cockrow Merle	Ch/Int Ch/Am Ch Tantivvey Diver of Pennyworth
			Cockrow Lady Kate
	Ch Dondelayo Ruanne of Charmoll	Ch Cockrow Tarquogan of Glenbervie	Ch Samarkand's Greenbrae Tarragon
			Cockrow Lady Kate
		Ch Dondelayo Rue	Ch Samarkand's Greenbrae Tarragon
			Linknumstar Lizard
Denorsi Tinkermoon	Int Ch Denorsi Moonduster of Glenbervie	Ch Cockrow Tarquogan of Glenbervie	Ch Samarkand's Greenbrae Tarragon
			Cockrow Lady Kate
		White Gorse of Glenbervie	Am Ch Cockrow Grouse
			Tarara of Glenbervie
	Denorsi Tinkerbelle of Glenbervie	Ch Cockrow Tarquogan of Glenbervie	Ch Samarkand's Greenbrae Tarragon
			Cockrow Lady Kate
		Ch Hillgarth Sunstar of Glenbervie	Hillgarth Snow Boy
			Hillgarth Spun Silk

Pedigree of Ch/Am Ch Hillsdown Repique.

It is interesting to note that the sire and dam of Ch Charmoll Mactavish were surrounded by consistent good breeding. Ch Baydale Cinnamon sired five champions. Ch Dondelayo Ruanne of Charmoll was one of three champions from the same litter, her sister Ch Dondelayo Roulette was breed record holder of her era and the litter brother was Ch Dondelayo Buckaroo who in turn sired ten champions. They prove that by breeding consistently within good lines from physically sound Whippets you should produce more of the same.

Ch Charmoll Mactavish.

After delving into the calculated breeding behind the sire and dam I expected, and was certainly not disappointed in, the excellent outcome of this mating. From the litter I kept

Ch Hillsdown Riosin (BIS) and her sire Ch Hillsdown Repique. Photo: Whimpanny

a red brindle bitch who was later to become Ch Hillsdown Tobique. She was my first home bred, owned and shown champion and holds a very special place in my memories. She had tremendous depth and all the elegance of her sire. Her movement was fabulous. Her photographs have never done true justice to her presence. It was particularly gratifying that she gained her title under three such well respected and knowledgeable experts, namely Mr R M James (Samarkand's), Mrs Anne Argyle (Harque) and Mrs Sheffield (Hillgarth). A repeat mating re-affirmed my judgement and produced Ch/Am Ch Hillsdown Repique. He had a rapid show career in England. From nine shows he was awarded 5 CCs and 1 Reserve CC. He, too, was exported to America. Fortunately before going he had already sired a litter when mated back to his dam. From this litter came Ch Hillsdown Riosin. As one would expect from such close breeding, Riosin was very much of Tinkermoon's type. She was a quality bitch of good size and a true mover but still did not have the length of coupling I would have wished for. Its a great feeling to breed a champion but one must always be looking to improve and go forward. Other success also came from these litters; Claire de Lune, from the first mating of Mactavish and Tinkermoon, was grand dam of Barnesmore Grey Owl, a CC winner. From the second litter came Hillsdown Fandango who sired Barnesmore Telegram Sam (Reserve CC winner) who, in turn, sired Ch Karnak Silver Tiger.

The next step for Hillsdown was to mate Tobique to a Baydale Cinnamon son. Hopefully, by doubling up on Tantivvey Diver and Tarragon, I would be keeping the consistency going. Ch Black Knight of Carmodian was a striking black brindle and had the physical attributes I was looking for. Although I thought him a little broad in skull I was confident that the breeding would come through and therefore this would pose no threat. Black Knight was sired by Cinnamon but his dam's lines would not match in until quite far back on the great grandparent line. In this litter was a red brindle dog named Moonraker of Lowglen who won a Reserve CC, a fawn bitch called Siobhan of Hillsdown, and the red brindle bitch, Pearl of Akonyte. These two bitches carried on the strong bitch line and came to be recognised as excellent brood bitches.

Around this time I went to look at a bitch puppy, for a friend, at the Oakbark kennels. Mr and Mrs Meakin had built up a most impressive

The late Bobby James (judge), Ch Hillsdown Tobique and the author.

Ch Black Knight of Carmodian	Ch Baydale Cinnamon	Ch Samarkand's Sun Courtier	Ch Samarkand's Greenbrae Tarragon
			Samarkand's Sun Cloud
		Cockrow Merle	Int Ch/Ch/Am Ch Tantivvey Diver of Pennyworth
			Cockrow Lady Kate
	September Girl	Highland Star	Allgarth Careless Rapture
			Gorcio Chavi
		Drabengro Petulengro	Hillgarth Selector
			Churchill Sherry
Ch Hillsdown Tobique	Ch Charmoll Mactavish	Ch Baydale Cinnamon	Ch Samarkand's Sun Courtier
			Cockrow Merle
		Ch Dondelayo Ruanne of Charmoll	Ch Cockrow Tarquogan of Glenbervie
			Ch Dondelayo Rue
	Denorsi Tinkermoon	Int Ch Denorsi Moonduster of Glenbervie	Ch Cockrow Tarquogan of Glenbervie
			White Gorse of Glenbervie
		Denorsi Tinkerbelle of Glenbervie	Ch Cockrow Tarquogan of Glenbervie
			Ch Hillgarth Sunstar of Glenbervie

Pedigree of Siobhan of Hillsdown and Pearl of Akonyte.

Siobhan of Hillsdown aged 10.5 years.

kennel. For some time I had admired the quality of the Oakbarks and so when Moving Picture was mated to Charmoll Mactavish I was more than interested in the outcome. Looking at the pedigree of this mating you will see Ch Deepridge Mintmaster and Ch Towercrest Flarepath Taurus are both sons of Ligonier. Mintmaster was then my all-time favourite Whippet. Here was the opportunity to introduce new bloodlines into my own kennel. To my great delight I was able to buy a young red brindle dog, and he went on to become Ch Oakbark Middleman (the other choice of name was for him was Middle for Diddle, which I'm told means bull's eye in Lancashire - this probably suited him more because a bull's eye he proved to be!)

Middleman was very attractive and masculine although not a big dog. His dark pigmentation was excellent. He was a true mover with daisy cutting action. If I were to be critical, in an ideal world I would have preferred a little more hind angulation. His comparatively short show record was impressive: he had ten CCs and ten Reserve CCs. He also sired three champions.

I had more than one litter from Middleman and Riosin and over almost two decades their joint qualities have regularly come to the fore. Between them they produced Barleyhorn Josie, dam of Ch Norwill Barley at Hammonds. Barley sired Ch Millwold Suntan who, when mated to Ch Pencloe Dutch Gold, produced the top winner Ch Millwold Gold Dust to Exhurst. Another from this litter was Millwold Hidden Gold at Permadon, a reserve CC winner who, when mated to Hillsdown Fergal, produced Ch

Permadon Golden Cascade. Penny Royal of Chilka is sister to Josie and she is the dam of Bizzie Lizzie of Hutaka who is dam of Ch Phinjani Pinball Wizard.

Riosin also had a litter by Hillsdown Fergal and she produced Irish Champion Hillsdown Sinead. Sinead is the dam of both Lazy Daisy of Hillsdown and Yesman of Hillsdown (1 Reserve CC and also sire of a CC winner). Lazy Daisy is grand dam of Fast Flo of Hillsdown (1 Reserve CC). When Fast Flo was mated to Pencloe Dutch Escort of

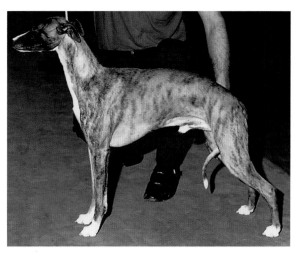

Ch Oakbark Middleman. Photo: Whimpanny

Ch Charmoll Mactavish	Ch Baydale Cinnamon	Ch Samarkand's Sun Courtier	Ch Samarkand's Greenbrae Tarragon
			Samarkand's Sun Cloud
		Cockrow Merle	Int Ch/Ch/Am Ch Tantivvey Diver of P.
			Cockrow Lady Kate
	Ch Dondelayo Ruanne of Charmoll	Ch Cockrow Tarquogan of Glenbervie	Ch Samarkand's Greenbrae Tarragon
			Cockrow Lady Kate
		Ch Dondelayo Rue	Ch Samarkand's Greenbrae Tarragon
			Linknumstar Lizard
Oakbark Moving Picture	Ch Oakbark Armfield Joker	Ch Deepridge Mintmaster	Ch Laguna Ligonier
			Deepridge Juliet
		Patjo Madam	Harque to Beaumont
			Dondelayo Gaiety
	Ch Oakbark Movie Queen	Ch Towercrest Flarepath Taurus	Ch Laguna Ligonier
			Flarepath Ravensdone Vega
		Flarepath Aquaria	Ch Lowglen Oakbark Masterminde
			Ch Laguna Ravensdowne Astri

Pedigree of Ch Oakbark Middleman.

Hillsdown she produced Ch Fawnbree Special Brew at Dumbriton, Ch Fawnbree Harvey Wallbanger and Fawnbree Bucks Fizz, a Reserve CC winner, all in the same litter.

I had a friend who had been in another breed for some years but was keen to have Whippets and so Siobhan and Tobique went to live with her for a while. Siobhan was shown and very rarely left out of the cards gaining a stud book number after being placed third in Open Bitch class. She was a very honest fawn bitch, feminine but not glamorous.

The last litter from Tobique was back to her grandson, Shergar of Wildglen. Shergar was brother to Ch Nicely Naughty at Birkonbrae. Any student of pedigrees will have noticed that grandsire to granddaughter often proves to be a successful mating and I could not see why the reverse shouldn't work just as well and the result speaks for itself. The mating produced Ch/Ir Ch Painted Pony who has sired champions, CC winners and Reserve CC winners.

Nicely Naughty went to the Andersons, already well known for their success in Bedlingtons, but I handled her throughout her career. It was decided to mate her to Samarkand's Sea Leopard and this produced the CC and Reserve CC winner Birkonbrae Fleur de Lys and Birkonbrae Coeur de Lyon, who was sire of Hillsdown Fergal. Her next litter was to Ch Samarkand's Beau Ranger and from this mating came Birkonbrae Beauson, who sired the Reserve CC winner Fast Flo, and his sister Birkonbrae Buttons 'n Bows. When Buttons was later mated to Fergal the results were wonderful. From the first mating came two English champions, the lovely bitches Ch Birkonbrae Everlasting Love and Ch Birkonbrae Forever Love, and two Swedish Champions Birkonbrae Summer Love and Birkonbrae Sweet Talking Guy. The second mating produced Swedish Champion Birkonbrae True Enough. Sweet Talking Guy and True Enough are proving to be top sires in Sweden.

Siobhan's talent as a brood bitch was brought to the fore when she was mated to Middleman. Her successful daughters were Ch Nicely Naughty at Birkonbrae, Rohanberry of Akonyte (1 CC and 1 Reserve CC), Moonbeam of Pencloe and Kienford (1 CC and 1 Reserve CC), Hillsdown Mollie, mother of several French, Norwegian and Swedish champions, and Hollyberry of Akonyte who was dam of Hillsdown Deniol (who won a Reserve CC and then went on to become a Norwegian champion). Hollyberry also produced Hillsdown Declan who went on to become a champion in Japan.

Rohanberry, when mated to Fergal, produced Tassle of Tarraday (1 CC) and China Rose of Tarraday (1 Reserve CC). Tassle was then mated to Ch Hillsdown Sorcerer to produce Ch Tarraday Magic Spirit.

Siobhan was mated to Coeur de Lyon, her grandson. From this mating came the prolific sire Hillsdown Fergal and Hillsdown Ciarran (later of Pencloe). Ciarran was dam of Barnesmore Centre Fold who won 1 CC and grand dam of English and Irish Ch Collooney Silver Fox.

Siobhan's last litter was by Blacque Legacy of Hillsdown (Ch Cherokee Lad x Ch Hino Legacy). In this litter was Hillsdown Blacque Rose, a physically unimpressive black brindle with white points. When considering possible sires I had to go for a dog with substance and length and so I decided on Ch Phinjani Pinball Wizard as he also had very good profile movement. He not only fitted the bill from the physical point of view but also

Ch Dondelayo Buckaroo	Ch Cockrow Tarquogan of Glenbervie	Ch Samarkand's Greenbrae Tarragon	Ch Laguna Limelight
			Ch Greenbrae Laguna Lucia
		Cockrow Lady Kate	Trevelmond Imp of Allways
			Laguna Little Lady
	Ch Dondelayo Rue	Ch Samarkand's Greenbrae Tarragon	Ch Laguna Limelight
			Ch Greenbrae Laguna Lucia
		Linknumstar Lizard	Ch Laguna Linkway
			Laguna L'Etoile
Ch Dondelayo Duette	Ch Samarkand's Greenbrae Tarragon	Ch Laguna Limelight	Ch Fieldspring Bartsia of Allways
			Ch Brekin Ballet Shoes
		Ch Greenbrae Laguna Lucia	Ch Runway Controller
			Ch Laguna Leading Lady
	Ch Dondelayo Roulette	Ch Cockrow Tarquogan	Ch Samarkand's Greenbrae Tarragon
			Cockrow Lady Kate
		Ch Dondelayo Rue	Ch Samarkand's Greenbrae Tarragon
			Linknumstar Lizard

Pedigree of Samarkand's Sea Leopard.

his breeding. His grand dam was of Hillsdown breeding, sired by Middleman and out of Riosin. His grand sire was Mactavish and there were also Black Knight and Oakbark lines in there. From the litter came Ch Hillsdown Sorcerer, Hillsdown Houdini (a winner in Germany) and Hillsdown Blacque Magique, who is grand dam to Ch Fawnbree Special Brew, Ch Fawnbree Harvey Wall Banger and Fawnbree Bucks Fizz, Reserve CC winner. I was thinking along the same lines when I subsequently mated Blacque Rose to the

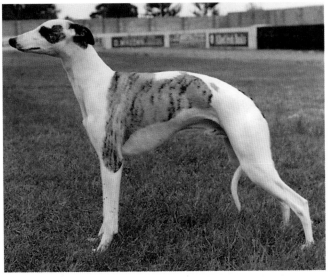

Ch/Ir Ch Painted Pony.

Ch Phinjani Pinball Wizard	Kaymark Mad Max	Ch Charmoll Mactavish	Ch Baydale Cinnamon
			Ch Dondelayo Ruanne of Charmoll
		Magic Silk	Ch Oakbark Mister Magic of Silkstone
			Palmik Star
	Bizzie Lizzie of Hutaka	Ch Carmodian Tawny Knight of Hutaka	Ch Black Knight of Carmodian
			Allgarth Countess Penelope
		Penny Royal of Chilka	Ch Oakbark Middleman
			Ch Hillsdown Riosin
Hillsdown Blacque Rose	Blacque Legacy of Hillsdown	Ch Cherokee Lad	Maluk Macgrath
			Chilka Delectable
		Ch/Ir Ch Hino Legacy	Ch/Ir Ch Painted Pony
			Barnesmore Blue Angel
	Siobhan of Hillsdown	Ch Black Knight of Carmodian	Ch Baydale Cinnamon
			September Girl
		Ch Hillsdown Tobique	Ch Charmoll Mactavish
			Denorsi Tinkermoon

Pedigree of Ch Hillsdown Sorcerer.

Amercian champion Fairways Riptide. I needed to introduce substance and length and from this litter came Hillsdown Americano of Showline, a champion sire in Norway. This was not the complete outcross it may at first appear to be as Riptide's sire is a grandson of the first champion I bred, Nevedith Nutcracker.

Pearl of Akonyte was very similar in make and shape to Siobhan but red brindle and probably a little more glamorous. She took first prize at a Championship show but never realised her true potential as unfortunately she sustained a broken leg. Mr and Mrs Jim Barker (Chilka) already had a young Hillsdown bitch and were looking for another foundation bitch and

Ch Hillsdown Sorcerer at Crufts.

Pearl of Akonyte.

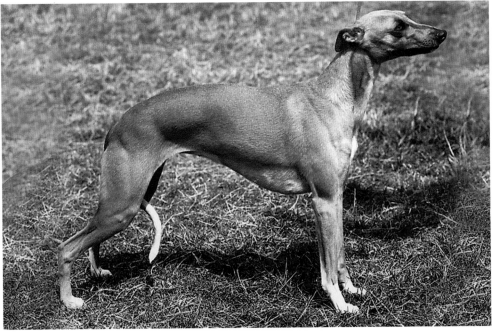

Ch Nicely Naughty At Birkonbrae. Photo: Whimpanny

		Nevedith Merry Monarch	Ch Akeferry Jimmy
Ch/Am Ch/Can Ch Nevedith Uptown Guy	Ch/Fr Ch Nevedith Paperweight		Trimar Trycolena
		Whitbarrow Minimist	Cockrow Saturn
			Whitbarrow Eustacia
	Sakonnet Alfalfa	Ch Akeferry Jimmy	Cockrow Partridge of Crawshaw
			Eegee Jane
		Sakonnet Black Mustard	Ch Black Knight of Carmodian
			Ch Sakonnet Sprig Muslin
Chilka Dairy Maid	Ch Oakbark Middleman	Ch Charmoll Mactavish	Ch Baydale Cinnamon
			Ch Dondelayo Ruanne of Charmoll
		Oakbark Moving Picture	Ch Oakbark Armfield Joker
			Ch Oakbark Movie Queen
	Pearl of Akonyte at Chilka	Ch Black Knight of Carmodian	Ch Baydale Cinnamon
			September Girl
		Ch Hillsdown Tobique	Ch Charmoll Mactavish
			Denorsi Tinkermoon

Pedigree of Ch Nutshell of Nevedith.

L to r: Ch Nutshell of Nevedith, Breed Record Holder and Reserve BIS Crufts 1990.
Ch Pencloe Dutch Gold, Top Dog 1991 and BIS Crufts 1992.

Hillsdown Fergal, sire of Ch Pencloe Dutch Gold, aged 9.

so Pearl went to them from Mr and Mrs Mason (Akonyte). When Jim Barker was ready for a litter from Pearl he came to me to use Middleman. It proved to be a good union and once more the strong brood bitch line came into play again. In the litter were: Chilka Deb's Delight (grand dam of Ch Carmodian Sampson of Dunarunna), Chilka Delectable (dam of Ch Cherokee Lad) and Chilka Dairy Maid (dam of Ch Nutshell of Nevedith). Nutshell had a glorious career and at this time is breed record holder with an astounding 44 CCs and seven Best in Show awards at Championship level. In 1989 she was Dog Of The Year All Breeds. In 1990 she was runner-up for the same award and was Reserve Best in Show at Crufts - no mean achievement.

Morag Bolton-Lockhart decided to bring Moonbeam back to Fergal to be mated, a half

Hillsdown Fergal	Birkonbrae Coeur de Lyon	Samarkand's Sea Leopard	Ch Dondelayo Buckaroo
			Ch Dondelay Duette
		Ch Nicely Naughty at Birkonbrae	Ch Oakbark Middleman
			Siobhan of Hillsdown
	Siobhan of Hillsdown	Ch Black Knight of Carmodian	Ch Baydale Cinnamon
			September Girl
		Ch Hillsdown Tobique	Ch Charmoll Mactavish
			Denorsi Tinkermoon
Moonbeam of Kienford and Pencloe	Ch Oakbark Middleman	Ch Charmoll Mactavish	Ch Baydale Cinnamon
			Ch Dondelayo Ruanne of Charmoll
		Oakbark Moving Picture	Ch Oakbark Armfield Joker
			Ch Oakbark Movie Queen
	Siobhan of Hillsdown	Ch Black Knight of Carmodian	Ch Baydale Cinnamon
			September Girl
		Ch Hillsdown Tobique	Ch Charmoll Mactavish
			Denorsi Tinkermoon

Pedigree of Ch Pencloe Dutch Gold.

brother sister mating, and the result created history in the modern Whippet show world. From the litter came the magnificent Ch Pencloe Dutch Gold, the only Whippet ever to win Best in Show at Crufts, an excellent ambassador of the breed both in the show ring and at stud. He was Top Sire in the breed over a number of years and also Top Hound Sire in 1995. To date he has sired nine champions and his progeny have gone on to produce more champions.

Fawnbree Harvey Wallbanger gained his title in 1997, shortly after his litter brother Ch Fawnbree Special Brew at Dumbriton. Studying his pedigree, it can be seen how the combining of the great dogs and bitches within the same lines in the '70s and '80s is still having an influential effect. It's a great feeling to see the names of Fergal, Siobhan, Tobique and Riosin in there in numbers and holding their own in such good company. As a breeder I get great pleasure and satisfaction from seeing other people breed successfully with Hillsdown lines and continually improve upon them.

Ch Pencloe Dutch Gold, winner of the Hound Group and Best In Show Crufts 1992.

			Birkonbrae Coeur de Lyon
Pencloe Dutch Escort of Hillsdown	Ch Pencloe Dutch Gold	Hillsdown Fergal	
			Siobhan of Hillsdown
		Moonbeam of Kienford and Pencloe	Ch Oakbark Middleman
			Siobhan of Hillsdown
	Hillsdown Magique	Ch Phinjani Pinball Wizard	Kaymark Mad Max
			Bizzie Lizzie of Hutaka
		Hillsdown Blacque Rose	Blacque Legacy of Hillsdown
			Siobhan of Hillsdown
Fast Flo of Hillsdown	Birkonbrae Beau Son	Ch Samarkand's Beau Ranger	Wellnigh Beau Belles
			Ch Samarkand's Subaru
		Ch Nicely Naughty at Birkonbrae	Ch Oakbark Middleman
			Siobhan of Hillsdown
	Hillsdown Josephine	Hillsdown Fergal	Birkonbrae Coeur de Lyon
			Siobhan of Hillsdown
		Lazy Daisy of Hillsdown	Ch/Ir Ch Painted Pony
			Ir Ch Hillsdown Sinead

Pedigree of Ch Fawnbree Harvey Wall Banger and Ch Fawnbree Special Brew at Dumbriton.

Ch Fawnbree Harvey Wall Banger.
Photo: Whimpanny

Chapter Ten

Planning And
Rearing A Litter

For the average pet owner the reasons not to have a litter far outweigh the reasons for doing so. Certainly before you take this irreversible step there are many issues to consider.

First and foremost why are you doing it? There are myths around that may lead you to believe a bitch is unfulfilled unless she has been a mother, or that her temperament will change after having a litter. These are wrong, your bitch will be perfectly happy never having had a litter. Her personality won't change any more so than it would with age and maturity. More important, not all Whippets make good, caring mothers. It has been known for a bitch to take very little interest in her litter causing much work for the owner and a possible very poor start in life for the puppies. Deciding to hand rear a neglected new litter is not a step to be taken lightly. It involves tremendous patience, dedication, and having the confidence in your own ability to know that you're sufficiently caring for the helpless babies in your charge. It is also a very time-consuming, demanding and a possibly stressful situation to embark on.

Assuming the mother is happy with her new charges, then do not imagine that she will take care of the puppies until they are old enough to go to their new homes. To believe this would be a grave mistake. Having a litter and taking proper care of both mother and babies is very hard work. Admittedly the mother feeds and cleans the babies for the first couple of weeks but she needs extra care and attention herself during this time. Once the puppies are starting to lap and eat then the work really starts. The amount of food that goes into a thriving little puppy's mouth can be pretty surprising but even more daunting is how much more seems to come out from the other end. A healthy playful litter have no aversion to rolling in what was yesterday's dinner and so keeping them clean can be pretty demanding work. Once they are fully weaned and in an established eating pattern it does get slightly easier but is still very time consuming and requires a regular pattern of sleeping, feeding and cleaning to be established.

The next question you must ask yourself is whether you have a suitable place for the bitch to give birth and rear the litter. It is grossly unfair to expect a house dog to be suddenly plunged outside into a kennel prior to the whole new experience of giving birth and then having to remain there until the babies are old enough to be left alone for any length of time. The average modern household doesn't exactly lend itself to becoming a whelping room and indoor kennel. Many experienced breeders will often have a litter indoors but their lives are built around dogs and their experience will have taught them

Puppies will require supervised time outdoors as they develop.

many handy tips to overcome potential problems - for example, the smells, cleaning, changes in the bitch's feeding and toilet pattern - without making too much of a major task of it, and not forgetting it is probably a labour of love for these people. You may visit a breeder who has a mother and young babies contentedly snuggled up in their bed, perhaps in a corner of the kitchen. Be warned this is not something that doesn't come with experience on the breeder's or new mother's part.

Have you any homes arranged for the expected puppies, and are you prepared to let them go? This can be quite a worry. I know of Whippet litters where there have been up to eleven puppies and all have survived. Whilst this is quite unusual, and its more likely to be smaller (maybe around five or six), you must be prepared for any number. Believe me, they will all be absolutely adorable. All puppies are, and Whippet puppies more so because of their easy natural fun-loving spirit and nature. It can be quite a wrench for the family when its time for the little ones to go to new homes, but they do have to go. Are you prepared to refuse potential owners if you think them unsuitable? More importantly, are you able and prepared to have back any puppies that haven't settled in their new homes? All these factors must be considered to save possible future heartache when its too late to do anything about it. As a final test, it may help dissuade you from proceeding if you were to pay a visit to a Whippet Rescue kennel; some of the poor unloved creatures that need help are quite the saddest sight.

Last and definitely not least, you may feel that you could make some money on a litter. After all you paid for your puppy, which was one of maybe six or seven, and so you may be anticipating a nice little four figure bonus. This is the worst possible reason for having a litter. Rather than anticipate a cash reward, any sensible person breeding a litter has money set aside for possible vet bills, and enough to ensure that all the pups can be fed and cared for whilst with you. A caesarean section is sometimes necessary and this alone can be a three figure sum.

If you're wanting a companion for your Whippet then you may be far better off buying one (perhaps from another breeder or Whippet Rescue) but if, despite all these reasons not to, I still haven't managed to put you off and you remain intent on having a litter after having carefully considered the above, then I hope I can prepare you for what is to come and that the rest of this chapter is both informative and useful.

I have explained how I decided which sires to use over the years in greater detail in the Hillsdown chapter. The following information is a guide to the physical and practical side of breeding and rearing a litter.

The average bitch has a regular season, often around every six months. This is by no means a rule and may vary between every eight months or even a full year. It doesn't mean anything is wrong with the bitch if she doesn't have one every six months, its just her cycle. Well before her season starts you should give great thought to which stud dog you would like to use. If you are unsure, then her breeder may be able to suggest a suitable dog. Do you particularly admire any stud dog? If so discuss him with your bitch's breeder. The main points to consider are the lines in her pedigree and what lines you wish to bring in. Does your bitch have any shortcomings that you would wish to correct in her offspring? These are questions that will help you decide on who should sire your litter. Once you have decided, contact the owner of the stud dog and ask if his dog would be available when your bitch is ready for mating. If you write, send a copy of your bitch's pedigree and maybe a photograph of her as this will help the owner decide whether or not to let the mating take place. If you telephone then have her pedigree handy so you can discuss how she is bred. The fee should also be discussed at the outset. For many matings an agreed stud fee is usually paid at the time of mating but sometimes other arrangements are made. The stud dog owner may prefer to have a puppy or two from the litter, which may be beneficial to you both. Whatever you decide should be agreeable to both parties. Be warned, if the agreement is for puppies and not a cash payment. It can be quite hard if the family have chosen a particular puppy that stood out from birth as a favourite and then this is also the one chosen by the stud dog owner. Be sure to get it clear before the mating. If the mating doesn't result in pregnancy for some reason then it could be due to one of several reasons. If the dog is a proven sire then it is usually considered that the failure is down to either bad timing or possibly something to do with the bitch. If a fee has been paid most reasonable stud dog owners, to show good faith, will let you have a repeat mating on the bitch's next season but they are not obliged to do so.

When your bitch starts her season then contact the stud dog owner again, even though you may have previously arranged a mating for an approximate time. The stud dog may have other bitches coming around the same time and also the owner may need to re.arrange his own time around your visit. I have found the ideal time to mate my own stock is on the tenth or eleventh day and then again on the thirteenth. Not everyone will agree to mating twice but I feel it leads to more successful matings. I usually offer this to anyone using my stud dogs as quite often everything is planned around the litter being born at a certain time of the year and so a missed pregnancy can cause a twelve month delay. Increasingly more people are having the bitch swab tested by the vet to determine the exact date on which to mate. This may be useful if you are a travelling a long way to the stud dog and therefore only one mating is possible. The bitch herself will often, by instinct, telegraph when she is ready to be mated. She will stand for a dog without moving and will lift her tail up and sometimes even over her back. If there is a dog nearby then it is quite handy to try her near him to test her reaction, but use extreme caution. An experienced dog can mate a bitch in seconds and it would be a disaster to have a litter from some silly mistake such as this. If by any chance your bitch is accidentally mated then you must take her to the vet within 48 hours. An injection to prolong her season and prevent any puppies can be given. However, this is an extreme remedy and repeated injections could lead to long-term womb damage, so take all possible precautions to prevent unwanted matings in the first place and never underestimate the amorous enemy!

The day arrives and off you go for the mating. Your job is to keep the bitch comfortable and calm throughout the whole procedure. The owner of the stud dog should do any necessary handling of the dog and you are there to hold your bitch steady enough to prevent her possibly snapping at the stud dog and, at the same time, reassure her. Some bitches, even though the mating is on the correct day and her body is reacting correctly, will still snap as the stud dog tries to mount her. This may be perhaps through nervousness at being under pressure away from home or the stress of all the sudden attention. A good experienced stud dog will mate in quite a short period, often a matter of minutes. Once the mating has happened, the dog and bitch 'tie' for some time; it can often be half an hour or longer, so ensure you are comfortable. When the penis is firmly inside the vagina there is a gland that swells like a bulb. This gland has to return to its natural state before the penis can be removed. To make them more comfortable the stud dog is turned away from the bitch to be positioned almost back to back. It is important that you hold onto the bitch to prevent causing injury to either of them. When the penis is eventually released its best to settle your bitch as soon as possible for the journey home. When you pay the stud fee you should be given a completed 'Kennel Club Application for Litter Registration by the Breeder' form signed by the stud dog owner, and a copy of the stud dog's pedigree. It is also a good idea to have a photograph of the stud dog if possible. The owner will very probably allow you to take one, so remember your camera.

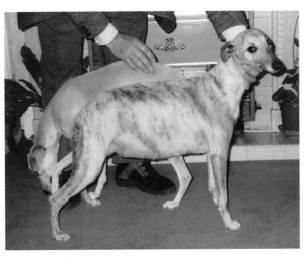

A pregnant Whippet two days before whelping.

Once successfully mated the bitch should go on to have puppies. Dogs don't have miscarriages but there can be other problems that result in no puppies. However, as a rule, the bitch will go the full term of around sixty three days before giving birth. Any such problems arising should only be dealt with by a qualified vet and so I offer no advice other than do not delay in contacting the vet if you feel there is something wrong.

You will see no changes in the bitch for what seems like an age. If you're really keen to find out whether the mating was successful then three weeks after mating is the best time to either have her scanned by a scanning professional (they advertise in the dog press) or take her to the vet who should be able to confirm her pregnancy.

The better you prepare her physically for the litter the easier she will find it all and the quicker she will get back her figure and condition. Carry on exercising her, possibly good walks rather than running. As always, feed her a well balanced diet and, as the date for whelping draws near, if you feel she maybe needs a tonic give some multi vitamins. Don't overfeed her but give her variety. Otherwise carry on as normal. Whilst there is no set timetable to events, at around 5 weeks your bitch will probably have thickened out across her back and her stomach dropped down slightly. As the due day comes closer she will get heavier and her lovely elegant brisket will seem to disappear, her teats will start

Another bitch two days away from whelping.

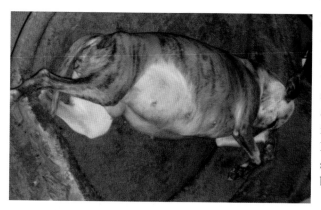

Having a rest before the puppies arrive.

swelling and you will begin to see the babies moving around trying to get comfortable. It can be quite fascinating to watch the little lumps burrowing away under her coat trying to get the best spot. Depending on her size and condition the bitch can be quite uncomfortable towards the end but she still does need exercising, albeit slowly. Also you should now have introduced her to the whelping box; its a good idea to get her used to sleeping in it before the time so it will be familiar. A good whelping box should be easy to clean, big enough for your bitch to lay out at full stretch and stand up in if the box is covered, and also it must be firm enough for her to push against whilst in labour. When you feel labour is starting its best to remove any blankets or bedding and have plenty of paper in the box. The paper can then be destroyed and changed quite easily.

I try to interfere with the birth as little as possible but am always on hand just in case. Its usually pretty obvious when the time is almost near. The bitch will become restless and pant quite heavily as she's wandering around. Her milk will start to fill into her teats and very possibly she will have diarrhoea. A sure sign the litter is on its way is the dam being edgy in general and not eating her meal. I have often found that my pups usually come during the night, why this should be I don't know. Whippets usually make excellent whelpers and mothers. However be warned they can be quite a handful once labour has started, howling, screaming, shredding and tearing anything in the way. That's where the paper in the box comes in very handy. This is one reason why I would advise against having the litter, say, in the dining room. Far better in a utility room or similar. There has been many a carpet or easy chair fall victim to a frantic bitch about to give birth. If the bitch has had the opportunity to become accustomed to resting and sleeping in the whelping box then she will be quite happy in there and as soon as the first pup has arrived you won't be able to coax her out!

Whelping Sequence

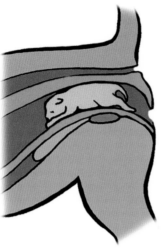

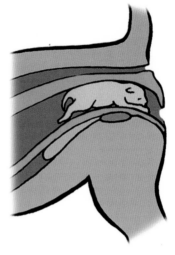

The pup may face forwards or backwards (as above) during the birth process.

Pup at the end of the birth canal ready to be delivered.

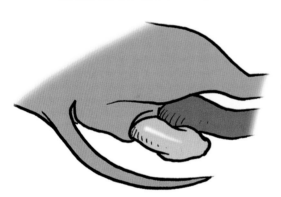

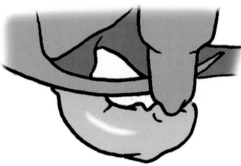

Pup emerging head first in its sac.

Bitch stimulating pup to breathe after the sac has been removed.

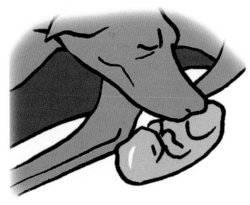

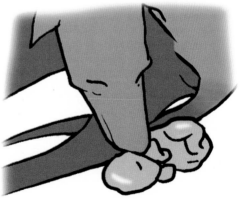

Licking the pup clean.

The pup is now ready to be placed on a teat.

The first sign you should see that means the first puppy is really on the way is a dark greenish fluid. The pup should appear within two hours of this but often sooner. Don't let it go for much longer than two hours without contacting your vet. Each puppy comes in its own birth sac and with its own placenta attached. In an ideal world, the puppy will be born head first and the bitch then breaks the birth sac and clears the pup's nose and mouth to allow breathing. Then she will bite the umbilical cord and eat up the placenta. She will then concentrate on licking and moving the pup around almost roughly until it is able to scramble to the nearest teat to suckle. Magically, this action then causes a message to prompt the next pup in line to start the journey to the outside world. The whole process is awesome and I never, ever fail to be moved and amazed at the strength and gentleness with which the new mother copes with what is happening. Take note the new baby will not look particularly like a Whippet; they have full rounded heads and a new born white one could be mistaken for a Bull Terrier or similar. The Whippet shape comes along almost unnoticeably.

However, as I mentioned, this is the ideal birth and although Whippets are usually good whelpers with few problems there can be some things to watch out for. Occasionally a first time mother can go into a panic state at what is happening to her during labour. Usually once the first puppy has appeared she gets down to the business in hand but sometimes a little help is needed to make the going easier. A long labour can tire the bitch and she may find it difficult for the final thrust to get the puppy out. If this is the case then you may need to gently but firmly ease the puppy out. Firstly, scrub your hands and lubricate them with petroleum jelly. Slide your fingers into the vagina to take a firm grip of the puppy's shoulders and then with the next contraction or contractions gently pull the puppy in a downwards direction. The placenta will follow. The mother then has to break the birth sac and clean the puppy's face quite quickly; if she doesn't then you must intervene. Pierce the sac around the head with your thumb nail and rub the face, neck and chest with a face cloth or towel; quite rough towelling material is best. Try putting the pup to the mother and she should now be licking it quite vigorously around the face and chest to stimulate breathing. If she is still not interested, hold the puppy firmly to support the neck and head then swing him from your chest in an arc to your knee, keeping his nose pointing downwards at all times. This should help clear his airways. Keep rubbing his chest and face for a few minutes then, when you are satisfied, place the puppy onto the mother's teat. Hopefully she will now have realised what is happening and her natural instinct will take over.

Sometimes a puppy will present itself feet first. This isn't too serious usually but don't let her struggle. Wasted effort will tire her out and cause possible danger to the puppies lining up in the birth canal. If you are unable to bring along the puppy with the contractions then you really need to call the vet.

Each puppy has a placenta attached to its own birth sac. When the mother bites the umbilical cord she will then eat the placenta. Let her do this. It may not appear very appealing to us but by eating this the bitch is re-introducing natural elements and vitamins into her system. Some modern thinking human mothers now emulate the animal

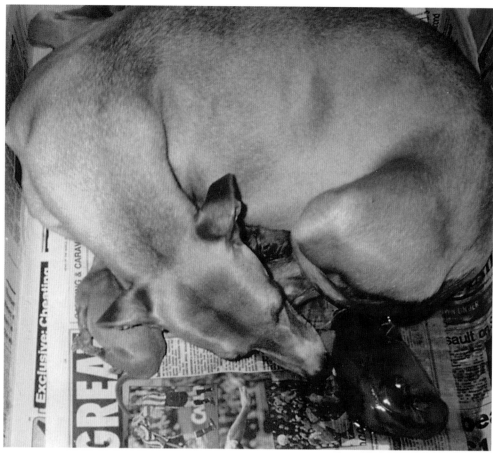

Pup in watery sac has just been delivered, the bitch instinctively turns to take care of it.

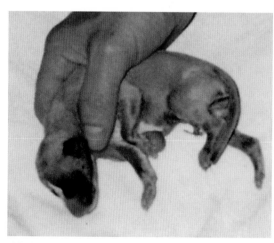

All cleaned up and ready to be placed on a teat.

world and eat the placenta following the birth of their children. Apparently the high vitamin B content is beneficial in preventing post-natal depression. One thing to watch out for is that there is a placenta for each puppy. It can sometimes become detached during the birth and it must be brought out. A vet would need to perform this task. If the mother has a large litter it is possible she may not eat all the placentas. If, after she has bitten the cord and attended to the puppy she doesn't show any interest, give her a

Once the litter have arrived safely, the dirty papers can be removed and replaced with clean bedding.

short time and then discreetly remove it. If the mother doesn't bite the cord within about ten minutes then you need to cut it for her. Take great care. Tie a piece of cord, fishing line or similar, quite tightly around it about half to three quarters of an inch from the tummy and then with sterilised scissors cut the cord.

In between each puppy the mother will busy herself with the new arrivals. The puppies can come at any interval and may sometimes follow each other in a matter of minutes or even delay for up to two hours apart. If your bitch seems to be going a long time between the puppies then she may want to have a drink of water or even go out to relieve herself. Its usually pretty obvious by the mother's behaviour when the last pup has been born. She goes into a more relaxed position and just busies herself with the new babies in between sleeping and maybe drinking, but you do need to check. Stand the bitch and gently feel all around her from above, going under to check there are no lumps or anything that feels unusual. Once all the puppies are delivered, change the bedding and make the litter comfortable. Its wise to still use newspaper as a bottom layer and on top use one of the thermal woolly type blankets available for dogs. This will be more comfortable for mum, help the puppies grip as they move around and also keep them warm and dry. Any wetness will go through to the newspaper. The mother may appreciate something light to eat at this time but don't overdo it. Ensure she has plenty of clean water and lots of milk throughout the first couple of weeks.

The new mother enjoying a well deserved rest whilst her puppies suckle contentedly.

As the new family settle down I usually feed her a light breakfast and a small fish meal around midday. This not only tempts the appetite but is also rich in calcium and vitamins which pass through the mother's milk to the babies. Then a meat and biscuit meal can be given in the evening. A new mother should be fed smaller amounts regularly to keep her fit and in condition whilst feeding her litter. A little scrambled egg is light and usually eaten up quickly for breakfast or supper. Cooked liver is excellent to tempt a flagging appetite at the beginning but do keep the amounts small at first.

After the birth there will be a discharge from the mother. This is dark brown, reddish in colour and lasts for around about a week or so before paling to a clear mucus that eventually stops. This is quite usual and nothing to worry about. However, if at any time you see a black, or greenish coloured or a bright blood coloured red discharge and possibly an unpleasant smell, then you will need to contact the vet for further investigation. Newspaper is still ideal, until the discharge has stopped, from a hygiene point of view. If you do use other things such as blankets or woolly dog bedding then make sure you keep it clean. For the first couple of weeks the mother will eat all the puppy excreta as part of her routine. Her licking and cleaning stimulates the puppies bodily functions. Keep an eye on the babies for little scabs. These can sometimes happen in a big litter or if the new mum hasn't cleaned them quite so well. It isn't any problem, all that is necessary is gentle bathing with cotton wool soaked in warm water and Savlon. Once you start weaning the puppies and separate them from mother for short periods you will need to clean the mess. Wherever possible remove the excreta straight away. If its left for any length of time then the pups will become curious and possibly start to eat it which is a terrible habit to get into and once started difficult to stop.

Between three and five days old, the puppies need to have their dew claws removed from their front legs. Many experienced breeders are able to do this for themselves but a novice should either take the pups to the vet or arrange for an experienced person to come in and do it. Its best to remove them as they are easily caught in grass and similar, causing injury and bleeding. Most show Whippets have them removed although it isn't compulsory. Hopefully everything is running smoothly and you will probably hear very little from the new mother in the first days as she will be totally absorbed with her young family. She should be calm and really just eating, sleeping and feeding her precious babies. Don't worry unduly if she seems to be off her food in these first few days and looks rather drained, it is understandable. As long as she has plenty to drink and small amounts of nutritious food and the babies are quiet and content then all is well. Let the bitch adjust and get her energy back slowly. Apart from an odd squeal the only sound you should hear from the babies is a soft contented mewing type of noise. A change will probably come over your bitch as she will now instinctively protect the litter from everything. Don't allow too many visitors as this can be quite stressful for her and also may risk infection to the babies. Even the most placid bitch can take a chunk out of someone or another dog if she feels they are a danger so its best not to tempt fate. Usually when the pups are older and running around most mothers will ease off a little. Its best to feed her quite light but nutritious meals regularly, usually three or four a day. In the first couple of weeks she will be loathe to leave the nest and will probably only do so to go to the toilet, racing back to do a head count with her nose of all the puppies. At about two weeks increase the amount and decrease the number of meals to be getting back to a more normal routine. Use common sense and judge by how well the bitch is looking.

A puppy's eyes will usually start to open somewhere between ten and fourteen days old. With the new found confidence this gives them, they will become more adventurous and, often before three weeks old, will be wobbling around the whelping box. As soon as they are able to stand quite steadily is the best time to start them lapping milk. Put a little slightly warm milk into a saucer or very low sided dish. Push the puppy's head gently but firmly down into the milk, release the head and then repeat. Usually after a few times the puppy has licked the milk from his nose and will have decided its good and worth a try to get some more. As with teaching anything, the best help really is patience. If I have a puppy that doesn't take to milk so easily then I will offer a tiny piece of meat and after a couple of pieces the little pup knows exactly what to do. Don't let them have too much.

Aged two weeks old and already moving about on their own.....

.....however their eyes are still closed and they are not yet able to hear.

What a difference a week makes! Three weeks old and standing to lap milk.

Increase the size of the meals you give them gradually. At first it's just a gradual process of introduction and also a slight relief for the dam, who can get pretty sore with the sharp claws and needle pointed teeth that start to appear. Once the puppies get to about 10 days it is helpful if you clip the tips of the sharp little claws away with ordinary nail clippers; they really can make a devoted mother quite uncomfortable.

Between three and four weeks old the pups are beginning to get into a more established routine of sleeping, feeding and playing. Take advantage of this time to let the dam have a rest too and, as the pups are able to have more substantial feeds from you, try to keep her away from them for longer periods starting with about an hour. The puppies will need worming at this stage. The best way of administering worming syrup is to use a small syringe. This way you are certain that all the required dose is taken and its so much easier to get the syrup right into the puppies' throats. The mother's instinct will be to try to get back to them as soon as possible but this rest time away from them really will do her good and also the pups won't be able to be constantly topping up with mother's milk and therefore should be more ready for what you are offering.

By around four to five weeks old you should be able to put down a bowl big enough for them all to get around and just stand back and watch, and listen. Its a great noise to hear them diving in for a good feed after a hearty playtime. Check that all the litter are getting enough. Sometimes the quieter, less bouncy puppy can be pushed out by a more boisterous sibling. The sooner you can get them fully satisfied the better for the mother, even though she may not believe you!

When the puppies are six weeks old they are tremendous fun. They should have finished taking milk from the dam and so her milk supply should be drying up. Its time for the puppies to be wormed again and also the dam. They really should be sleeping away from her and only be with her for very short periods during the day if she absolutely demands it. At this age a puppy should be on four meals a day. A breakfast of milk or

Aged five weeks. Back onto newspaper again as more cleaning up after them is required now that they are older and almost weaned.

Always supervise children and dogs. Introducing the pups to children will help with their socialisation.

cereals; a meal at lunchtime of either fish or meat with biscuit; a similar meal early evening; and, at supper time, milk and/or cereals again. If you chose to feed one of the complete puppy diets then follow the instructions to the letter as they are carefully researched to give a balanced diet. Their day will consist of waking, eating, playing, sleeping and so on. A content puppy of this age will collapse anywhere and fall asleep after a hectic play.

From about six weeks old the puppies are interested in anything and everything that's going on around them and there's nothing better than introducing them to the human

Aged six weeks and tired out after a play session. Note the variety of articles provided for their amusement.

Enjoying outdoor life in the safety of a puppy pen.

The breeder of this litter decided to keep the fawn dog, Digby. We shall trace his (and his litter sister Fuschia's) progress over the first twelve months in the following photos.

race in general. Young children and puppies are a great mix for each other and supervised play is most beneficial to the puppies as a confidence builder.

Play needs to be supervised to prevent youngsters being too rough. Although puppies are lively and enjoy rough and tumble, they are still quite vulnerable. Give them lots of toys to play with. The pups in the picture overleaf would have had quite a lot of fun with the egg box and a knotted piece of rope is great for them to have tug-of-war competitions with. Whatever they have you must be sure that it won't splinter and hurt them. The earlier young puppies learn to mix, the more confident they will be with strangers. Also now, if you haven't already decided, its time to decide who you will be keeping from the litter - not always very easy!

At twelve to thirteen weeks a puppy is usually starting to shape up and resemble a Whippet and you can probably have a good idea of what to expect in the way of development in the immediate future.

From the profile photo of Digby, you can see that, although still a baby, the outline is taking shape. This dog has good length, he's well proportioned with a good spring of pastern. The front picture shows that he has good strong bone, a clean front and full chest. He also has lovely dark pigmentation and a good expression. In fact, all in all, a very promising puppy.

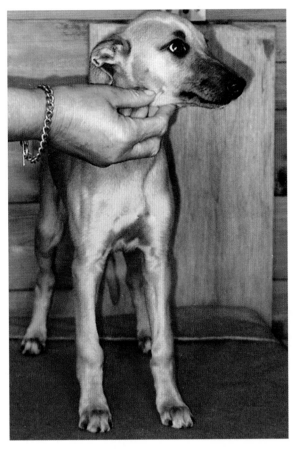

Digby learning to stand quietly on the table.

Digby in profile aged 13 weeks.

In the photo of Digby and Fuschia together (aged 5 months) you can see that they are shaping up and fulfilling the promise they had when much younger. Very similar in type and both with good true fronts.

The photo of Fuschia taken from the front shows good ear carriage, pigmentation and expression. Her front can also be seen to be good and clean. The picture of Digby at the age of six months shows that he still has the good length and proportions promised in the earlier picture; in addition he still has good spring of pastern and maturity is bringing him good angulation.

The final picture is at one year old and almost fully mature, another six months should just about finish them.

If you compare the picture of these two to that of the 1966 photograph of the two Cockrow bitches, who can be found way back in the youngsters' pedigrees, you will find them not too dissimilar and that thirty years or so hasn't after all really made much difference to the type.

Digby and Fuschia aged 5 months old.

Fawn bitch, Fuschia (litter sister to Digby), aged 6 months.

Digby aged 6 months.

One year old and almost fully mature.

Cockrow Tarantara and Cockrow Taradiddle.

A General Timetable of Events

Finally, there are no hard and fast rules as to what happens when, and not every litter will be exactly the same, but the following is intended as a loose guide.

(A whelping table can be found on page 252.)

Peak of season	Mating
21 days into pregnancy	Scanner/vet is now able to confirm pregnancy if required
35 days into pregnancy	Bitch starting to lose elegant outline and become wider
49 days into pregnancy	Introduce bitch to whelping box. Review bitch's diet and general condition
63rd day of pregnancy	Estimated delivery day
Pups aged 3 - 5 days old	Remove dew claws
At 10 days old	Trim the sharp ends of the puppies' nails
At 14 days old	Eyes should now be opening
At 3 weeks	Start weaning. Worm puppies
At 5 weeks	Worm again. Lengthen periods away from mother
At 6 weeks	Separate from mother. Allow people to visit and permit some handling of the puppies
At 8 weeks	Puppies should now be fully weaned. Ready to go to new homes. Worm the bitch

Chapter Eleven

Health And Welfare

This chapter is written as a guide to maintaining a healthy life for your dog and to perhaps be of help and reduce panic in the event of an accident or emergency. It is not intended to be an all-embracing bible for the health of your dog for life. Hopefully if you spot symptoms soon enough, major health problems can be sorted out before causing too much pain and suffering to your dog. If your dog is unfortunate enough to need veterinary treatment then this chapter may help you alleviate some of the pain and discomfort until professional treatment can be carried out.

Fortunately there are no serious genetic problems in this breed, as can sometimes be found in other breeds, and providing you are sensible with diet and exercise you can expect your Whippet to be around for a good few years. The basic guideline to remember is that you are as responsible for your dog as a parent is for a child in these matters and so common sense must prevail. Whilst many health problems can be remedied at home, if you are in any doubt whatsoever then you must always consult your vet.

Once you have your puppy, a visit to the vet should be the first thing. This way you can be sure that the puppy is healthy and at the same time also get to know the vet and staff at the clinic. It's important that you feel comfortable with the vet and happy with any treatment your dog receives at the surgery. Always ask questions if you are unsure of any treatment being recommended, it is far better to be safe than sorry. When deciding on which vet to use it's advisable to ask around friends and neighbours to see where they go, but do bear in mind that everyone has their own preferences and experiences so opinions will vary.

There follow some pointers as a general guide as to whether your dog is healthy or otherwise. Always remember, never take chances or let symptoms persist untreated.

The Birds And The Bees

Mating and related issues are explained in detail in the chapter relating to breeding and rearing a litter but something to watch out for in summer are wasp and bee stings and other insect bites. They can be quite troublesome and cause discomfort. The trouble is most Whippets I know still think it a great old game to try to catch them and will pursue it to the end. The stings will usually leave a large swelling which is painful and irritating. If your dog is allergic to the sting then the consequences can be quite serious with regard to breathing, so go straight to the vet for treatment. In milder cases remove the sting, wipe with alcohol and bathe with cool water until the anger is out of the swelling. You may hope that your dog has learned a lesson, but don't expect it!

Most dogs get fleas from time to time and it's advisable to have a regular search out and destroy plan to keep on top of them. Signs of infestation are itching and inflammation, skin problems, restlessness and distress in your dog and also bites on the owner. There is a wide selection of sprays on the market which make life much easier. If fleas are left to live on a dog then it will have a very poor effect on his general health and, I would imagine, popularity! Fleas can also be responsible for the transmission of tapeworms. Once a flea lands on a dog it remains there until removed or until the flea dies. Once a female flea has bitten she produces a great number of eggs within a few days. These eggs fall from the dog and hatch out and then the warmth of a nearby dog will stimulate the flea into jumping on to him, perpetrating the whole cycle. It's a frightening thought that a single flea can produce over 2,000 eggs in a lifetime so, in summary, I would advise that fleas are something to keep well clear of. It will help if each time you have a de-fleaing session you change your dog's bedding right through, and of course regular vacuum cleaning in his favourite cosy places will be most beneficial in keeping the invaders at bay.

Bladder

Try to get your dog to drink plenty of water from an early age and make sure clean, fresh water is always available.

Almost any problem with the waterworks that I can think of needs treatment by a vet and so much can be identified from testing the urine that I feel no irregularities should be left without consulting the vet. It would be most useful when your dog has a problem if you are able to take a sample of fresh urine to the surgery with you. It can be quite tricky obtaining a sample but luckily the build of a Whippet makes it much easier than getting a sample from something like a Yorkshire Terrier. When you go for the sample try to get it first thing in the morning because usually the urine has built up overnight and so you should be able to obtain enough for a sample. You will need to take quite a shallow container with a wide top out with you when exercising and then slide it into the stream of urine when either your bitch squats or dog cocks his leg. The wide neck allows you to catch more but don't forget to transfer the sample into a more manageable container such as a screw top jar to take to the vets.

Bowels

A well balanced regular diet is the best way to prevent any bowel disorders. All dogs are different; some can and do eat almost anything with no ill effect and others thrive better on a plain diet. If your dog is generally healthy and fit then you can be confident that you are feeding correctly but if your dog has bouts of diarrhoea or constipation seemingly for no reason then maybe you ought to rethink his diet. As with the waterworks, it isn't advisable to let any bowel irregularity continue untreated for any length of time.

Probably the most common problem is diarrhoea. This can be due to a number of causes, often eating too much of the wrong food. This shouldn't last for any length of time.

Do not feed but make sure fresh drinking water is available. If the diarrhoea lasts 24 hours or more then consult the vet without further delay. If vomiting and a temperature accompanies the diarrhoea then do not wait, consult the vet as soon as possible as these could be symptoms of something serious. A Whippet can dehydrate very quickly when losing body fluids and this means swift action is essential.

Dry hard stools are a sure sign of constipation and once again this can be caused by the wrong diet or sometimes the result of an intestinal blockage. Whilst the dog's digestive system is built to cope with bones (only give him marrow bones or roast bones), sometimes they can cause a blockage. If this happens then consult the vet immediately. Try to get the dog to drink water and if you are worried that your dog may be dehydrating before you get to the vet then squirt water right down the dog's throat a little at a time.

Ears

Possibly the first sign that you will see of any ear trouble is your dog shaking his head or rubbing and scratching the ear repeatedly with the paw. Ear problems shouldn't be left as these can quite soon turn into something more serious and difficult to treat. The best way to prevent ear problems is by keeping the inside nice and clean by regularly cleaning with cotton wool buds and warm water or warmed olive oil. Don't 'dig' into the ear but gently turn the bud into it. This way you will be able to lift anything lurking in there out rather than push it further in. As with the nose and eyes, foreign bodies in the ears can cause problems but any deep probing should be done by the vet.

If the ear has a brown waxy substance on the inside and there is a discharge, probably accompanied by an unpleasant smell from the ear, then its quite possible that the dog has Canker. Do not attempt to treat this. Go to the vet as soon as possible.

If your dog is repeatedly scratching around the ear accompanied by a discharge which is more dry than waxy, then have a look with a magnifying glass. If you can see tiny white insects then your dog has ear mites. Drops can be bought from the pet shop to remedy the problem but if it doesn't clear up in accordance with the guidelines for the drops then consult your vet.

To apply ear drops, hold the head tilted slightly to one side in a firm but reassuring manner. Squeeze the drops into the ear canal and then gently massage to spread the medication around the area.

Eyes

Just as in humans, a healthy dog should have clear, clean bright eyes and similarly a dog's eyes are just as delicate. Sore or runny eyes should be cleaned and bathed and then inspected closely for possible causes. A fairly common cause is a foreign body in the eye but in some cases this could be an indication of an infection such as Conjunctivitis which will need treatment from the vet. If the eyes are mattering or weeping and there are other symptoms such as a runny nose then go to the vet immediately.

If you can see a foreign body then very carefully try to remove it using a cotton wool bud but if you are not able to get it out easily then bathe and apply eye ointment to help move the object. The safest eyewash is simply boiled water left to cool to blood heat. If this doesn't help after a couple of attempts then go to the vet without further delay as an object can cause permanent damage if allowed to work its way into the eyeball.

If the eyeball is injured then you can make your dog a little more comfortable before you get to the vets by bathing the eye in castor oil and covering it with cotton wool soaked in castor oil, but this should only be a temporary measure until professional treatment can be administered.

Applying eye drops is similar to nose drops, the most important thing to remember is to be firm but reassuring. Tilt the head as far back as comfortably possible, apply the drops from a short distance to the inner corner of the eye and hold in position for a short time, allowing the drops to spread around the eye.

Maturity

If your Whippet bitch is with you purely for companionship then you may be well advised to have her spayed quite early on. This will prevent any accidental matings, which would result in unwanted puppies, and also be much easier on your home. Whippets are very clean but there will be blood and natural smells which will mark your home and furnishings. Also, even worse, you may be the victim of unwelcome attention from eager neighbourhood Romeos picking up her scent after being exercised. Often the seasons are every six months and last for about three weeks so it could be quite a nuisance.

This Nylaring will keep the dog amused whilst exercising his teeth and gums.

Discuss with your vet the best time to perform the operation. Don't feel guilty as you're not depriving her of anything. If you have a dog and a bitch living with you then it really is essential as the poor dog will go almost out of his mind and could turn into an obsessive demon just to get to her for a mating. Even the loveliest, most obedient chappie will winkle his way into rooms where you think your bitch will be safe.

Mouth

A dirty mouth on a dog is really very unpleasant and is usually accompanied by bad breath. A healthy mouth should be pink with strong white teeth. Any dullness is a sign of plaque. Plaque is a mixture of leftover food and naturally produced bacteria that adheres to the enamel coating of the tooth. As it remains and hardens calculus is formed and plaque then forms onto this and so on it goes. All this growth will cause the gums to be quite painful and inflamed and if not remedied can lead to gingivitis and periodontitus. If allowed to build up, removing the plaque can cause unnecessary bills at the vets. A child's tooth brush or a rag soaked in salt water or very diluted hydrogen peroxide is all that's really necessary to keep the mouth clean if your dog has a healthy diet and plenty of things to chew on. Don't use human toothpaste as the taste and sensation is not pleasant for a dog, but canine toothpaste is available. If calculus or tartar does build up

Enjoying a nylon dental floss which helps to keep teeth free from tartar.

then it can be removed with a dental pick but most inexperienced owners find it easier to let the vet remove it. There are a wide variety of chews made from processed hide easily available quite cheaply from supermarkets and pet stores. Most dogs love grinding them down to nothing and at the same time they are cleaning their teeth. A well boiled large marrowbone is also great for this and lasts ages - not quite so colourful to look at though. These bones can be bought ready prepared from pet stores or fresh from the butchers. Fresh ones need to be boiled for a long time to harden them to prevent the bone splintering. Do not give your dog bones that splinter such as chicken and chop bones, they can cause untold damage. Any broken or bad teeth should be treated by the vet as soon as possible.

Excessive saliva and dribbling isn't usually a problem in Whippets so a sudden increase in the amount of saliva or dribbling could be an indication of some other problem. The first thing to check for is - yes, you've got it - foreign bodies. Quite often a piece of wood or bone can break off and get stuck behind the teeth and these can be usually be removed with patience and a pair of tweezers. If you are unable to dislodge the piece then, once again, the vet is better equipped to get in and remove the offending piece. For something deeply embedded it may be necessary to anaesthetise your dog so as to give the vet full access without causing your dog too much stress or discomfort. If you are unable to trace a foreign body but there are other symptoms such as bad breath or a sore mouth then it would be advisable to visit the vet as prolonged symptoms could be an indication of some form of infection.

Nose

The old wives' tale of a wet nose being a sign of good health is pretty near the mark but not the only criteria. A warm nose doesn't necessarily mean anything is wrong. The nose should always be clean. A watery clear secretion is perfectly normal but any thicker or coloured discharge should be checked out as soon as possible. As with humans this could be a symptom of a complaint connected with the chest or respiratory system and so the vet will check the lungs, temperature and general condition for further signs of an illness. Dogs do sneeze from time to time but if this comes on suddenly and is persistent then it could mean that there is something stuck in the nose. Here again you will need the vet. It isn't easy to remove a foreign body from a dog's nose and could quite easily cause pain and damage to the dog, so take no chances. Dogs are like humans and suffer allergies but the symptoms are able to be eased so here again a visit to the vet is necessary.

If nose drops are recommended then the following method will probably cause the least fuss. Be firm but reassuring with the dog. Using one hand tip the nose upwards so he can't see, but do keep talking to him while at the same time dropping the medication onto the nose from a short distance away. Do not let the dropper enter into the nostril, the drops will run down because of the angle at which you're holding the head. It's probably easier if done by 2 people with one person giving the drops and the other holding the dog firmly around the shoulders and again reassuring him.

Sticks and stones....

Whippets' bones are no more brittle than any other dogs but because of their build and often lively temperament, broken legs are something that do occur. Most Whippets under 3 years old seem to believe that they can fly and insist on trying. After this age most, but not all, have usually have come to terms with the fact that they are without the necessary equipment.

If your dog is unfortunate enough to experience a broken bone then the first thing to do is to make the bone secure by applying a splint, firm enough to support the bone whilst at the same time causing no extra pain. Don't attempt to set the bone but as soon as your dog is comfortable and supported enough to be moved, go to the vet. Fortunately many breaks can be mended with little after-effects and life can carry on as normal in a relatively short time, but unfortunately there are no rules or guarantees that everything will be fine. Here again you really need to be able to talk honestly and openly with your vet about the possible outcome. I know of some show Whippets that have had broken limbs and have made a wonderful recovery and the mend is not visible unless you have the inside knowledge to know exactly where the break happened. This obviously comes at a price. The cost of a specialist setting a break, albeit almost invisible, can run into a four figure sum. Many vets can do a perfectly adequate job on breaks and the dog be perfectly comfortable and mobile afterwards at a fraction of the price. Prevention is far better than surgery so it does help if you don't encourage your dog to be "wild", leaping about from

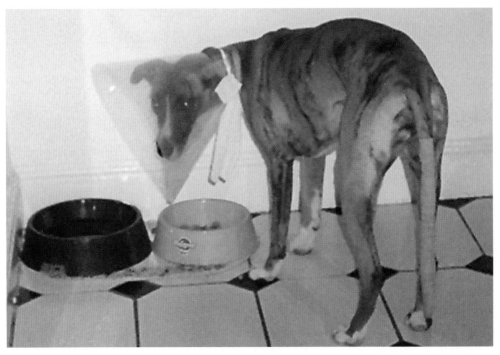

A plastic head cover will prevent the dog from removing her dressing and re-opening the wound.

furniture to floor and such and over walls and hedges, but it can be quite an impossible task with some. Broken limbs are usually set in plaster and a comfortable but annoying restraint put over the head to prevent the pot being nibbled and licked away. It probably takes around six weeks for the leg to heal sufficiently for the plaster and support to be removed but this all depends on each individual case.

Worming

Almost all puppies are born infected with roundworm. Dormant larvae in the bitch's tissues become active with pregnancy and are passed on to the unborn puppies through the placenta. The new mother can also pass the larvae through her milk until the pups are around 6 weeks old. Some of the general signs of infestation are digestive problems and coughing, a pot belly and yet failing to gain weight elsewhere. In extreme cases death can be caused to very young puppies and a highly infected bitch may subsequently give birth to "fading" puppies or still births. Worms are quite easy to pick up but thankfully relatively easy to treat. A breeder will generally have wormed the litter twice before the puppies leave for their new homes and they will need worming again at around ten weeks old. If you chose to use a worming syrup rather than tablets you may find it easier to use a syringe. This will enable you to measure the correct amount out and then ensure that the full dose is directed straight down the throat. Once mature, I really feel that your dog is the best guide as to how often to worm him. If he is looking "down" or showing any of the symptoms mentioned then treat him for worms first of all. It's quick and painless and your dog should show an improvement in a very short time. If the treatment doesn't make any difference then you need to investigate further for possible causes.

Caring For The Older Dog

As I've said previously, Whippets are very adaptable and can be quite hardy, so you can expect to have one with you for a good few years. They can suffer from much the same sort of problems as we ageing humans do: diabetes, arthritis, rheumatism, cancer, heart conditions and pretty much anything that can wear out the body with the passing of years.

I have always found that the first sign of old age in my Whippets has been a stiffening in the back legs, much as with old people. Similarly as with human arthritis sufferers, the condition can be eased by gentle exercise. Regular walking, even for a short distance, can help keep the legs and back end more supple. Medication can be given by the vet but as its a permanent condition I prefer to use a natural remedy suggested by a herbalist. Celery seed tablets I found to be very effective but they do have a diuretic effect so are probably not practical if your dog lives in a densely carpeted area in the house. Pearls of garlic and kelp are very good and worth trying. The main thing to remember is that old Whippets are really just like old relatives. They eat less, sleep more, don't feel the need to run anywhere very often and sometimes just need extra thought from you.

Whilst I feel strongly about teaching good, no nonsense eating habits at a very early age I do think that it's fine to perhaps give in to whims for the old ones. I have had older

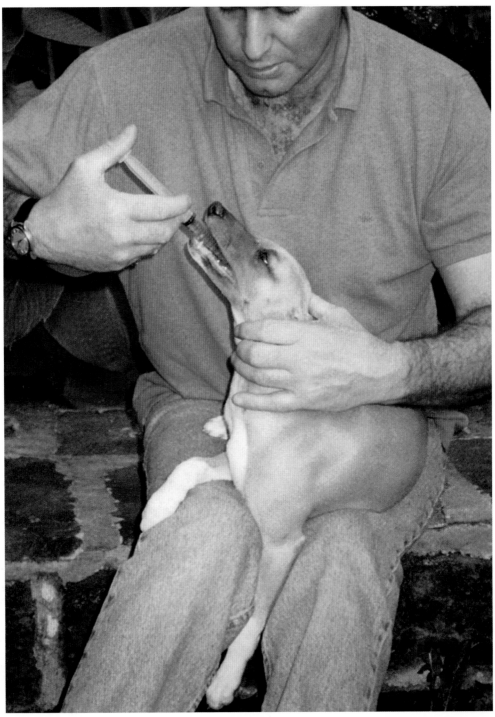

Administering worming syrup or any type of oral liquid medicine is much easier with a syringe.

ones who have "spread" with age. Usually these were the ones who always cleared everything in the feed bowl at one go in younger days, carrying on in the same way as they aged. I've also had the more choosy ones who ate sufficient when they were hungry but knew when to stop. Siobhan, always a good well built bitch, was quite a slow dainty eater and in later years "kept her figure". Fergal was of the same temperament and, latterly, quite bony. Blacque Legacy, unfortunately, was quite the reverse and unless kept in check would have ballooned. The best guide lines for the more delicate oldies is to feed nutritious food in smaller portions, cut down the bulk and perhaps offer more variety. Leave it down longer so they can have some and then come back for more. There aren't many Whippets that I've come across who don't love milk. Most of my dogs love rice pudding, porridge and the like.

Elderly Whippets may be indulged a little more in their feeding habits.

It is really important to remember that you're doing your dog no favours by letting him get overweight. If your old dog is still happy on one meal a day then don't worry about it, carry on as normal. We are all different with our own habits and how our bodies react to what and when we eat, and so are the dogs. As long as the dog is happy and healthy then you're doing it right. If things change then have a slight re-think on his diet to see if things improve.

The senses usually become duller too in an older dog. You probably won't notice your dog's hearing deteriorating until its quite bad. Nothing can really be done about it but be more vigilant when out with him as although Whippets are sight hounds, they also depend on sound to be aware of what is going on around and about. Failing eyesight is also something that is inevitable the older a dog gets, so special care whenever the dog is away from his kennel, home or familiar surrounding is necessary.

I've found with many Whippets which I and friends have owned, it very often has to be your decision when your dog is at the end of his days. It's a very hard decision to have to make but the prime consideration has to be for the dog and his quality of life. My own yardstick is while an old dog still enjoys food, still greets myself and others with a wagging tail and knows when to go "to the toilet", no matter how doddery, then they're okay. Once they're unable to do these basic things then, sadly, I feel you owe it to the dog to make the decision. It is heartbreaking but it's cruel to prolong your dog's life for the selfish reason of wanting his company. A faithful friend is entitled to love and dignity. I feel, when making the decision, that it is "better done a day too early than a minute too late". If this happens to you then your vet may come to your home or you may need to take your dog to the surgery. It is quite painless and the dog literally goes to sleep very quickly. If you ask, you will be able to take him home after he has been put to sleep. We have our oldies buried at home and Fergal is in a lovely spot in the garden just away from the kennels. I would suggest that if you do need to go to the surgery you ought to ask someone not too closely involved with the dog to drive you as this is a very stressful event and you could be a risk on the road to yourself and others.

Agility is an enjoyable way of keeping your Whippet fit.

Chapter Twelve

Whippets Worldwide

Whippets are a truly cosmopolitan breed and can be found in many corners of the world, naturally enjoying differing levels of popularity in different countries. Top British kennels have exported stock all around the world for many decades up to the present day. When researching this book it was most interesting to discover the same kennel names occurring in many corners of the world. This has surely strengthened the breed globally and, in fact, many of the icons in our breed have successfully contributed to the breeding of the top specimens around the world today. I have, without exception, been impressed when discussing breeding plans and programmes with enthusiasts from abroad. These people have a true love for the breed and this has ensured that good, sound specimens are produced, often despite being a minority breed in their country. The research, care and sensible planning that is behind their eventual litters is something to be admired and although we are the 'mother' country of the breed it isn't always the case that such thought is given over to planning a litter here in Britain.

Current winning bitches in Italy: l to r, Rivarco Incredible Desire and It Ch Rivarco First Lady.

Italy

Over the years, Italy has imported a host of foreign stock, mostly British. Mrs Paulo Bianchino Spardo of the Sant'Alessandro Whippets was one of the first to introduce Laguna and Dondelayo lines. In the early 1960s she imported Martindale Fennel, who was mostly Dondelayo bred and produced a number of champions in the 1960s. At around the same period Mr Luca Consolini of the Dell'Enza kennel was very successful in bringing together Laguna and Shalfleet lines with the European lines already present in Italy. Some of his breeding laid the foundations for some of the top kennels today, most notably the Rivarco Whippets of Mr Gaetano Turrini. Another prominent breeder of the early 1970s was Mrs Uta Kukavicic. Mrs Kukavicic imported a number of British lines, for example, Laguna, Ruegeto, Courthill and Glenbervie. Around this same period Mr Paulo Dondina imported Ch Twigairy of Glenbervie who was the first in line of a whole host of British champions going to Italy. Twigairy was closely followed by White Frost of Glenbervie, Novacroft Starbright, Savilepark Sweet Harmony, Denhills Delectable, Ch Nutcracker of Nevedith and Nevedith Bright Beret.

Multi Ch Almaglo Minuette.

Ch Savilepark Sweet Harmony was imported by Mr Mauro Carpone of the Almaglo affix and, when she was mated to Samarkand's Sigma, produced Multi Ch Almaglo Minuette who was one of, if not the, greatest Italian winners in the breed. She was awarded the staggering amount of over 50 Best In Show awards.

Baron and Baroness Renai della Rena bought a number of Dondelayo dogs and also Denhills Delectable from Mrs Knight. Delectable had already produced an important dog in her litter to Dondelayo Mosaic before leaving

Ch/It Ch Denhills Delectable.

Britain. The dog was Ch Dondelayo Statue who went on to be a very important sire in Australia. Delectable was also unrivalled in the show ring. The Renais later imported from the French kennel Manoir de la Grenouillere, belonging to Mrs Bourdin. Another French kennel that has been imported to Italy is the Sac a Malices belonging to Karen Mesavage.

Although the breed isn't widely popular in Italy there is a hard core of enthusiastic exhibitors. The most recent imports are Nevedith and Hillsdown from Britain, Le Manoir de la Grenouillere from France, the Signum lines from Sweden and also Sporting Fields from America. Probably the most successful modern day kennel in Italy is Rivarco, belonging to Mr G Turrini who has brought in bloodlines from a number of these kennels.

Belgium

Belgium has a small but thriving Whippet fraternity attracting between sixty and seventy dogs at their major shows. As could probably be expected, quite a lot of their dogs are from French bloodlines. Currently, the leading kennel is probably the Di Mahana Whippets of Mr and Mrs Delabelle.

Denmark

Denmark has only a handful of enthusiasts. The first one to come to mind is the Fairway kennels belonging to Mrs B Warmberg. Her dogs have been consistent winners for many years. Mrs Warmberg is a respected figure in the show ring and has judged here in England and at the famous Skokloster show in Sweden. Another consistent winner in recent years in Denmark is Mrs V Vamberg. Her Vibes kennel has been built on a lot of Oakbark breeding.

Holland

For many years breeders in Holland have produced top quality Whippets. One of the dominant kennels is Samoem's, belonging to Tim Teiller. Ch Samoem's Silent Knight was imported to the Shalfleet kennels in Britain by Mrs Wilton-Clarke and became the first foreign bred Whippet to gain his English title. The Epicurian kennels of Mr Frank Samper have been consistent winners for many years and the backbone of his lines are Int Ch Statesman of Silkstone and Int Ch Dondelayo Paint Tin. The top winners of most recent times are the Gulleyridge kennels of Mr Frans Boers and the Of Herlaers Town Whippets belonging to Mr T J Van Essen.

Japan

The Whippet is not a particularly popular breed in Japan. However, there are a small number of conscientious Whippeteers who strive to promote the breed and ensure the quality is of a high standard. It was interesting to discover that the first Whippet was introduced to Japan as far back as 1928.

It is impossible to keep abreast of Whippets worldwide and so the following information has been written by well known, respected breeders and judges in the countries where the breed enjoys most popularity.

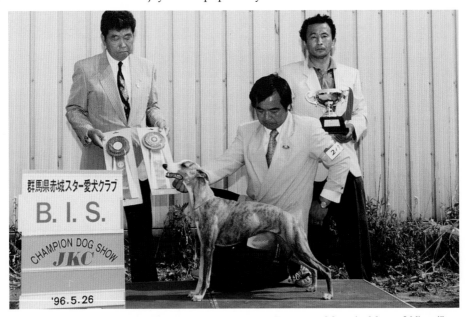

Jap Ch Lumbini Imperial FCI (Jap Ch Hillsdown Declan x Maggie Mae of Himeji).

Canadian bred Lady Beatrice, the first known Whippet to be exported to Japan.

AUSTRALIA by Frank Pieterse

The development of the breed in Australia since the 1950s has been dominated by a number of outstanding English imports. Since the late 1980s however, the English influence has been tempered somewhat by the arrival of American lines both directly and via Scandinavia. Until the mid 1990s Australian Quarantine regulations have favoured imports from the United Kingdom. This, together with historical ties between the two countries, has probably been the main reason for the bias towards English imports.

The Early English Influence 1950-1970
Around 1950 the Flashing kennels of Mr and Mrs T McGorien were successful with their Aust Ch Flashing Claire de Lune and the record Best In Show (BIS) winning Calpin Bartic Coquette, who was subsequently eclipsed by her son Aust Ch Flashing Cyclone with over 13 BIS.

Mrs M Burnside of South Australia (Allstars) started in 1950 with Allways, Laguna and Wingedfoot lines. Allstars in turn provided foundation stock for Mr and Mrs Wilson (Wingstar) from 1965. Using Briarcliffe and Waddellie lines together with Carmodian, Baydale, Nimrodel and Shalfleet lines, this kennel produced show ring and track winners.

Ch/Aust Am Ch Lowglen Oakbark Masterminde.

During the 1950s and '60s, Miss M Waddell of New South Wales imported eight Allways Whippets from England and she was to have a significant effect on the breed through her Waddellie affix. Ch Playmate of Allways (born 15.4.59) was generally considered to be her best import. The Waddellie imports and their progeny were used by a number of breeders including Mr and Mrs L Bright of Queensland (Zipity), Messrs I Payne and J Karas of New South Wales, (Amersham), Mrs D Stewart of Victoria, (Rosiel), and Messrs I Doherty and T Crowley of New South Wales (Martinique). In addition to campaigning the record winning Aust Ch Flashing Cyclone, Messrs Payne and Karas imported another stud dog, Aust Ch Briarcliffe Rameses, and made up many champions including Aust Ch Waddellie Rendezvous and the Specialty BIS winning Aust Ch Waddellie Supreme Atom.

Mrs D Stewart's Rosiel kennels were strongly influenced by Waddellie and Amersham lines. Her Aust Ch Amersham Ability, in addition to winning over 10 BIS and 15 Best Opposite Sex In Show awards, was the dam of some 5 Rosiel Australian champions. Mrs Stewart's puppy Rosiel Royal Sign won Best Puppy In Show at Melbourne Royal. He was closely related to Ch/Am Ch Courtney Fleetfoot of Pennyworth. In the late 1970s Mrs Stewart enthusiastically bred to the imports Ch/Am Aust Ch Lowglen Oakbark Masterminde and Ch/Aust Ch Allgarth Envoy.

In Queensland Mr and Mrs L Bright of Zipity kennels bred the almost unbeatable red fawn dog Aust Ch Zipity Wonderland on Waddellie lines ex Allways and Brekin. In the mid 1970s Mr and Mrs Bright imported Arthur Nicholson's lovely Glenbervie bitch, Glenbervie Sky Belle. Bred to Ch/Aust Ch Dondelayo Statue shortly after he came to Australia in 1977, she produced Australian champions Zipity Tartan Piper and Zipity Tartan Statuette. Piper sired the multi BIS Champion Martinique Moon Bright. Mated to her father, Statuette produced Aust Ch Kylebay Key West for Mr J Lockwood of New South Wales (Kylebay). She also had the distinction of beating her father for BOB at Brisbane Royal and won Reserve in Group whilst only just out of puppy class!

The English Influence In The 1970s - Masterminde, Envoy and Statue
The mid 1970s was arguably the most important period for the development of the breed in Australia with the import in 1973 of Ch/Am Aust Ch Lowglen Oakbark Masterminde, Ch Allgarth Envoy (1975) and, in 1977, of Ch Dondelayo Statue. Masterminde was bred along impeccable lines by Mr and Mrs D Meakin of Oakbark kennels. Starting as Oakbark Masterminde he was purchased by Mr Fred Nicholas who added his Lowglen kennel name. Mr Nicholas subsequently sold Masterminde to the Martinique kennels of Mr I Doherty and Mr T Crowley. Masterminde comfortably made up his Australian title and won BOB at Sydney Royal, but otherwise was not extensively shown.

In over a decade before the arrival of Masterminde, Messrs Doherty and Crowley, strongly influenced by the Waddellie lines, consistently won Royal CCs, BOBs in group and Group awards with such dogs as Aust Ch Waddellie Lancer, Aust Ch Waddellie Mighty Atom, Aust Ch Martinique My Fair Lady, Aust Ch Waddellie Lucy Gray, Aust Ch Waddellie Vienna and Minakin Make Me A Star. Their Aust Ch Martinique Tequila, bred along Laguna and Waddellie lines, was a highly successful show winner.

During the 1970s and '80s Masterminde, both in his own right and when his progeny were crossed with Statue, gave this kennel a spectacular series of Australian champion Whippets and wins at Championship shows and Royal shows. The Masterminde offspring Aust Ch Martinique Calico Haze, Aust Ch Martinique Calico Kate and Aust Ch Martinique Calico Hero were all top show winners at BIS and Specialty level.

In 1975 the young Ch Allgarth Envoy was imported to Australia by F M Pieterse (Statuesque) and B McCowage (Andiamo). Envoy quickly became an Australian champion and followed this with a successful show career which involved numerous BIS and many other Group awards. Envoy was the sire of Andiamo Columba, the foundation bitch for the Rothbury Kennels of Dr and Mrs I Affleck in Victoria. He also sired Aust Ch Andiamo Sabreur, who in turn sired Aust Ch Allswell Just A Dream, the top winning BIS Whippet to date in Australia. Whilst Masterminde was making his mark as a sire in Australia, in 1977 F M Pieterse imported Ch Dondelayo Statue who had quickly made up his English title, including the CC at Crufts and Reserve BIS at WELKS. Statue was to make a great mark in the show ring and as a sire, siring 43 champions and being the grandsire and great grandsire of many more. He won 4 Whippet Club Specialties, BIS, BOB, Sydney and Melbourne Royal, another 8 BIS and many Groups.

Whereas Mrs Knight's Dondelayos were tightly linebred on Ch Samarkand's Greenbrae Tarragon, Statue was somewhat of an outcross in that his dam was Ch Denhills Delectable. The Ch Laguna Ligonier grandchildren - litter brother and sister Oakbark Pyramid and Oakbark Ballerina - were the grandsire of Statue and dam of Masterminde respectively. Possibly this had something to do with the fact that Masterminde/Statue crosses were very often particularly successful. Statue sired the first Statuesque BIS winner, Aust Ch Statuesque The Sting, as well as Aust Ch Martinique Paper Mache (Best Opposite Sex in Show at Sydney Royal), Aust Ch Martinique Paper Drum (Best In Group Melbourne Royal), Aust Ch Statuesque Res Anibrow (Best In Group Sydney and Melbourne Royal and twice Specialty BIS winner), Aust Ch Statuesque Res a Loan (Specialty BIS winner) and Aust Ch Bellendene Rupert Bear (Best in Group Spring Fair, at which Statue had won BIS in 1977).

In Sydney, Mr and Mrs M Beasleigh (Bellendene) linebred strongly on Statue for many years and were rewarded with a number of outstanding champions, amongst them Aust Ch Bellendene Rupert Bear, Aust Ch Bellendene Sea Gypsy, and Aust Ch Bellendene Grey Owl.

The 1980s English Imports

In the early 1980s Messrs Doherty and Crowley imported Ch Solotown Simeon. Sired by Ch Oakbark Mr Magic of Silkstone, this brindle particolour dog was used extensively at stud in this country. Simeon's champion offspring included Aust champions Martinique SS Showpony and Siesta, and the 7 Dachlah Australian champions Bass, Flute, Piano, Harp, Bell, Drum and Tenor Solo. Mated to the Statue daughter Aust Ch Stormbay Thisbe, by Ms Y Lorenzi and Ms J Welsh, Simeon sired the top winner and Whippet Specialty RUBIS Aust Ch Stormbay Lillico and her brother Aust Ch Stormbay Flin who, campaigned in the United States by Phoebe Booth, also became an American champion.

In 1980 F M Pieterse imported the English twice-winning BIS All Breed winner, Ch Dondelayo Reinette. Mated to Statue, Reinette produced Aust Ch Statuesque the Squire who, when mated to the Envoy daughter Andiamo Columba, produced Australian champions Rothbury War Dance and Rustbucket, two highly successful show bitches for Dr and Mrs I Affleck's Rothbury kennels. Judging the Specialty in Sydney in 1986, Mrs Anne Knight (Dondelayo) awarded War Dance BIS and War Paint the Dog CC.

The Rothbury kennels went on to become one of Australia's most successful kennels by mixing Statue, Envoy and Reinette progeny judiciously and later adding their American import, Am Ch Delacreme Dragonslayer. Champions from this kennel include the Statue children Replica (who also became a Canadian champion) and Hotlips. The Dragonslayer offspring include Aust Ch Rothbury Snow Chief, Aust Ch Rothbury Storm Boy, Aust Ch Rothbury at the Ritz and Aust Ch Rothbury Bone Crusher who went to Norway and became an International Champion.

In 1986 F M and L H Pieterse imported the young Ch Cottonmere Personality of Oakbark, bred by Mr and Mrs Greenwood, and campaigned to his English title by Mr Dennis Meakin and his daughter Julie Greenwood Meakin. Personality, mated to Aust Ch Statuesque Sundancer (an

Int Aus NZ Swd Nor Ch Statuesque Personalised.
Photo: Trafford

Envoy daughter and Statue granddaughter), produced Australia's first International champion Whippet: Int Australian New Zealand Swedish and Norwegian Champion Statuesque Personalised. Campaigned by Petter Fodstad and Nenne Runsten-Fodstad in Norway and Sweden, Personalised won BIS both days at the Skokloster Sighthound Specialty in 1990. On his return to Australia he won 4 BIS All Breeds, BIG Brisbane Royal and was then campaigned to his New Zealand title by Nicole Colquohoun. Person was Top Sire in Sweden in '91 and '92.

Aust Ch Cottonmere Personality of Oakbark also sired Aust Ch Statuesque Silver Bullet, winner of Reserve BIS Sydney Royal 1992. Silver Bullet's dam was the result of a father/daughter mating on Statue with Masterminde on the tail female line.

Kennels of Note
The Allswell kennels of Mr and Mrs D Mudge, South Australia, campaigned Aust Ch Martinique Calico Star who was Top Whippet in South Australia for four consecutive years. This kennel produced Aust Ch Allswell Chit Chat (a Statue daughter and BIS winner) as well as Aust Ch Allswell Deal Me In, a multi BIG winner, Aust Ch Allswell Evening Star, winner of BIG Melbourne Royal and Aust Ch Allswell Just A Dream.

Mr and Mrs B Wilson's Noholme kennels have incorporated Statue/Masterminde and Simeon lines. Their dogs include Aust Ch Noholme Electric Blue, Aust Ch Noholme Shady Lady NZ Aust Am Can Ch Noholme Beauling Alli, who completed his American title with a major under the well known international judge Dr Espen Engh, and the great sire of the '90s Aust Ch Noholme Pepper Mill.

In South Australia the Skyeway kennels of Mr J and Mrs A Gunn have produced and campaigned many champions and BIS winners including Aust Ch Skyeway Yankee Sigma (winner of 4 BIS at the South Australian Specialty), Aust Ch Skyeway To The Stars (BIS at two Whippet Specialties) and their Aust champions Skyeway Movie Star and Hooray for Holly.

In New South Wales Ms M Deerfoot's Aust Ch Deerfoot Cameo Cabaret has taken BIS from puppy class at the NSW Specialty under the respected Swedish international judge

Aust Ch Noholme Pepper Mill.

Magnus Hagstedt. This bitch was to have an important influence on Mrs Rule-Steele's Taejaan kennels, when mated to Aust Ch Noholme Pepper Mill, producing such stars as Aust Ch Taejaan Tia Maria who in turn was to be the dam of Sydney Royal BIS winner Aust Ch Taejaan Ms Margarita. Ms Deerfoot, (who actually changed her name from 'Holmes' to 'Deerfoot') campaigned the young bitch Aust Ch Alltalk Hot Shoe Shuffle to BIS at the Sydney Specialty under American specialist Michael Dougherty.

In Queensland Mr G Swan's (Ryeford) Aust Ch Ryeford Billy Brag, bred along the Martinique lines with Statue/Masterminde influence, was just one of his numerous top show winners. His Aust Ch Martinique Seventh Ave won Best Opposite Sex In Show Melbourne Royal 1986. Also in Queensland Mr and Mrs T Cooney's Shalique kennels have produced many champions including Mr and Mrs Baxter's Shalique Satin Touch, winner of Best In Group Melbourne Royal, and litter sister Mrs Rule-Steele's Aust Ch Shalique Satin Layce, winner of Best In Group Sydney Royal. Both were sired by Aust Ch Noholme Pepper Mill.

In Sydney Mr and Mrs M and J Fleming's Meilandina kennels have been a strong force for some 15 years. Their first dog Aust Ch Zaretan Bedouin Sheik (again from Masterminde/Statue lines) started them strongly with a BOB Sydney Royal. Continuing on these lines, and including Aust Ch Rosiel Touch of Tan, they produced the highly successful Australian champions Meilandina Reason to Rave and Meilandina Reason to React, the latter being a prolific BIS and Group winner as well as having won a Specialty BIS under Mrs N Runsten.

In New South Wales, Ms B Daines (Dachlah), Ms M Hoy (Moonwind), Mr and Mrs H Jadezak (Dachswyn), Mr G Skene (Shearwind) and Mr and Mrs J Walker (Tischamingo) are respected breeders and exhibitors. Messrs Jones and Caruana bred the bitch Aust Ch Acrefair Applause, on Masterminde/Statue and Simeon lines. Owned by Mrs B Kelly (Cliffburn) of Victoria, she won BIS at the Sydney Specialty on 3 occasions.

Mr and Mrs Slayter (Calahorra) have, since the mid '70s, bred with Nimrodel, Allgarth, Dondelayo, Solotown Simeon, Baydale and Nevedith lines producing several Australian champions. Their Nevedith bred bitch Aust Ch Calahorra Toffee Apple has recently been mated to the American import Aust Am Ch Sporting Fields Irish Derby, and a puppy from this litter has taken a CC from Puppy class.

In Victoria, Mrs S Delaney (Alltalk) and Mrs N Harris (Bonnymead) are respected breeders. Mrs Delaney bred the Specialty BIS Aust Ch Alltalk Hot Shoe Shuffle and Aust Ch Alltalk In The Mood who won BIS at the Victorian Specialty under Mr D Meakin (Oakbark) in 1995. Mrs N Harris (Bonnymead) bred Aust NZ Ch Bonnymead Red Pepper and Aust Ch Bonnymead Simply Summer who took the Dog CC and Bitch CC (and BIS) respectively, at the Victorian Specialty under Mrs D McCleod (Peperone).

In the late 1980s Mrs P Adam of Queensland (Grau) imported the young English dog, Denhills Deligate. As an Australian champion and multi BIS winner, Deligate dominated the Queensland show ring and sired BIS winners. Deligate was influential in the breeding program of Mrs J Marks from Queensland (Oakway). A mating to her Parkette Presteena, (Masterminde/Statue/Martinique lines) produced the BIS Aust Ch Oakway Swing Time who, mated in turn to Int and Multi Ch Statuesque Personalised, produced the Australians champions Oakway Centre Stage and Oakway Magnafique. Centre Stage, in 1996, won the Queensland Contest of Champions and 2 free trips to Crufts for Mrs Marks and her co-owner Mr I Rasmussen. Magnafique won BOB and Runner-Up in Groups at Melbourne Royal.

Aust Ch Taejaan Ms Margarita, handled by Sonia Turay.

The late 1980s saw the move into Whippets by the kennels of Mrs Rule-Steele (Taejaan). Previously highly successful in Afghans, Mrs Rule-Steele started with some promising Noholme stock. The cornerstone of this kennel was to be Aust Ch Noholme Pepper Mill (Cricket), born in 1986, who has sired over 24 champions and 17 BIS including 6 Specialty BIS winners. These include Aust Ch Taejaan Make Mine Mink, Aust Ch Shalique Satin Layce, Aust Ch Taejaan Tia Maria and Aust Ch Taejaan Read My Lips. Mrs Rule-Steele has bred some 21 champion Whippets and made up titles with another 6. In 1995 in partnership with Mrs Anne Knight (Neilhurst), she imported the lovely young bitch Dumbriton Endless Love from Mrs

Aust Ch Allswell Just a Dream.

Aust Ch Silkstone Jewel In The Crown. The only
Whippet ever to win BIS at the Sydney Royal.

Gilmour. Endless Love quickly made up her Australian title with her wins including a Specialty BIS and an All Breeds BIS. In 1997 Mrs Rule-Steele capped an already outstanding career in the breed - including several Sydney Royal wins and a Melbourne Royal Group win - by winning BIS Sydney Royal with her Aust Ch Taejaan Ms Margarita, handled by Sonia Turay.

Aust Ch Taejaan Tia Maria (the dam of Ms Margarita) was sired by Aust Ch Noholme Pepper Mill out of Mrs Anne Knight's Aust Ch Deerfoot Cameo Cabaret. Mrs Knight is herself a prominent breeder and exhibitor, having imported the Ch Phinjani Pinball Wizard son (ex Ch Daleforge Carmen Jones), Aust Ch Daleforge Dancing Brave.

At the time of writing a Pepper Mill daughter, Ms J Ginnich's Aust Ch Arjai Fields O Passion, has won 25 BIS.

The top BIS winner of all time in Australia is of Envoy/Statue/Masterminde breeding, Aust Ch Allswell Just A Dream. Owned and campaigned by Mrs Denise Tuck of South Australia, this bitch has won 34 BIS and 59 Best In Group awards as well as being 5 times Top Whippet in South Australia and BIS Canberra Royal.

In 1994 Mr and Mrs Pieterse (Statuesque) imported the young Ch Silkstone Jewel In The Crown. Bred by Mrs Roma Wright-Smith (Silkstone), this bitch was the first champion daughter of Ch Pencloe Dutch

Gold. 'Joy' was Top Puppy UK 1992, Top Whippet UK 1993 and Reserve in the Hound Group 1994. In addition to winning 3 BIS All Breeds shortly after her arrival in Australia, in 1995 Joy (handled by Mrs L Pieterse) became the first Whippet to win BIS Sydney Royal. Joy's first litter in Australia was to NZ Aust Am Can Ch Noholme Beauling Alli, which produced Aust Ch Statuesque Jewel Thief, BIS at the 1997 SA Specialty.

The Scandanavian Influence
In the early 1990s Messrs Doherty and Crowley imported Airescot Chaconne from Mr Fodstad and Mrs Runsten Fodstad of Norway. Chaconne became an Australian champion and was used extensively at stud. Messrs Doherty and Crowley, in partnership with Mr R Barwick and Mr and Mrs Fleming, then imported Chaconne's sire, the International and Multi Ch Airescot Waistcoat, from Sweden on loan. Handled by Mr Barwick, Waistcoat made up his Australian title with several BIS on the way and was also extensively used at stud during the 14 months he was in Australia. Waistcoat's first champion progeny, Aust Ch Statuesque Pillow Talk (campaigned by Messrs S Thomas and D Sidebottom) made up her title as a junior of 14 months. Pillow Talk's dam, the Norwegian import Airescot Party Dress, is sired by Person out of Mrs Runsten's Skokloster BIS winner the American bitch Aust Ch Bohem Callas of Whippoorwill (also Waistcoat's dam).

These imports reflect the earlier mentioned American influence coming in via Scandinavia, although Callas was very closely bred to the English dog Am Ch Greenbrae Barn Dance through Mrs Barbara Henderson's American Whippoorwill lines. The most successful Chaconne offspring to date have been Messrs Doherty and Crowley's Aust Ch Martinique My Marimba, a multi BIS winner with a Specialty BIS to her credit, and Mr and Mrs Fleming's Aust Ch Martinique My Flamingo, a BIS winner.

The American Influence
The increasing interest in American lines has been demonstrated by the import of Am Ch Delacreme Dragonslayer and, more recently, American champions Airescot Chaconne, Waistcoat and Airescot Party Dress. In 1995 Mr and Mrs D Hiltz (Starbuck and Torbay) imported further American lines from the Bo Betts and Sporting Fields kennels. The handsome young dog Am Ch Sporting Fields Irish Derby, who was sired by Mrs Runsten's Int Ch Sporting Fields Irish Mist has, at the time of writing, produced 3 litters. This includes one to his kennel mate, Aust Ch Sporting Fields Foreign Affair, who has also been successful in the ring with a RUBIS and several Group awards. In 1996 Mr and Mrs Pieterse imported Mr Bo Bengtson's young bitch Bohem Critic's Choice (Am Ch Delacreme de la Renta ROMX out of Am Ch Bohem Of Thee I Sing) who was in whelp to the famous American sire Am Ch Starlines Reign On. Critic's Choice quickly became a champion with 2 BIS and 4 Best In Groups and, in 1997, the Specialty BIS under Mrs D Gardner of England (Novacroft).

Australian Whippet people are keen competitors and enthusiastic breeders who are prepared to experiment with lines from all around the world. The American National Specialty in 1996 was visited by a number of Australian Whippet breeders who were anxious to learn more and get to know their international counterparts. Although Australia only has 2 pure Specialty Clubs, the members consistently raise funds to bring international Specialists to judge their shows. These efforts have been rewarded with the breed being a consistent winner in the Hound Group and BIS level, both at Championship and Royal shows.

CANADA by Linda Buchholz

(An explanation of Canadian titles can be found on page 250.)

The vastness of Canada means that Whippet fanciers are well spread out from coast to coast, making it difficult for breeders to be aware of what is happening across the country. In 1993 the National Whippet Club was formed to try to bridge the gap and bring breeders and fanciers together. The NWC holds an annual National Specialty show which is hosted in a different region each year and publishes an informative newsletter. Their current project is the revision of the Canadian breed standard.

Can Berm Ch Alery Astrologer's Antares.

Although records of early Canadian Whippets are sketchy, it appears that the first two Best In Show wins for Whippets in North America occurred in Canada in the 1920s in Winnipeg and Toronto. Rag racing also appeared to be a popular pastime right up to the start of World War II. In 1925 Whippets were exhibited at the Pacific National Exhibition in Vancouver with Whippet racing as the feature grandstand attraction, drawing an entry of 25-30 racers. By the 1960s Whippets were steadily gaining popularity in Canada and breeders were becoming well established. At that time, the most influential breeders on the West Coast were Joyce Anson and her daughter, Pamela Arthur, under the kennel names of Rockabye and Sonna. Their most notable dogs were Can Am Ch Sonna Rockabye Baby CD, her daughter Can Ch Rockabye Ember Of Course ARM and the Best In Show winning Can Am Ch Rockabye Folly. Mrs Anson and family had moved to

Canada from England bringing with them 3 bitches: Prudence of Conevan, her daughter Can Ch Rockabye Peace Pipe and the black Tinribs Tiger Rag.

Richard and Barbara Webster's Urray kennel enjoyed great success and was mostly based on outcrosses of English/Canadian stock to the United States import sire Am Ch Stars and Stripes of Suntan (a son of Am Ch Eyeland Double or Nothing). In 1963, in the East, Martine Collings returned to Canada to establish the famous Winterfold kennel which would have a great impact on Canadian and American Whippets. Her English import Ch Coveydown Greenbrae Wayfarer (litter brother to Am Ch Greenbrae Barn Dance) produced many outstanding winners on both sides of the border, the most famous being the lovely Am Can Ch Winterfold Bold Bid (out of Stoney Meadows Bold Queen), herself a producer of note with 14 American champions for the MorShor and Sporting Fields Kennels in the United States. Winterfold Whippets were the foundation of several Canadian and American kennels.

In Ontario, Alan Pepper and Terry Tafft established their Alery Kennels with Can Ch Winterfold Shining Hour (Tantivvey Diver out of Stoney Meadows Bold Queen) as their foundation bitch. When bred to the Barn Dance son Am Ch MorShor's Whirlaway, she produced top winning Can Am Ch Alery White Warlock, Canada's Top Whippet for 1971.

Warlock was bred to Lorricbrook Fandango and produced the first Canadian owned Whippet to win an American Whippet Club Specialty: Can Am Ch Astrologer of Alery, Top Canadian Whippet of 1980. To continue the line, Astrologer sired Can Bermuda Ch Alery Astrologer's Antares who became the Top Whippet for 1982. Antares traces every line of his pedigree to Ch Greenbrae Laguna Lucia, with the exception of one, which goes back to Am Ch Stoney Meadows Snow Queen. Mr Pepper is now judging whilst Mr Tafft has continued breeding

Can Am Ch Baccarat Bon Chance.

under the kennel name Baccarat and has enjoyed success with offspring from his United States import bitch Am Can Ch Bohem Delacreme Chevrotain (litter sister to the top American winner, Demoiselle). Her daughter, Can Am Ch Baccarat Bon Chance (sired by Can Ch Woodsmokes All Ablaze), was Canada's Top Whippet for 1993.

Max Madger's world famous Lorricbrook kennel in Ontario has produced many champions in Canada, the United States of America, the United Kingdom, Europe and South America. The United Kingdom lines have had great influence in this kennel. Mr Magder's great import dog Can Ch Dondelayo Buccaneer (by Buckaroo out of Duette) enjoyed great success in the show ring as a multiple Best In Show winner and as a top producer in both Canada and the United States of America. A later British import, Can Ch Shalfleet Statesman, has also made his mark as a stud dog of note. A grandson of

Can Ch Rothbury Replica.

Can Ch Woodsmoke Applaud Th' Obvious.

Can Am Ch Nineveh Royal Derby.

Statesman, and great grandson of top United States producer Can Am Ch Misty Moor's Chalmondoley, Can Am Ch Lorricbrook Runaway at Shalfleet was imported by Mrs Wilton-Clark and gained his English title in 1983.

Pat Miller's Woodsmoke kennel, located in New Brunswick, has consistently produced Best In Show winning Whippets. Founded on the Winterfold lines and bred back to Barn Dance, her outstanding foundation was Can

Am Ch Night Talk of Woodsmoke, one of Canada's top winning Whippets for several years and holder of many breed records. Night Talk in turn produced extremely well for Woodsmoke. The Australian import Can Ch Rothbury Replica and the United States import Ch Anteres Perlier (daughter of America's top producer Ch Delacreme De La Renta) were added to Woodsmoke and have produced many American and Canadian champions. One Replica daughter, Can Ch Woodsmoke Share A Moment, won 17 Best In Shows, a record for Canadian bred Whippets. Current top winner is Can Ch Woodsmoke's Applaud Th' Obvious, a Best In Show winner at 6 months of age. A recent acquisition is the New Zealand import Can NZ Ch Noholme Beau Lemova, co-owned with Rachelle Descent of Kwikasair kennels in Alberta.

Can Am Ch Nasusa Raise The Curtain F Ch.

Photo: Mikron Photos

The Nasusa kennel of mother-daughter team, Susan and Carla Badick from Calgary, Alberta has produced some outstanding winners. Their foundation bitch, the multiple

Can Am Ch Swiftsure Happy Daze ARM Am Can F Ch.

Specialty winning Can Am Ch Nineveh Royal Derby (sired by a litter brother of Am Ch Sporting Fields Clansman out of a daughter of Am Can Ch Misty Moors Chalmondoley) was bred to the top United States producer Am Ch Saxon Shore Amber Waves and produced several Speciality and Group winners, finishing championships in both Canada and America. Canadian Specialty winners Royal Derby and her son, Am Can Ch Nasusa Taymarc Dalcregan West, have both won Awards of Merit at American Whippet Club National Specialties. Derby was later bred to an Amber Waves son and produced the Best In Show winning Can Am Ch Nasusa Raise The Curtain F Ch. A son of Raise The Curtain, Am Can Ch Nasusa Cacique, was awarded Best of Winners at the 1996 American Whippet Club Specialty show.

Can Am Ch Swiftsure Out of Africa, aged 9, winning his 12th Specialty Best In Show.

Heather Dansereau's Devonair kennels in Ontario has produced many lure coursing and Show Champions. Her foundation bitch Can Ch Dress Circle Devonair Jane UD F Ch was the first triple titled sighthound in Canada. It is rare if there are not several Devonair Whippets in the Top Ten lure coursing Whippets in any given year. Some notable dogs produced by this kennel include the Specialty winning Can Am Ch Devonair's Mitchell Frank F Ch X Am F Ch (a son of English import Ch Nevedith Uptown Guy) and the all time lure coursing point winners Can Am Ch Devonair's Incanta Odin F Ch X Am F Ch and Devonair's Phoebe F Ch X LCM.

The Swiftsure kennel of Steve and Linda Bucholz in British Columbia has produced winners in racing, lure coursing and showing, and is another kennel that competes successfully on both sides of the border. In the 1970s they imported Am Can Ch Marial's King Arthur from the United States. He was a proven producer of top dual purpose dogs. His son, the Specialty winning, top Canadian racer and lure courser Can Am Ch Swiftsure Happy Daze ARM Can Am F Ch, produced many dogs with show, coursing and racing titles. A Happy Daze daughter, Am Ch Roving Roulette Am F Ch (out of Am Ch Stoney Meadows Miss Julia) was Best In Show at the American Whippet Club National Specialty in 1989. Happy Daze was bred to Am Ch Surrey Hills Savannah (litter sister of the top United States producer, Houston) which resulted in the multiple Best In Show winning Can Am Ch Swiftsure Out of Africa. Canada's Top Whippet from 1990, Out of Africa, has won a record 12 Specialty Shows including the 1996 Canadian National Specialty from the veteran class, as well as 4 Awards of Merit at American Specialty shows.

Loughren Quick Silver F Ch X Am F Ch.

David Markus and Rob Lindey (Aikersaill) in Manitoba have produced several Canadian and American Show Champions. They have been successfully combining their Canadian lines with Whippoorwill. Dr Janet Lalonde (Flyte) in Ontario has also produced several American and Canadian champions, working mostly with the lines of Lorricbrook and the American kennel Surrey Hill. Dr Lalonde (breeder-owner) handled her lovely Can Am Ch Flyte's All That Jazz (Can Am Ch Flyte's Hot Buttered Rum x Can Ch Surrey Hill's Blonde Venus) to Best In Show at the first Canadian National Specialty show in 1994.

Several inactive kennels which must be mentioned for their contribution to Canadian Whippets are the Denroc kennels of Tuck Turner in the West, the Sirhan kennels of Audrey Benbow, and the Gambit Whippets of Victor Nunn, both in the East. Denroc produced many show and lure coursing champions, most notable being the Best In Show, number one lure coursing dog, Can Ch Denroc Hell on Wheels F Ch X (a son of Am Ch Misty Moor's Chalmondoley). While Sirhan were well known for their famous Borzois, they also produced some top Whippets including one of Woodsmoke's foundation bitches the Best In Show winning Can Ch Sirhan Great Expectations CD. Although not active for very long, the Gambit kennels produced several beautiful champions including the Best In Show winning Can Ch Gambit Vitesse, a grand-daughter of the top American sire Chalmondoley.

Lure Coursing

Lure coursing is an extremely popular pastime for Canadian Whippet fanciers. Canadian lure coursing was organised in the Spring of 1976 in Victoria, British Columbia under the banner of Canadian Sighthound Field Association. Although many were content with CSFA coursing, others desired the title and sport to have more official status and the Canadian Kennel Club was approached to accept lure coursing as an official CKC event. In 1982, the CKC officially adopted the sport under their sanction and adopted the CSFA rules. The titles of Field Champion Excellent are issued by the Canadian Kennel Club and appear on official pedigrees.

Many of Canada's top lure coursing Whippets are also Show Champions, with Specialty and Best In Show winners often appearing in the Top Ten on the coursing field. Several have even earned Top Ten Show and Coursing placements in the same year. Many of the top show kennels actively lure course their dogs. In order to promote this dual purpose aspect, the Canadian Kennel Club recognises an event unique to Canada called a 'Field Trial Conformation Specialty'. This event is held immediately following a CKC lure course and only those dogs that have earned a qualifying score in the preceding lure course are eligible to be shown for CKC show points.

Canada's 1996 Number One Lure Coursing Whippet was Loughren Quick Silver F Ch X Am F Ch from British Columbia. He was bred and owned by June Harrison and Lorne Hawkins and is from a combination of Wyndsor racing lines from California with those of the German import Flyer of the Crackerjacks ARM ORC F Ch. A total of 256 Whippets competed in lure coursing across Canada in 1996.

Flat and Oval Racing

As stated previously, rag racing enjoyed great popularity up to the start of World War II. In 1965 a group of Whippet fanciers held Canada's first National Point Race Meet under the rules of the American Whippet Club, in British Columbia. This meet was won by Urray Chieftain, owned by William Turpin Sr. Currently, the BC Whippet Racing Club and the Vancouver Island Whippet Club host several meets each year under the auspices of the North American Whippet Racing Association and the National Oval Track Racing Association. In 1996, NOTARY Oval Racing was introduced to Ontario where they are now successfully hosting meets.

Bill and Alice Turpin's Of Course kennel was enormously successful in the 1970s and 1980s. Their Can Ch Rockabye Ember Of Course (Pennyworth Tumbleweed x Can Am Ch Sonna Rockabye Baby CD) was the first bitch to win the American Whippet Club's Award of Racing Merit title (ARM). Her son Can Ch Emberson Of Course ARM (sired by the United States bred show winner Am Can Ch Stars and Stripes of Suntan) was one of the top racing Whippets in North America and both were very influential as producers.

Since the mid 1980s, the James Ringdove Kennel on Vancouver Island has emerged as the dominant racing kennel in Canada and many parts of the United States. Their racing line is based on the English import bitches Cockymoor Genee and Besaps Cockymoor Queenie and the German import dog, Flyer of the Crackerjacks. Ringdove Merlin R Ch SORC was named the Number One Oval Racer in North America by the NOTRA for 1996 and Ringdove Black Adder SR Ch SORC was the NAWRA's Number One Flat Racer in North America.

FINLAND by Sampo Miettinen

The first Whippets were imported in 1920 from Denmark and the first litter was born on 27 July 1925. Before the Second World War, Whippets were not very popular in Finland.

1959 saw the beginning of a new era in Whippets. The Finnish Sighthound Club imported a bitch called Allways Dawn of Test from the United Kingdom. She was mated to Fin Ch Robmaywin Stargazer of Allways and whelped a litter of nine.

Between 1960 and 1965 seven males were imported from the United Kingdom and two from Sweden. Mrs Tuulikki Stockell and her 'of Streamline' affix was one of the well known breeders of this period and is probably responsible for introducing the breed to Finland.

Int Nord Ch Sopisco Sally.

From the 1970s the breed gradually became more popular and in 1982 The Finnish Whippet Club was established. Some of the important sires around at the time were Int Ch Bohem Lekain, Int Ch Bohem Filipin, Int Ch Dondelayo Jonty, Int Ch Fleeting Flamboyant and Fin Ch Colt's Crown Point.

Mrs Aune Maatta of the Sopisko affix took top honours in showing, racing and coursing. Her Int Nord Ch Sopisco Sally won numerous Best In Show awards and was Top Whippet in Finland twice.

Another major winner at this time was Mrs Sirkka Vartiainens with her Tuulikeron Whippets. Her breeding plans were mostly based on the dogs she imported from the United Kingdom. These were predominantly

Int Ch Autumn Terra Bella I'm Redee.

Denorsi, Dondelayo and Samarkand lines. Mrs Hannele Takkinen of Flaming Hill Whippets was one of the top winners in the '70s and '80s and her Int and Nord Ch Colt's Better-Be-Good, bred by Mrs Ingela Kyrklund and imported to Finland from Sweden, was Top Whippet in Finland three times. Mrs Vuokko Kaarianen still enjoys success in the show ring from starting out with her Sokovintin Whippets in the '70s. However, her strength is her knowledge in breeding for success on the racetrack. Year after year her breeding has won almost every honour with excellent times and, some years ago, one of her bitches in Holland was mated to a super racing male and the subsequent litter were the fastest ever in Finland.

One of the most influential breeders in Finland is Mrs Asta Aho of the Jakais affix and, indeed, many of today's top Finnish breeders have started with Mrs Aho's dogs. In 1980 her Int Ch Jakais Adimir was Runner-Up in the Dog of the Year competition. Mrs Aini Kastinen successfully bred her Metsanreunan Whippets which could not be missed around the show ring because of their obvious type. In the late '80s Mrs Kastinen bred a litter sired by Fin Ch Woodbrook's Feeler and each one of the litter gained their Finnish title, some accomplishment. Feeler, out of two of Mrs Aho's Jakais dogs, was Top Whippet in 1982. Mr Unto Timonen and, later, Mr Sampo Miettinen of the Woodbrook's Whippets, have enjoyed great success from the '80s continuing through the '90s. Fin Ch Woodbrook's Pick-Bee was Top Whippet in 1986. Int and Nord Ch Nevedith Ring Dove was imported to the kennels from the United Kingdom and she took Top Whippet in 1985. Two years later the honour was awarded to her son Fin Ch Woodbrook's Safe Way Home.

In the early '90s the breed was at an all time high in popularity. Considering Finland is not a big country (although long) with about five million inhabitants, the registration of up to 280 puppies in a year was, perhaps, rather too much. Fortunately, this number seemed to be the peak and now the breed appears to have settled down to a more reasonable number of about 170 - 180 puppies registered each year. The Whippet is still the most popular sighthound in Finland and many owners are interested in showing, racing and coursing (which is even more popular than racing).

From the '80s and '90s there have been a number of influential imports of stud dogs into Finland, which have helped greatly to improve the quality of the breed. The most influential being Int Ch Nevedith Xray, Int Ch Peperone Pilsner (both from the United Kingdom), Int Ch Bohem Flight Time, Fin Ch Autumn Sky At Dawn (both from the United States) and Int Ch Gaugin du Manoir de la Grenouillere from France.

A very important stud dog has been Int Ch Play A While at Peperone. Although he lives in Sweden, some Finnish breeders have used him with good results. Over this period the number one in the breed has been the imported American bitch, owned by Woodbrook, Int Ch Autumn Terra Bella I'm Redee. She was bred by Virginia Huffman and Jeanette Puzzi in the United States out of Am Ch Whippoorwill Fanfare by Am Ch

Int Ger Ger KC Swiss Ch Flic Flac Amazing Grace.

Chelsea Drakkar of Oxford F Ch ROMX. Her record speaks for itself: Top Whippet four times, Top Sighthound and twice Runner-Up in Dog of The Year. She has also won the Finnish Whippet Club National Specialty an amazing four times. Her daughter, Int Ch Woodbrook's Wonderful Life, carried on the success when she became Top Sighthound in 1995.

Ms Sirpa Jarvinen (Quatrain's) imported Fin Ch Seaspell's Blue Mesa from the United States and has bred from her wisely, producing the Top Whippet in 1991 - Ch Quatrain's Admira. Blue Mesa has put a strong stamp on her descendants.

Ms Helja Manninen (Zigetty's) has been a succesful long term breeder. She started out with Swedish lines and then later Peperone, including the influential Int Ch Peperone Pilsner. Her imported bitch Peperone Peugeot was very successful and took Top Winner in 1990.

The Plaudite kennels of Ms Pirjo Aalto and Mr Timo Jutila were built on two Zigetty's bitches. They now have a very even type having stuck mostly to Peperone lines.

Ms Anita Backlund (Kipin Kapin) has done little breeding but had an excellent litter out of Bohem Flight Time, each one going on to become a champion. One of the litter, Am Ch Kipin Kapin Goldilocks, was exported to the Whippoorwill kennels in the United States. There have been other successful exports from Finland to the United States and Europe and, pleasingly, these have done extremely well in their new countries.

In Finland today American breeding is very visible and strong. However, Finnish breeders have not forgotten the country of origin, the United Kingdom, and are skilfully mixing the British based and the American based lines with excellent results. Luckily, Finland has breeders with good knowledge and a genuine interest in the breed.

GERMANY by Thomas Münch

Whippets were registered in Germany from as early as 1903 but did not become popular until the 1920s, when track racing was invented. Apart from a couple of early imports, which mostly went back to Ch Manorley Maori, there were hardly any connections with Britain up to the 1950s when two extremely successful and influential dogs were imported. One of them, Martyn of Allways, was the brother of Douglas-Todd's celebrated Ch Wingedfoot Marksman of Allways in England. The former gained his International Championship as well as the Federal Track Racing Championship (Bundessiegerrennen) twice. This dog was living proof of the fact that show bred Whippets can also race successfully.

Amongst others, Martyn sired the famous brother and sister Famos and Fatme v. Schlesierland, both again excelling in the ring and the track. Atom's Flash of Allways (Ch Fieldspring Bartsia of Allways x Ch Red Atom) was another successful import. Through his famous son, Olaf vd Cloppenburg, his dominant influence as a sire of exceptional racing winners can be traced in many pedigrees of top racing Whippets on the European continent.

With approximately 250 puppies registered each year, Whippets have slightly risen in popularity in recent years. The average owner still much prefers racing to showing their Whippets, so maybe it is not surprising that, over the years, a particular 'beauty and performance' type of Whippet has emerged of which some critics say it is neither typical nor particularly fast.

There are two national championships for dogs in Germany: a club championship (usually referred to as the 'German Championship') as well as the German Kennel Club Championship.

Doris Kleineberg's v Kleinen Berg kennel must rate as one of the most successful Whippet kennels in Germany ever. She started off with a bitch of old German breeding in the late '60s but her present winners are almost entirely based on Tim Teiller's famous Samoem strain. Mrs Kleineberg has bred numerous champions over the years. Countless Bundessieger and Europasieger titles have been won by her dogs, mainly solid reds, but it was left to the blue brindle Furioso v Kleinen Berg (by Ch/Am Can Dutch Ch Lorricbrook Runaway at Shalfleet) to win the title of World Champion under Shirley Rawlings in Bern, Switzerland in 1994.

Helmut and Colette Senkbeil's Black Magic breeding establishment is almost entirely based on dual purpose German breeding. A number of successful blacks and blues carry their affix.

Joachim Kiack's Almansor's Whippets are almost entirely based on British bloodlines. In recent years Ch Silkstone Finesse has been imported and quickly gained her German and International Championships. A new acquisition is the young dog Oakbark Midnight Mint (Ch Cobbyco Cavalier x Ch Moonlight Model at Oakbark) who has already begun a successful show career.

Andreas Reschke's Nevedith Fire Opal (Ch N. Zippy Zimmer x Ch Nutshell of N.) is another successful British import easily finishing her National Championships.

My own FlicFlac Whippets have successfully competed since the second half of the '80s. The fawn brother and sister FlicFlac Angel Cake and Amazing Grace are both multi-

Int Ger Ger KC Ch Hammonds Simple Simon.

Multi Ch Jake du Manoir de la Grenouillere.

titled champions as are F. Camelot (by Ch Lorricbrook Runaway at Shalfleet) and F. Flying Flame (by Ch Hammonds Simple Simon). Ch Hammonds Simple Simon (Ch H. Sebastian x Lydia of Hammonds by Hillsdown Fergal), imported from Angela Randall, has not only excelled in the show ring, he is also a sire of significance. Other successful imports are Ger Ch Courthill Conquering Hero (Ch Pencloe Dutch Gold x Crown Affair at Courthill), bred by Roger Stock, and Hillsdown Houdini (Ch Phinjani Pinball Wizard x Hillsdown Blacque Rose), both good sires in their own right. My latest import is Int Ch Pencloe Dutch Amber (Ch Pencloe Dutch Gold x Hillsdown Blacque Magique), bred in Scotland by Morag Bolton-Lockhart. This dog has enjoyed a fantastic two seasons in '95 and '96, finishing her national and international championships with more Best of Breeds, Group wins and placings than one could hope for.

Another successful British import is Oschinski's Courthill Crystal Ring (same breeding as Conquering Hero) who has also easily finished her National and International Championships.

Wolfgang and Verena Baumann's id est Whippets were a leading force in former East Germany. Their new, entirely British bred bitch Jade de Nikolaiev (Ch Hillsdown Heartbreaker x Mithrandir Coin of the Realm, litter sister to Ch/Ir Ch M. Panning for Gold) made history by going Best In Show at Leipzig All Breed International Championship Show in September '96. This was a truly fabulous win for the breed in Germany!

FRANCE by Thomas Münch

Fr Ch Paris Panther
(Sporting Fields Man In Paris x Paris Pauline).

Nowhere in Europe is the Whippet more popular than in France. Annual registrations have topped the 1,000 mark and a couple of years ago the breed was ranked among the 20 most popular breeds in the country. Like in many other parts of Europe racing and, in recent years, lure coursing are very popular with Whippet enthusiasts. The top French racers regularly trouble the European competitors at the very popular international race meetings. On the show side some of the best known and most successful kennels anywhere can be found in France.

Over the years, Karen Mesavage has produced some outstanding specimens carrying her Sac a Malices affix. She started off with a bitch of French breeding but has combined British, American and continental European bloodlines to create a distinctive type. She has produced numerous champions all over Europe including Scandinavia, where Magnus Hagstedt's Int Ch So Proudly We Hail du Sac a Malices (Pub Crawler du Sac a Malices x Wilpat French Connection) has left a lasting impression on the breed there, as well as in North America and South East Asia.

Currently, Karen Mesavage enjoys great success with her United States import Fr Ch Paris Panther (Sporting Fields Man in Paris x Paris Pauline), bred by Sharon Sakson, and his offspring. One of Panther's many wins was BOB as well as BIS at Skokloster in Sweden '96, a tough act for anyone to follow!

Equally successful are the Manoir de la Grenouillere Whippets of Jackie Bourdin. Jackie also started off with a bitch of French breeding but has enjoyed the most success with her homebreds, almost all of which are linebred to two British imports: Ch Sandlena Astronomer (Ch Newbould Muffinman x Oakbark Merry Maid) and Hillsdown Mollie (Ch Oakbark

Int Fr Sp Ch Julie du Manoir de la Grenouillere.

Middleman x Siobhan of Hillsdown). More recently, Danish Ch Normandy Social Standing, an American import, has contributed to her breeding programme, again with remarkable results. Like Karen Mesavage, Jackie has parted with some top class Whippets who, consequently, have become champions in many European countries, as well as further afield.

Claude Rebourg's d'Escala Whippets are a combination of some of the finest British bloodlines. She has enjoyed a lot of success with her imports carrying the Lowerdon, Tamsmorna and Chyton affixes as well as their offspring.

Bernard Fischer has used British blood from another source with notable results. His homebred Fr Ch Honey Honey du Tadjoura, sired by Ch Nevedith Dawn Dazzler (Nipper of Nevedith x Nav Anna of Nevedith), has twice been World Winner (in 1995 and 1996).

The Countess de Saint Seine and her de Grillemont Whippets are a French institution. Her early British imports include some most successful Lagunas. In recent years the unusually coloured Fr Ch Sunsalve Heatwave at Hutaka (Fr Ch Tawny Knight at Hutaka x Lowglen Songbird) has contributed to the Countess's breeding programme of tri-coloured Whippets.

Mr Gayraud's XR de Chambord affix represents yet another influential kennel. Mr Gayraud has used Nevedith and Dondelayo breeding with some outstanding results.

Danielle Lempereur's Blue Springs Whippets exclusively stem from her British foundation bitch Int Ch Barchellee Blue Lagoon (Ch Blue of Longacres x Liberty Bell of Barchellee). Her homebred champions Blue Springs Alizee and Blue Springs Hadrian (by Ch Lorricbrook Runaway at Shalfleet) are both multi-titled, classic fawns.

Dorianne Bernard had started a remarkable breeding programme before her untimely and tragic death. Some early d'Escala winners were her foundation but she also imported some influential dogs and bitches from the United Kingdom carrying the Pardee, Novacroft, Mithandrir and Daleforge affixes. Amongst others, her import Novacroft Emperor (Ch Harque to Equerry x Novacroft Merriment) sired David Coppel's homebred Fr Ch Dixmoor give me the Moon (Ch Nevedith Paperweight x Fr Ch Dis Merci a La Dame du Sac a Malices), a top winner and good producer in her own right.

SWITZERLAND by Miss L E Gut

Whippet breeding began in earnest only after the Second World War, and the first imports in the '50s came from Germany. Then, after 1960, Miss Wettstein (now Mrs Champendal) imported two blue dogs. The first was Boughton Blue Beau (by Marksman of Allways) whose daughter Zamba vom Tierlipark became an International Champion, but he himself proved unsatisfactory at stud. Later the kennel name was changed to 'Liberty'. Next Miss Wettstein imported Vahlay Musk Rose, dam of five International Champions, and also Vahlay Burnt Amber. Recent imports came from Tim Teiller's Samoem's kennels, namely Samoem's Solidity and Samoem's Spring Lily. Elfe of Liberty, a granddaughter of Lorricbrook Runaway at Shalfleet, now has a pretty litter by Hillsdown Houdini.

Mrs Helmy Ranft imported the pure white Shalfleet Pollyanna (Ch Peppard Topflight out of Shalfleet Story) who became an International Champion and also the black bitch Ladiesfield Spade (Ladiesfield Bedazzled x Ladiesfield Black Shadow). However, only Spade produced a litter which contained a beautiful black bitch; otherwise the breeding was discontinued.

Int Ch Laguna Lady Lightfoot.

At about the same time, the begining of 1960, Miss L E Gut imported Laguna Lady Lightfoot (Ch Laguna Limelight x Ch Laguna Leading Lady) and also Laguna Lancelot (Ch Laguna Ligonier x Laguna Lunette, 2 CCs). Both were very successful and became International Champions with 7 and 5 CACIBs respectively. The progeny of these two Whippets were very lovely but they all went to pet homes as people were not interested in showing at that time.

Miss Gut was responsible over the years for fifteen imports from England, 6 alone from the Laguna kennels. Unfortunately Miss Gut had to give up breeding for health reasons.

Later, in the '70s, Eva Holz (Fleetewing) imported Courthill The Crofter and Dondelayo Ballad. It was especially the former and his progeny that 'put her on the map'. They were lovely quality Whippets.

Eva Holz started her kennels with a bitch named Lightstep Noyna from Miss Gut. Noyna was a winner at both shows and races but, after a number of years, Mrs Holz also gave up breeding.

Today it is mainly Mrs Edith Lauper who breeds regularly and, from time to time, includes English

Int Ch Laguna Lancelot.

exports. Some of her Whippets are quite successful and again a great number of pups went to pet homes.

Finally, Whippets in Switzerland wouldn't be complete without mentioning Mrs Gertrud Brunner, our most senior Whippet breeder, having started in 1948. Her interests, however, have always lain more with racing than the showing side.

WHIPPETS IN IRELAND
by Margaret Martin

Athough never very numerous, Whippets in Ireland have always enjoyed a faithful and loyal following and, over the years, many animals have been imported from Great Britain covering various strains. Most notable would be Whippets from the Dondelayo and, latterly, Hillsdown lines. In the late 1960s Mrs Wendell Howell of the Great Circle Whippets in America came to live in Ireland and brought several Whippets with her. These dogs were shown extensively in Ireland and won well at Championship Shows. Several well known British exhibitors have made up Dual Champions (that is, under IKC and KC rules) including Jack Peden of the Denorsis before he emigrated to South Africa.

Ch/Ir Ch Collooney Silver Fox. Photo: Crawford

Whippets in Ireland very often tend to be second breeds for exhibitors perhaps better known in other breeds. For example, the Ingrams of Tirkane Boxer fame also exhibited Whippets very successfully several years ago. Walter Thompson of the Moirabank Irish Setters also had a great deal of success in the breed, mainly from dogs

Ir Ch Barnesmore Painted Lady.

purchased from the late Anne Knight's Dondelayo kennels and the late A B Nicholson's Glenbervie lines. From these early imports Walter bred several Irish champions. Tommy Agnew (Tacavonoff Borzois) has also been a keen Whippet exhibitor in the past and still maintains his interest in the breed today. Marian Sloan (Seltaeb and Austrene Whippets), who was a great friend and admirer of Anne Knight and her Dondelayos, over the years

Ch/Ir Ch Barnesmore Circus Paint
(Ch/Ir Ch Painted Pony x Ir Ch Barnesmore Mercedes).

had several top winners from this kennel including Dondelayo Marianette of Seltaeb who was the dam of Ch Dondelayo Reinette and grand-dam of Ch Dondelayo Bandelero. Marian also had one of the last line in the shape of Samarkand's Vitessa bred by the late Bobby James and Anne Knight. Vitessa was mated to Ir Ch Barnesmore Manta (Ir Ch Carmodian Tawny Knight of Hutaka x Ch/Ir Ch Hino Legacy, a Painted Pony daughter) to produce a litter which are behind many of today's winners.

The Barnesmore Whippets of sisters Margaret Martin and Lucinda Thompson have been most successful in recent years with dogs from this kennel gaining titles in several different countries. The kennel dates from the 1970s with the purchase of Van Olreim Vanessa from Philip Moran-Healy. This little monkey brindle bitch by Dondelayo Lysander out of Hillsdown Pandora was a great mover and is behind all the present-day Barnesmore Whippets directly on the bitch line.

In 1983 the particolour dog Painted Pony (Shergar of Wildglen x Ch Hillsdown Tobique) was purchased from Philip Moran-Healy. This dog, as well as having a very successful career in the showring (gaining both his English and Irish titles), also proved to be a most successful sire with champion daughters and grand-daughters. A legend in his own lifetime, Paint was a dog for the big ring and excelled himself in Group and BIS placings. An eye-catching colour with movement to die for, he made a big impact on the Irish show scene which his children and grandchildren continue today. Ch/Ir Ch Barnesmore Circus Paint, his daughter, was IKC Showdog of the Year in 1996 and also won the Hound Group at Leeds Championship show in 1997, and so the line goes on. Although limited in the number of bitches he was used on (mainly Barnesmore bitches),

Paint managed to stamp his type most firmly on the breed in Ireland and is behind most of the dogs in the ring in Ireland today. Today, many good winning dogs are now bred in Ireland but the bloodlines all trace back to these well known and respected forebears. To date there have only been four Irish owned English champions namely Painted Pony, Hino Legacy, Circus Paint (all owned by the Barnesmores) and Albert and Marlene Richie's Collooney Silver Fox. All four also have their Irish title too. Silver Fox is Breed Record Holder in Northern Ireland with nine CCs.

In recent years many United Kingdom residents have shown Whippets in Ireland and several have now won their dual Irish and KC titles including Pip Campbell's Ch/Ir Ch Mithandir Panning for Gold and Mr and Mrs Bird's Ch/Ir Ch Pennybeck Silver Sixpence. The Irish 'Circuit' is popular with exhibitors from the mainland as they have the chance to enter five championship shows in a space of eight days and many champions are made up on the Circuit each year .

Showing and Judging in Ireland

Judging at Championship shows in Ireland is quite different from that on the mainland in that rarely does one get a specialist judge for one breed. In no breed would one get the number of exhibits found at Championships in Great Britain so therefore a judge will normally be asked to do several breeds in the Group in which he/she judges and the best one can hope for is a competent all-rounder or hound specialist. Numbers at the shows here would not warrant or support specialist judges in each breed and therefore this system seems to work best for us.

Points for a championship title are awarded through Green Stars which are the equivalent of Challenge Certificates. A dog needs a total of forty points to gain his title. Maximum points at any one show should be ten and anything from five or over is a major. A dog needs four majors included in the total forty points to gain his title, that is, you cannot amass points in ones and twos - you must have at least four majors. Points are awarded on an Index system which is updated yearly by the Irish Kennel Club according to the numbers of the breed registered the previous year. Depending on the Index, Green Stars at any one show will be worth from one to ten points. If a dog wins BOB with a five point Green Star and subsequently goes on to win the Hound Group, then he automatically gains the highest number of points which have been awarded to any other dog in that Group. So a Group win almost always brings a total of ten points to the winner. However, a dog can only use one Group win towards his championship title.

The most notable difference in our judging system is the fact that with the lack of specialist judges, most judges revert to all-rounder type judging and no matter how nice or close to type your Whippet is, if it does not move right (is unsound) then you are wasting your time showing here. Also, size seems to make a difference; too big or too small and you look out of place.

The Northern Ireland Whippet Club holds a Championship show under IKC rules every March and, to date, has always tried to obtain the services of a breed specialist or at least a recognised hound specialist for the breed. This show is always well supported by exhibitors from Scotland and further afield which helps keep the entry respectable.

Whippet Racing in Ireland

Whippet racing has had its ups and downs over the past thirty odd years. Depending on the interest, the NIWC has been involved in several different racing venues and in the late

'70s and early '80s Pat Johnson and Rosie Gault of the Patros Whippets ran a most successful racing programme for several seasons, latterly at Crawfordsburn Country Park which was a great venue. This venue was unfortunately lost to building work and the racing itself seemed to die a death after this. However, many Whippet owners in Ireland are keen hunters and their Whippets can give a very good account of themselves in the field of pursuit of rabbits.

NEW ZEALAND by Nicole L J Harrison

Unlike the United Kingdom system, New Zealand has a system that awards Challenge Certificates at every Championship show. To earn the title of Champion eight Challenge Certificates are required under 5 different judges. The newest ruling regarding this title of 'Champion' is that it does not matter how many Challenge Certificates are gained under the age of 12 months, one must be recorded over the age of one year to earn the title 'Champion'. There is also a new title to be gained - that of Grand Champion. To earn this prestigious award a dog must win 50 Challenge Certificates and 3 All Breeds Best In Show awards (under 3 different judges). New Zealand has seen only 2 Grand Champion Whippets who are both now deceased: Grand Ch Woollahra Smooth Dude, owned by G

Gr Ch Woollahra T For Tartan (20.6.84-12.5.97),
New Zealand's top winning Whippet bitch.

and C Henderson and Grand Ch Woollahra T for Tartan, owned by Nicole Harrison and Rae Kersey. Both were bred by Phil and Rae Kersey. These two Whippets are also the top winning male and female in New Zealand to date.

Also available in New Zealand are 'Racing' Challenge Certificates. There are only 6 per year awarded (3 in the North Island and 3 in the South Island). The three are divided into one per year in each of the three weight classes. To qualify for a Racing Challenge Certificate, a dog must record the fastest average time from three of his fastest races in his weight class for that particular year.

NZ Ch Martinique Rag Trumpet.

To become a Racing Champion he must win a Challenge Certificate for two consecutive years. If he misses a year then it's back to square one.

New Zealand currently has 5 Dual Racing and Showing Champion Whippets: Rac/NZ Ch Highlife Hurricane owned by P Edbrooke and J Pettitt; Rac/NZ Ch Highlife Let's Dance owned by S Pearson; Rac/NZ Ch Highlife White Wedding owned by P Edbrooke and J Pettitt; Rac/NZ Ch Upstage Too Hot To Handle owned by J and E Lyon and Nicole Harrison; and Rac/NZ Ch Kana Ka The Artful Dodger owned by J and P Newton.

The Whippet world in New Zealand has seen many breeders come and go. However, some of the successful originals are still involved in breeding, for example Phil and Rae Kersey who together were Woollahra. Both have new partners and new kennels - Phil and Polly have Upmarket and Rae now breeds under the Upstage affix. Peter and Jackie Newton are still enjoying success with their Kana Ka kennels; Karen and Vic Hall own the Hatherleigh Whippets whilst the Tee family have the Gainsfield kennels. Then there is Priscilla Edbroke and John Pettit with Highlife Whippets, Brian and Sandy Wilson's Noholme Whippets (now owned by Sandy), M and D Powley's Shenkhan Whippets, Nicole Harrison's Devine kennels, Hendersons' Arcon kennels, Eva Ekstam's Ronndal, Graeme Duncan's Dash Whippets, Alan Bradshaw's Bards, Dale Spears Wildarra, Yvonne Taylor's Silkwood, Molly Measor's Sonnenheim, and Lynda Watson's Shenace Whippets.

New Zealand kennels who have gained the honour of breeding All Breeds Best In Show winners in New Zealand are: Arcon, Devine, Kana Ka, Hatherleigh, Upmarket, Weathertop, Highlife, and Woollahra. All those Whippets who win All Breeds Best In Show awards qualify for the annual Best In Show Winners competition. To date no Whippet has yet won this award. The same applies to All Breeds Best Puppy in Show winners who then compete for New Zealand's Top Puppy. In 1991 NZ Ch Devine Designer Genes (daughter of T for Tartan) won the All Breeds Puppy of the Year competition.

The popularity of the breed has improved in the show arena with Whippet numbers topping the Hound Group. The quality of the breed has ensured that Whippets often take top group awards and, occasionally, Best In Show wins.

Unfortunately this beloved breed does not share the same popularity in the 'pet' stakes that breeders enjoy in the United Kingdom. Many litters have to be culled back to potential show prospects as pet homes are few and far between. It is a sad affair when the only people willing to pay for pet Whippets are pig hunters and then purely to mate with their Mastiff or Terrier breeds to improve the speed of their pig dogs. The breeders in New Zealand have a huge PR exercise to educate people to the attributes of this wonderful breed. The main stumbling block is that most New Zealanders just don't know what a Whippet is!

There are a number of specialist breed judges who breed, exhibit and judge Whippets. These include Nicole Harrison, Phil Kersey, Polly Middleton-Kersey, Eva Ekstam, Heather Tee, Graeme Duncan, Alan Bradshaw, Merle Powley, Dale Spear, Maree McKenzie, Brian Wilson and Sandy Wilson.

There have been several dogs who have made an impact on the breed in New Zealand, the most notable sires being NZ Ch Noholme Electric Blue and NZ Ch Martinique Rag Trumpet who are both Australian imports. The honour for top dam would fall between two New Zealand bred bitches: NZ Ch Noholme Shady Lady and NZ Ch Antoinette of Kana Ka.

It is interesting to note that behind most of the top winning stock of today are Ch Dondelayo Statue, Ch/Am Aust Ch Lowglen Oakbark Masterminde and Ch Solotown Simeon - all United Kingdom imports and three of the most influential sires that Australasia has seen.

Int Ch Rothbury Bonecrusher and Nor Ch
Memoars Lobelia of Librium.

NORWAY by Espen Engh

Even though the first Whippets were imported to Norway soon after the turn of the century and the first two gained their Norwegian champion titles in 1917 and 1919 respectively, the current strain was introduced by Mrs Madeleine Rieber Salvesen in 1936. Her first two imports came from Britain, the pure Willes-bred male Sir Peter and the fawn bitch, Tiptree May. The latter qualified for both her Norwegian and Swedish championships in 1939. Mrs Rieber Salvesen imported two additional foundation bitches for her Brenna Whippets from Denmark and Sweden, introducing the blue colour through the Danish bitch Skjoldhoys Tenna.

Brenna bred their first Whippet litter in 1937 and crowned their first

Int Nor Swed Dan Ch Emotion du Manoir de la Grenouillere.
Top Norwegian Bitch All Breeds 1992.

Int Ch Dumbriton Emotion.

homebred champion, Nor Ch Brennas Mona Lisa, in 1946. Sixty years after their first litter, Brenna is still active in the breed and may possibly be the oldest Whippet kennel in the world. From the start up until 1962, the entire breeding program was based solely on these original four imports from the 1930s for as many as seven generations. By the early 1960s the strain had become intensively in-bred, but had produced a number of champions, the majority of them being blue in colour. The highlight was probably Nor Ch Brennas Blue Pixie Best In Show at the Oslo International Show in 1952 under W Lewis Renwick. He was sufficiently impressed to include a photo of Blue Pixie in his book on the breed. Another important dog was Nor Ch Brennas Boy, sire of the Swedish bred Tundrans Kenna who is found in the bitch tail line of a number of famous Swedish kennels, notably Seeberga, Memoars, Gardsjon and Colts.

By the late 1950s it became obvious that outcrosses were needed. Int Ch Spinning Lariot of Allways became the first addition of new blood in 25 years of breeding and 43 Whippet litters. The outcross resulted in no less than three champions: Nor Ch Brennas Mike, Monty and Lady Blue, all important for future generations. Mrs Hjordis Espeland, starting out as a kennel maid at Brenna in the 1950s, soon took an active part in the breeding. After Mrs Rieber Salvesen's death in 1965, Mrs Espeland became responsible for the Brenna breeding program. A 1967 breeding to Int Ch Laguna Leader produced Int Ch Brennas Sheik and Int Ch Brennas Shirin. This famous brother and sister team dominated the Norwegian show rings for many years. A repeat breeding produced additional champions.

In 1974 Thurma Easter Rose arrived at Brenna as the first of a string of imports from Anne Knight's Dondelayo Kennels. She was soon followed by Int Ch Dondelayo Jonty, himself a top show dog and the leading sire in Norwegian history with at least 18 champion offspring. With Nor Ch Dondelayo Spellbound he produced the highly influential Brennas 'S' litter containing Norwegian champions Brennas Silvert, Speedy, Simona and Sontana. Later Dondelayo imports such as Nor Ch Starry of D., Nor Ch Silverstar of D., Nor Ch Doriel D. and Nor Ch Lounell Lavinia of D. were not only successful in the show ring but each produced several champion offspring.

By far the predominant kennel in the history of Norwegian Whippets, Brenna has produced at least 47 homebred champions, the latest crowned in 1996. Several other kennels have based their breeding on Brenna bitches, most notably the Incarvill kennels of Malfrid Baasnes and the Con Moto kennels of Inger and Ole Steen. Incarvill has produced 24 Whippet champions by blending Brenna with Dondelayo since the first litter in 1974. The highlight of the kennel was probably the pure Dondelayo bred Int Ch Incarvill's Brilliant Pearl, Norway's Top Whippet in 1988 and 1989 and BOB at the famous Swedish Skokloster show. Con Moto produced a string of champions from similar lines, including Int Ch Con Moto Fanitulla, Top Whippet in 1987. Her daughter, the Con Moto-owned Nor Ch Showline Statuette was Top Whippet in 1995. Also from the predominantly Dondelayo pedigrees, the Pendahr kennel of Ingunn Ohrem and Hanne Torkildsen and the Moscow kennels of Tom Ringnes and Erik Granmark have produced a number of champions.

Breeding along slightly different lines, combining Nevedith with several Swedish strains, the Librium kennel of Anne-Grethe Sonesen and Gerd Rossland, the Siprex kennel of Berit Grotterud and Morten Andersen and the Frifart kennel of Eva and Sven Svendsen have all been highly successful.

From the early 1990s, the Norwegian Whippet scene has been dominated by new imports from several countries, but usually with mainly or at least partly British pedigrees. The Australian import Int Ch Rothbury Bonecrusher was Top Whippet in 1990 and 1991. He was followed by several French imports including Int Ch Emotion du Manoir de la Grenouillere, Top Whippet 1992, '93, '94 and her half-brother Int Ch Diorissimo du Manoir de la Grenouillere, a champion in a record number of countries. Both Bonecrusher and Emotion have won BOB at Skokloster. The English import Int Ch Dumbriton Emotion completely dominated the show rings during 1996 and 1997 with 24 BOBs from 27 outings.

In the late 1990s Whippets are not as popular in Norway as in neighbouring Sweden and Finland. On average no more than 60 or so Whippets are registered annually with the Norwegian Kennel Club. Show entries vary a lot between different areas of the sparsely populated country, but rarely exceed 50 at any one show. Other Whippet activities, such as coursing and racing, hardly exist. In general, the Norwegian Whippets are still strongly dominated by British strains, the American influence being much less evident than in Sweden and Finland.

SOUTH AFRICA
by Bryan Kelly and Jo Robertson

Probably the most famous Whippet ever to come into South Africa was Ch Wingedfoot Claire-de-Lune imported by Mr and Mrs Sadler (later Mrs Anna Katsounis). Claire arrived in whelp to Wingedfoot Indigo Imp, a mating arranged because Anna had an interest in blue and white.

Around this time, Mrs June Pretotious imported Folkline Sticklepath Sailor Boy who was to prove a valuable addition. However, it was the later purchase of Ch Denorsi Moonduster of Glenbervie by the Tula kennels of Anna Katsounis which was to have the greatest impact on Whippets here and it would be true to say that almost every Show Champion bred in South Africa has at least one line to 'Dusty' in his pedigree.

Moonduster won 17 All Breed Best In Shows before being retired.

During this time Mrs Pretotious imported Dondelayo Hijack who was unlucky to meet Moonduster in the ring on many occasions. However, he also made his mark and sired champions for June and notably Gertie Modder van Gellicum. Other imports followed: Ch Dondelayo Minuette of Oldwell (who was tragically lost to them after a year), Ch Denorsi Dancing Belle, Barmaud Lord Halifax of Savilepark and then came Ch

SA Ch Smithvale Galaxy.

SA Zim Zam Ch Buckland Augustsong of Ravilais.

Beseeka Knight Errant of Silkstone (Whiskey), who had a fabulous show career which he topped by going Best In Show at the 1980 World Show in Italy. The immediate progeny of Knight Errant were a little mixed, probably the best of them being Gertie Modder Van Gellicum's big winner SA Ch Jukskeiriver Satin. However, Whiskey's grandchildren fared better and a clearer type emerged in the Tula and Alut Whippets of the late Mrs Sheila Fitchet.

SA Ch Barmaud Lord Halifax became another champion for the Tula kennel and was also a Best In Show winner. SA Ch Oakbark Mastermark of de Gratton belonging to Neil Kay was imported. He is a litter brother of Ch Oakbark Milord and Ch Oakbark Movie Queen. Mastermark sired Best In Show winners for Neil Kay and Rosemarie Cabion of the Sleepy Hollow affix. Their bloodlines were based on the imported bitch from Anne Argyle, of Harque fame, namely SA Ch Harque to Yvette who was by Ch Dondelayo Buckaroo out of Ch Harque the Lark. Yvette was mated to Denorsi Moonduster and produced two outstanding bitches for this kennel, namely SA Ch Sleepy Hollow Silver Star and litter sister SA Ch Sleepy Hollow Morning Star, both of whom were Best In Show winners. It was the mating between Silver Star and Oakbark Mastermark which produced a further Best In Show winner for this kennel - SA Ch Smithvale Galaxy.

During the early '90s, the Brejen kennel of Jackie Jackson saw the arrival of Nevedith Call Me Casper who, although he never attained his championship, produced three champions out of Armore Ultimate Sucess of Brejen (a daughter of SA Ch Smithvale Galaxy).

The first half of 1993 saw the arrival of SA Ch Silkstone Kings Ransom (Ch Pencloe Dutch Gold x Ch Firedance at Silkstone) from Roma Wright-Smith. He has proved to be a valuable acquisition to the Whirlwind Kennel under the partnership of Juliet Duthie and Rosemarie Cabion. King attained his championship with ease and has continued to hold his own in the ring. He has also proved to be a valuable sire and has produced champion progeny. He is a litter brother of Ch Silkstone Kantara.

Pascal Botella with his Sol Y Sombra Whippets is a recent immigrant to South

SA Ch Silkstone Kings Ransom of Whirlwind.

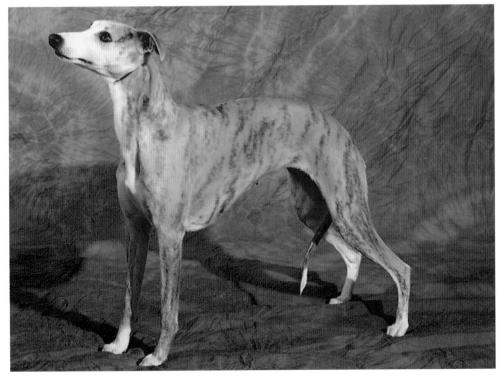

SA Ch Courthill Country Music.

Photo: Visual Concepts Photography

Africa and has done well with his homebred progeny especially Int Ch Sol Y Sombra Angel Eyes, by SA Am Ch Chelsea Drakkar of Oxford out of Int Braz Ch Dyanne du Manoir de la Grenouillere. He has also imported from Jackie Bourdin in France, Pat Miller of Woodsmoke in Canada and, more recently, the Alleri kennel in the United States. These recent imports will certainly leave their mark in time to come and hopefully we will hear more about them in the future.

Bryan Kelly imported a bitch from Barbara Robinson, namely Savilepark Soft Breeze of Cottoncove, a litter sister to Ch Savilepark Saucy Shrimp of Oakbark. Although a little different in the ring, Breeze became a South African champion and, when mated to SA Ch Smithvale Venture of Merlanjo (SA Ch Smithvale Galaxy x SA Ch Smithvale Shere Khan), produced 5 worthy South African champions from one litter. Two of these have Best Puppy In Show wins to their credit. Breeze's grandchildren are also winning in the ring at present, so Breeze has certainly proved to be a worthy acquisition to this kennel. SA Ch Smithvale Shere Khan is a granddaughter of a previous import, namely Chyton Miss Print from Shirely Rawlings.

During 1993 Bryan Kelly imported from Roger Stock SA Ch Courthill Country Music of Cottoncove (Hillsdown Fergal x Ch Courthill Crown of Gold) who easily achieved her championship and has gone on to become a Group and All Breed Best In Show winner.

Top winning Whippets in the last 10 years have been:
- SA Ch de Gratton Tarquin (Neil Kay), a grandson of SA Champion Oakbark Mastermark of de Gratton, was a Best In Show winner in the 1980s.

- SA Ch Brejen Heracles (Jacki Jackson) by SA Ch Baal of Merlanjo (son of Moonduster) out of SA Ch Brejen Sunmist (Moonduster's daughter).

- SA Ch Buckland Giselle of de Gratton, bred by June Lynos and owned by Neil Kay, by Shirin Moon Magic of Wonderval (a Moonduster son) out of SA Ch Umtengi Disa of Buckland.

- SA Ch Tula Spanish Lily of Alut by Tula Conquistador out of Tula Fleur de Lys (a Double Knight Errant granddaughter) owned by the late Mrs Sheila Fitchet.

- SA Ch Jukskeiriver Brocade by SA Ch Jukskeiriver Snomist out of SA Ch Jukskeiriver Satin, owned by Mrs Gertie Modder van Gellicum.

- SA Ch Smithvale Galaxy (Rosemary Smith) by SA Ch de Gratton Mischief (Oakbark Mastermark of de Gratton) out of Smithvale Stardom (SA Ch Brejen Heracles).

In addition to being a top sire and grandsire of numerous champions, Galaxy has been a multiple Group Winner and has All Breed Best In Shows wins to his credit. At that time he was perhaps unlucky to come up against another top winning Whippet of more recent times, the lovely fawn and white SA Ch Buckland Augustsong of Ravilais. Bred by June Lyons, by SA Ch Brackenhill Milesia of Buckland out of Buckland Nova and in the ownership of Ian Allison, 'Aria' won her SA title plus Zambian and Zimbabwean titles. At All Breed levels, she won 3 Best and 4 Reserve Best In Shows, numerous Hound Groups and was Top Hound for two years. Her granddaughter, SA Ch Ravilais Guilletta - also owned by Ian Allison and a daughter of SA Ch Smithvale Venture of Merlanjo out of Ravilais Norma - was another successful show dog with Best In Show wins to her credit plus her Zimbabwean title.

L to r: Swed Ch Gardsjons Charlotta, Swed Ch Gardsjons Beathe-Christine, Swed Ch Gardsjons Aslog, Swed Ch Gardsjons Carolina, Swed Ch Memoars Astarte.

SA Ch Silkstone Kings Ransom of Whirlwind, although not a Best In Show winner, has won numerous Hound Groups and has proved to be forceful competition.

Likewise, SA Ch Brejen Polly Flinders by Nevedith Call Me Casper has done her fair share of winning for the Brejen kennel with numerous Groups to her credit.

SA Ch Courthill Country Music of Cottoncove has become a multiple Group winner and All Breed Best In Show winner for Bryan Kelly.

South Africa has recently seen a number of lovely imports from the Irish kennel of Lucinda Thompson (Barnesmore). Hopefully the young progeny who are making their name in the ring will continue to be an asset to future South African bloodlines.

SWEDEN by Magnus Hagstedt

The first Swedish Kennel Club stud book was published in 1893, whilst the Swedish Kennel Club was founded in 1889. In 1904 the breed name is listed in a register, together with other Sighthound breeds. Whippets are included for the first time in the stud book in 1914. Three bitches of Danish breeding are listed under the heading: 'Whippet, small English Sighthound'.

In 1911 a 'Toy Sighthound' is included in the stud book. This male was owned by Mr T Nyren whose affix Whip Graceful is the first Whippet registration in Sweden. The following year a bitch called Donna, of German breeding, is listed as an Italian Greyhound. Donna's daughter Bella was the first Whippet to be listed in the Swedish Kennel Club stud book!

Swed Ch Bohem Mome Rath.

In 1914 Whippets are presented in a large feature in the Swedish Kennel Club magazine. All dogs included are of Danish/German breeding. These bloodlines have long since been lost in the Swedish Whippets of today.

A new era for Whippets started after the Second World War in the 1940s, when the Fleet Foot kennels owned by Agnes Nilsson imported new stock from England. These came from the Sagaland kennels with lines to the breeding of Tiptree, Watford and Willes. Descendants from these dogs still feature, albeit way back, in the pedigrees of some of the current dogs.

Following the dominance of the Fleet Foot Whippets is Tony Horberg, another important breeder. She was most active with her Tundran dogs throughout the 1950s, '60s and well into the '70s. Her foundation bitch came from Fleet Foot and was very successful when bred with the United Kingdom Wingedfoot imports,

Swed Ch Freeline Flame, a dog who both shows and races successfully.

most notably Wingedfoot Cream Cracker. Tony Horberg also owned two imported Bellavista Barry daughters and, as a result of clever breeding, became one of the most successful breeders ever in Sweden.

Many breeders have based their programmes on Tundran stock. One of the most important ones was Walter Akerstom's High Speed kennels. They are remembered mostly for a string of solid blue Best In Show winners, including the classic Swed Ch High Speeds Blue Sheik. These dogs are also good representatives of the multipurpose Whippets generally bred in Sweden, where several top winning champions have also done well on the race-track.

The most prestigious award for Swedish breeders is the Hamilton Plaque which is awarded by the Swedish Kennel Club to breeders with a distinguished record. So far only five Whippet breeders have been awarded this trophy: Tony Horberg's Tundran kennels in 1958; Marta Zetterstom's

Swed Ch Colt's Cocktail Bird.

Swed Ch Houghtonhill Orbit. Photo: Hjalmarsson

L to r: Swed Ch Marash Melody of Bayard and 4 of her offspring : Swed Ch Balzac Opsis Kalpo
Swed Ch Balzac Galago, Swed Ch Balzac Fria Tider, Swed Ch Balzac Cafe Existens.
Photo: Hjalmarsson

Bojar kennels in 1968; Mary Ansell's Seeberga kennels in 1975; Bo Bengtson's Bohem
kennels in 1983; and Catharina Ostring's Gardsjons kennels in 1985.

Notable Kennels

Bojar
The Bojar kennels were based on partly Swedish lines and partly British imports, mainly
Tinribs and Allways. One of the most important brood bitches was Samarkand's
Dragonfly of Test. Later, they also co-owned Swed Ch Shalfleet Starbuck with Bo
Bengtson.

Seeberga
The Seeberga kennels started with a bitch from Tundran and later used other imports from
England, including a co-ownership of Swed Ch Badgewood Mark Twain with Bo
Bengtson, as well as Swed Ch Baydale Bronze Miller.

Bohem
Bo Bengtson's Bohem kennels has played an important part in the development of the
modern Whippet in Sweden, partly as a successful breeder on a small scale but also for a
string of successful imports from England. Of these the Ligonier son Ch Laguna Leader
was most important in the 1960s but perhaps even more influential, later in the 1970s, was

Ch Fleeting Flamboyant, a Diver son. His homebred males Swed Ch Bohem Lekain and Swed Ch Bohem Filipin enabled Swedish breeders to closely follow the development of the breed in England.

Gardsjons

The Gardsjons dogs of Catharina Ostring have an unequalled record in All Breed competition. Over the years the production of a long line of homebred champions with a strong family look has done much for the general status of the breed. Dominating the very popular competitions with Breeders' Groups at All Breed shows, the Gardsjons kennels reigned supreme for many years, culminating in the Swedish Kennel Club naming Catharina the 'Breeder of The Year' in 1985.

Swed Ch Birkonbrae Summer Love (Hillsdown Fergal x Birkonbrae Buttons n' Bows).

Above: Swed Ch Gardsjons Gota (Swed Ch Hi Tor's
Baryshnikov x Swed Ch Gardsjons Birgitta).

Above: Swed Ch Fennaur Delacroix (Swed Ch Birkonbrae Sweet Talking
Guy x Swed Ch Fennaur Bella Bartok).

Skokloster 1995.
L to r: BIS Swed Ch Signum Dolce and Gabbanna; Res BIS Accents Little Limerick.
Judges: Mrs S Thompson (UK) and Mr E Engh (Norway).

There are many more active breeders in the breed in Sweden than those singled out for mention. Over the last ten plus years the following have all enjoyed success in the ring: Accent's (Monica Jonsson); Airescot (Nenne Runsten); Bokella (Siv and Helen Ogren); Balzac (Anna Lena Backvall-Hallin and Dick Hallin); Carmodey (Lena and Peter Hjalmarsson); Colt's (Ingela Kyrklund); Delaklin (Marianne Ekwall); Equus (Margaretha Martensson and Kim Bengtson); Fennaur (Christer Wik); Foxys (Monika and Peter Wounder); Freeline (Kirtsen Ronne); Hjortonblommans (Anna-Lisa Pekkari); Kapriol (Agneta Kapper-Karlsson); Klenod's (Inger Carlsson); Memoar (Mayvor Lindfors); Per-Mo'bile (Tina and Tommy Permo); and Signum (Magnus Hagstedt).

The Swedish Whippet Club was founded in 1976. The same year saw the first two-day Sighthound extravaganza at Skokloster. The first Sighthound show had been the previous year and was judged by Molly Garrish from the United Kingdom. The first Whippet Club Breed show, held in 1976, was judged by Bobby James (also from the United Kingdom). Ten years later this weekend event was well enough established to stage the largest Whippet show ever in the world. Three hundred and ten dogs were entered and the judges were Bo Bengtson and Mary Lowe from the United Kingdom. Skokloster judges read like a 'Who's Who' in Whippets, the majority being from the United Kingdom.

An average of 250 Whippet puppies are registered with the Swedish Kennel Club each year. Three Challenge Certificates are required to become a Swedish champion. The qualifying one must be won after the dog has reached two years of age. The Swedish Kennel Club is a member of the FCI and use a translated version of the British standard

Skokloster 1997.
L to r: BIS Harling's Swed Ch Play A While at Peperone;
BOS de Gans' Swed Ch Dance of Fire of Herlaers Town.
Judges: K Thomas (UK) and F Pieterse (Australia).

for Whippets. The Swedish Whippet Club publishes an illustrated newsletter, Whippet Bladet, and has produced a complete set of Swedish Whippet champions in two volumes, as well as year books. The club also organises seminars, teach-ins and regional breed shows.

Other Whippet activities in Sweden are oval track racing and straight track racing. The latter of these two is numerically the largest and very popular with breed fanciers. Interest in lure coursing is growing although coursing with live game is illegal in Sweden. The Swedish Whippet Club promotes multi-talented Whippets and a couple of years ago began awarding the 'Triple Diploma'. This is an award given to dogs with merits from three different categories: show or conformation; race or lure coursing; obedience or agility. Only a few dogs have qualified so far and it is a very prestigious award. The Swedish Whippet scene has become very international over the past decade. Top winning and well producing imports have come from near and far, incorporating new bloodlines from Australia, the United States, and Continental Europe together with the more established British lines. This is the situation as Swedish breeders prepare to take the breed into the new Millenium.

THE UNITED STATES OF AMERICA
by Mary Beth Arthur

Phil Moran-Healy writes:

"When planning this book, I realised that it was essential to have the articles from other countries written by people who "knew their onions" and would be able to give an all-round acount of the breed in their particular country.

America is vast and Whippets now enjoy widespread popularity across the country, so it was to be some task to condense the research. I asked several people whose opinions I respected who they thought would be capable of such a task and the same name cropped up, that of Mary Beth Arthur. Happily, she agreed to cover the breed in the United States for me, despite several personal commitments at the time. The completed manuscript I

Judith Shearer handling Am Ch Meander Mocking Bird.

received was excellent, interesting and informative but, alas, far too much to fit within the space constraints. Rather than omit large pieces, I decided to put together a summary of the whole manuscript.

Here is the result, which I sincerely hope covers the broad spectrum of the breed in the United States from the very early days up to the present times and I truly regret not being able to present it to you in its entirety. "

(An explanation of the abbreviations of American terms can be found on page 250.)

Lucky Number of Mardomere.

The breed was first registered in America in 1888. This was prior to the official recognition of the breed in England. As in most other countries, racing was the major interest with showing becoming increasingly popular over the years. The strength of the racing fraternity ensured the survival of Whippets in America as a true sporting hound.

The first Show Champion, Am Ch Bayview Pride, was born in 1902. Bayview was a leading kennel at that time and many pedigrees in the United States can be traced back to these bloodlines.

Influential Kennels

Meander

The Shearer sisters (Meander) were probably to have most influence in determining the 'American' type of Whippet. From the 1920s through to the 1940s there were very few changes to their uniformity, being solid colours with a dark eye. In outline they resembled a miniature version of a true English-type Greyhound.

Julia and Judith Shearer were total enthusiasts and were involved in the running of the American Whippet Club for many years. In fact the breed standard was written around their dog Am Ch Mica of Meander.

Mardomere

Mardomere Whippets, owned by Mrs George Anderson, were kept very much within their own kennel. Mrs Anderson rarely allowed her stud dogs to be used on outside bitches and hardly ever sold her puppies. Consequently, they aren't prominent in today's Whippets. Mardomeres were probably at the height of their success in the early 1940s and there was tough competition between Mrs Anderson and the Shearer sisters for top honours, other exhibitors almost always losing out to one or the other of these well stocked kennels. They were quite distinctively different in type. The Mardomeres had smaller, shorter bodies and were mostly parti-colour.

Mrs Anderson imported some good stock from England. These and the progeny they produced were some of the finest Whippets at the time. The most noteworthy were: Best In Show Am Ch Fiornell Glamorous (Tiptree Monk x Tiptree Christine), Am Ch Lady Bibi, Am Ch Madam Superb, and Am Ch Laguna Lucky Lad (Ch Laguna Liege x Ch Brekin Ballet Shoes). Lucky Lad won the Hound Group at Westminster and also proved himself at stud, siring at least eleven champions. Litter brother to Glamorous, Am Ch Tiptree Noel was also imported by Mrs Anderson and, when mated to the outside bitch Am Ch Frosty Morn of Meander, he sired the Best In Show bitch Am Ch Picardia Polkadot. Polkadot went on to produce Am Ch Picardia Fieldfare who became a sire for the Meander kennel.

Pennyworth

Margaret Newcombe first registered her Pennyworth kennels in 1940. However she was no stranger to the breed. Her mother owned the Clairedale Kennel which the then single Mrs Newcombe was managing quite successfully. As often happens, the cycle goes on and Mrs Newcombe's daughter, Claire Newcombe, is active and successful in the breed today with her Specialty winning Am Ch Willcare's Aged in Wood, Am Ch Pennyworth Light My Fire and Am Ch Patric's Personal Agenda.

It was the Mardomere Whippets that first caught Mrs Newcombe's imagination when she began her lifetime love and involvement with the breed from the 1940s through to the present day. She has also imported a number of Greyhounds along with Whippets. Her foundation stock was from the Mardomere kennel of Mrs Anderson and one of her early

Am Ch Patric's Personal Agenda. Photo: Bergman

successes was the BIS winning bitch Am Ch Pennyworth Blue Iris (by Impressive of Mardomere x Am Ch Seagift Penniesworth). Blue Iris also went on to be a good producer. Mrs Newcombe acquired from Mr John Hutchins an already successful male imported from Britain. His name was Ch/Am Ch Fleeting Falcon (Fleeting Father O'Flynn x Fleeting Oldown Snipe). He not only proved himself in the show ring but also his worth as a stud dog, producing a number of champions. Mrs Newcombe's most successful import and probably her best known dog was Ch/Am Ch Courtenay Fleetfoot of Pennyworth (Ch Bellavista Barry x Myhorlyn's Anita). Fleetfoot had a storming career in the show ring, including the coveted title of Best In Show at Westminster Kennel Club Show. This great dog was also a top producer, siring 45 champions. He is there in many of today's winners.

In 1966 Mrs Newcombe imported Ch/Am Ch Tantivvey Diver of Pennyworth (Ch Laguna Ligonier x Fleeting Fancy Free). Diver sired 25 champions and appears in many pedigrees including Am Ch Pennyworth Would You Believe, out of Am Ch Pennyworth Burning Dream. Falcon, Fleetfoot and Diver are also in the pedigrees of a number of Award of Racing Merit winners. Ch/Am Ch Nevedith Uptown Guy (Ch Nevedith Paper Weight x Sakonnet Alfalfa) is Mrs Newcombe's latest English import.

Mrs Newcombe is very generous in her praise and gratitude to all who have been involved in the success she has enjoyed in the breed, in particular the breeders in England who enabled her to build Pennyworth on solid foundations with the lovely dogs who became part of her family.

Stoney Meadows

Another kennel starting around the same period belonged to Mr and Mrs Potter Wear whose first Whippet was Meander Topaz. As very often happens the world over, making the decision to have a Whippet as a family companion often leads to much more. Topaz was the foundation of the influential and successful Stoney Meadows Whippets. When she was mated to Saddlerock

Ch/Am Ch Courtenay Fleetfoot of Pennyworth, a record breaking winner in the early 1960s.

Sho'Deed E'Does, she produced the BIS Specialty winning male Am Ch Stoney Meadows Masquerade. Mrs Wear brought in Am Ch Fashion of Mardomere (Am Ch Tiptree Noel x Am Ch Border Fly) and these bloodlines successfully combined with Meander lines to produce Stoney Meadows Epic (Stoney Meadows Madrigal x Stoney Meadows Make Believe). Epic was to be an influential sire and is behind many of the top dual purpose Whippets of the 1960s, '70s and '80s, including National Select Am Ch Marial's Padneyhill Illusion CD ARM, Am Ch Marial's Whitewater CD ARM ORC, and Am Ch Marial's Monte Carlo CD ARM. Am Ch Stoney Meadows Snow Queen, an Epic daughter, was the dam of top producing and top winning dog Am Ch Stoney Meadows Royal Fortune. Mrs Wear developed the Stoney Meadows Whippets through in-breeding and line-breeding and then she introduced lines from English imports and other American kennels to produce many successful Whippets which are still influential in the pedigrees of today.

Whipoo

Mr Eugene and Mrs Sybil Jacobs became involved with Whippets in the late 1940s under the kennel name of Whipoo. A few years later their enthusiasm turned to participating in the revival of Whippet racing in America. The revivalists' goal at that time was to breed and promote dual purpose specimens of the breed. The revivalists probably reached their zenith in the '60s when ten of the most competitive Whippets in the United States were pitted against one another at the Chicago International All Breed dog show. Of these ten, nine were conformation champions. Am Ch Whipoo's Whimsey CD was the winner on this occasion and on several subsequent occasions at the same site. Mr and Mrs Jacobs are true fanciers of the breed who set themselves unfledging goals to produce the functional animals they so admire. They were involved with obedience training and Mrs Jacobs excelled in this discipline, training and handling several Whippets to good results at meaningful competitions. They were also heavily involved in the production of the Whippet News when in its infancy.

The Whippet News was the official publication of the American Whippet Club and was started by Louis Pegram in 1956. It was a welcomed, useful publication that promoted wider communication across the breed nationwide, being both helpful and informative. The current Whippet News and Whippet News Annual are as a result of the increase in popularity of the breed from around the mid '70s and the careful dedication of the editors over the years. It is an important part of the United States Whippet fancy.

Gold Dust

Another couple who started out with a Whippet as a loving pet but got hooked on breeding and showing are Bob and Joan Goldstein of the Gold Dust Whippets. They acquired a Mardomere bitch purely as a pet. She came with no papers but the seed was planted and whilst at a dog show they were greatly impressed by Dianne (Moore) Bleeker's Am Ch MorShor's Whirlaway. They decided that their next Whippet would be just like him in colour and temperament and so bought a bitch sired by Whirlaway out of Am Ch MorShor's Hop-To-It-Girl (by Am Ch Seven League Sunday Best). The bitch was Am Ch MorShor's Oriesta CD. They only had approximately 15 litters in over a period of 35 years and always had Whirlaway as their ideal.

Their first litter was Oriesta bred to Am Ch Seyberne's Gallant Fox and this produced Am Ch Gold Dust's All That Glitters, who then produced the 'Glitter Litter' sired by Am Ch MorShor's Bold n' Courageous. In the litter was Am Ch Gold Dust's Florentine, Am Ch Gold Dust's Dazzling Double Take and of course Am Ch Gold Dust's Twenty-Four Karat. Each bitch was very successful in the

L to r: Miss Judith Shearer, Eugene Jacobs and Sybil Jacobs with 5 Whipoo bred Whippets.

show ring, but Twenty-Four Karat won Best Of Breed at many Specialties. 'Kari' was bred to Am Ch Stoney Meadow's North Star and produced the successful sisters Am Ch Gold Dust's Satin Finish and Am Ch Gold Dust's Limited Edition. These are behind some of the top winning Whippets of today.

Bohem

Bo Bengtson of Bohem Whippets is well known throughout the Whippet world as an exhibitor, breeder, judge and correspondent. He is the former editor of the Sighthound Review and yet all this involvement is from someone who saw no delight in the first Whippet he came across! This was in the 1950s but his opinion of the breed certainly took an upswing when he saw a photograph in a Swedish dog magazine of Am Ch Laguna Lucky Lad when he won the Group at Westminster. Bo was then smitten and all thoughts of his previous experience with the breed were forgotten. He contacted Mrs McKay (Laguna) in England and subsequently bought a 2 month old puppy. This was in 1961 and the puppy went on to become Am Ch Laguna Locomite. He was Best In Show at Stockholm show in 1963 and became one of the all-time top winners in Sweden. Bo became close with the Lagunas and, over a period of time, purchased more dogs of similar bloodlines which he has remained with to the present day. He still considers Lucky Lad as being close to his ideal and attributes his success to the early dogs and the solid foundations they gave him to build on. There have been a number of Bohem champions both in Sweden and America.

Highlight

In the early 1960s Mrs Clare Hodge wisely imported from England the Best In Show winning Ch Selbrook Highlight (Ch Robmaywin Stargazer of Always x Porthurst Creme De Menthe) and the top winning and top producing Am Ch Greenbrae Barn Dance (Ch Laguna Ligonier x Ch Greenbrae Laguna Lucia). Barn Dance is in the pedigree of most of the top winning and top producing Whippets in America today. He sired an amazing 63 champion offspring!

Marial

Another mother and daughter involvement was that of Bernice Strauss and Mary Beth Arthur. They acquired their first Whippet Sege Little Silver in 1963. The following year they purchased Group winning Am Ch Forest Slim Jim CD (Am Ch Red Letter O'Lazeland x Harbridge Lovely Lady). At the time they had a lease bitch Am Ch Eyleland Paisley (Stoney Meadows Epic x Meander Ribbons) and, when the two were mated, they produced a litter that was to be the foundation stock for many dual purpose standouts in the '70s, '80s and '90s. The most notable in the litter was Am Can Ch Marial's King Arthur CD ROM who sired dual purpose standouts in both the United States and Canada.

Runners

Isabell Stoffers Speight started her Runners Whippets in 1964 with English bloodlines, an Allways dog and a Ladiesfield bitch A mating from these two produced her first champion and racer. Later came a solid brindle from a mother/son bred bitch named Am Ch Tesque of Flying W (Am Ch Tonto of Flying W x Am Ch Homestead Cinderella). Tesque became the foundation for Runners and produced the Best In Show bitch Am Ch Runner's Our Own Charisma ROM. One of Charisma's famous offspring is Best In Show

Am Ch Runner's He's The Continental by Am Ch Misty Moor's Royal Huntsman. He's The Continental was number one Whippet in the United States for three years.

Am Ch Martinique SS Shamrock was then brought to the Runners kennel from Australia. Her sire was Aust Ch Solotown Simeon and her dam Aus Ch Martinique Calico Park. Shamrock went on to become a Specialty winner. Isabell Stoffers Speight is a serious breeder who knows what results she wants from a mating and only really breeds for herself. The sires she chooses are always complimentary to her bitches, albeit not the 'dog of the day'. She also researches the puppies that the stud has previously sired for soundness. The overriding factor that the stud must provide is versatility. Her Best In Show winning bloodlines are also title holders in racing, coursing and obedience.

Morshor

Dianne T Bleeker and the MorShor Whippets have a strong reputation for breeding sound show winners and producers. In 1965, out of a mating by Am Ch Greenbrae Barn Dance to his daughter Am Ch Hills Harvest Moon Dance (Barn Dance x Seven League Snowscape) came Am Ch MorShor's Whirlaway. He had an impressive show career and was Top Whippet in 1967. His show career was cut short by injury. However, he proved himself to be an excellent stud, siring 57 champions. Dianne Bleeker has bred a number of top winners which include Am Ch MorShor's Appraxin Ariel ROMX (Am Ch MorShor's Bold n' Brave x Am Ch Winterfold's Bold Bid). Ariel is the sire of the all-time top American brood bitch Am Ch Misty Moor's Chalmondoley.

Sporting Fields

The Sporting Field Whippets were started in 1968 by Mr and Mrs James Butt and today this kennel still enjoy success in the ring in the hands of their daughter Dionne 'Debbie' Butt. Am Ch Winterfold's Bold Bid was certainly a good acquisition for the Sporting Fields kennel. She was bred by Martine Collins in Canada from English import Ch Coveydown Greenbrae Wayfarer x Stoney Meadows Bold Queen and came to the Butts from Dianne Bleeker. Bold Bid was not only a top winner in the show ring but also produced at least 14 MorShor and Sporting Fields champions.

Another very important Whippet to come to Sporting Fields was English import Ch Charmoll Clansman (Ch Baydale Cinnamon x Ch Dondelayo Ruanne of Charmoll). He had a great show career and was also a top producer, siring the Sporting Field's next winning dog, Am Can Ch Sporting Fields Clansman, who became the ranked number one show Whippet for several years and also carried on the healthily successful producing lines. He is the double grandsire of Am Ch Sporting Fields Strider (out of Am Ch Sporting Fields Oh My). Strider enjoyed much success in the show ring and he also sired the National Specialty winner Am Can Ch Sporting Fields Kinsman. His dam is Shilo's Avia of Sporting Fields, sired by Am Ch Delacreme De La Renta. Kinsman has an enviable show record and he too has sired champions. Currently carrying on the successful reputation for the Sporting Fields is BIS Am Ch Sporting Fields Jazz Fest (Am Ch Topaz Jazz Singer x Sporting Fields Simplicity).

Hound Hill

Cora Nunnally Miller's Hound Hill Whippets emerged in the 1960s. She and Larry Shaw (Kirklea) co-bred a litter sired by Courtnay Fleetfoot which produced her foundation stock. Her foundation bloodlines were a combination of Pennyworth, Stoney Meadows

Am Ch Delacreme De La Renta, sire of 107 champions.

Am Ch Whippoorwill Tanager.

and the lightly used dog Bismarck of Frisia (German import Lars vom Burgfried x Am Ch Eyleland Julia). In 1979, feeling that the public should be aware, Cora Miller announced that she had encountered an unusual type of cataract in several of her Whippets, which was detectable at a very early age. The Hound Hill kennel was then closed and test breedings done to try and establish the mode of inheritance. After working with Cornell and the University of Pennsylvania, it was determined that it was a genetically emerging factor, a mutation which could have happened in any bloodline, and it probably did not exist before. After she got a handle on the situation, there was never another case of cataract at Hound Hill and the kennel was once again opened up.

In Cora's own words:

"Performance defines this breed. It etches the muscles that follow the sweeping lines of leverage........the force that impels the double suspension stride and the beautiful reaching side gait."

Hound Hill Whippets have been of consistently high quality and enjoyed much success. Cora's philosophy on this success is:

"Sentiment should never govern breeding choices. This is sometimes a hard edict under which to function but it is absolutely necessary to the health of the breed and the very continuance of the breeder. There must be positive reasons why a bitch is selected to breed and why the stud was chosen above all others. The dog cannot do it alone, although he is often expected to do so. Every dog has his weak points but if he is strong where the bitch is weak and the bitch can answer his soft points not only with good quality on her part but strength throughout the line, he should certainly be considered further. There shouldn't be many weak points on either side. Affection for an individual animal should be regarded most warily in the breeding context. Without question, the most difficult habit to imprint upon one's brain and eye is objectivity. The next, nearly as tough, is the proper place for sentiment."

Whippoorwill

The Whippoorwills were started in 1971 when Barbara Henderson VMD purchased her first, Jessica of Whippoorwill. Jessica was sired by Am Ch Highlight's Eidolon out of Moen's White Rose. Her grandfather was Am Ch Greenbrae Barn Dance and when she was mated back to him she produced the first of over seventy champions for Dr Henderson. Amongst these there are a number of obedience title holders, LCM's Specialty winners and five Best In Show winners, three of which came from the same litter! Dr Henderson has imported English lines and combined them well with American bloodlines. Am Ch Whitbarrow Parsley was brought into Whippoorwill and had two litters, producing a champion in each. In her litter by Am Ch Blue Fox at Whippoorwill she produced Am Ch Lady Blair of Whippoorwill. Her other champion was Am Ch Fenwick of Whippoorwill. Lady Blair had an excellent show career and both these two offspring also went on to be known as good producers in their own right. In 1982, in co-ownership with Bo Bengtson, Dr Henderson imported from England Am Ch Hardknott Maestro of Bohem. Maestro bloodlines fitted in well with the Whippoorwills and he was well used at stud, siring 40 champions. Maestro features in many pedigrees and Whippoorwill Whippets have been very influential in the United States and elsewhere. Dr Henderson has the sound goal, when breeding, of producing a quality Whippet, sound in structure and temperament and adhering to the Whippet standard.

Am Ch Hamrya's Lucky Charm F Ch SC and Am Ch Hamrya's Four Leaf Clover.

Multiple Best In Show-producing Am Ch Bo-Betts Divine Dessert and her dam Top
American Whippet brood bitch Am Ch Misty Moor's Divine Pleasure ROMX.
Original pastel by D Fitzgerald

Merci Isle

Iva (Cottrell) Kimmelman's first fancy for Whippets was taken in 1964 when she saw a photograph on the cover of Life Magazine of a Whippet. It was Margaret Newcombe's Am Ch Courtenay Fleetfoot of Pennyworth. However, as is often the case, it was some years later before she owned her first, Verdi. Not surprisingly, she was a granddaughter of Fleetfoot as well as another English import Am Ch Ringmore Finisterre.

When Am Ch Merci Isle Hot Flowers was mated to Am Ch Delacreme De La Renta, the litter produced the National Specialty winner Am Ch Merci Isle Meridian JC ROM. Meridian's son Am Ch Merci Isle Burncoat Babylon SC (his dam was Am Ch MorShor's Appraxin Sheree) emulated his father in being a National Specialty winner. Some distinction for this kennel who usually average one litter per year.

The breeding programme for Merci Isle, although different bloodlines are incorporated at times, centres around two bitches: Am Ch Merci Isle I See Delight LCM and Merci Isle A Distant Mirror SC. Although both are from different dams they do have a common link with Am Ch MorShor's Majestic Dell LCM ROMX and other greats. Iva Kimmelman is happy to concentrate her breeding on Meridian purely for temperament, as he also seems to have the ability to pass on his physical attributes along with it.

Delacreme

Mary Dukes became active in the breed in the mid '70s. She enjoyed success in the show ring with Am Ch Runnner's Creme Da La Creme (Am Ch Misty Moor's Chalmondoley ROMX x Am Ch Runner's Our Own Charisma). Creme Da La Creme was mated to Am Ch Saxon Shore Amber Waves and went on to produce Am Ch Delacreme De La Renta ROMX who was a Specialty winner and also a top producer. He sired the huge total of 107 champions including two National Specialty winners. He was co-owned by Mary Dukes and Doris Bandoian.

Bo-Betts

Carol Parker Harris purchased her first Whippet in 1979. She was by Am Ch MorShor's Whirling Home and named Triple Times Tara. Tara gained her title and the seeds of love for the breed were planted. The next puppy to be purchased by Carol Parker Harris was Am Ch Bo-Bett's Luke Skywalker, bought for her daughter. He was a strong red brindle and white who luckily completed his title in a short time as, shortly after doing so, he damaged his tail in an accident and lost half of it. This was not to be the end of his success, though, as he had other strings to his bow and went on to gain his LCM in coursing, a CD in obedience and also ROMX as a breeding dog. He sired Am Ch Bo-Bett's Wild Willie who, in turn, sired Am Ch Bo-Bett's Wild Tobiano and BIS Am Ch Bo-Bett's Wild Waylon. Luke has also sired many other functional champions.

Luke has a special magic when mated to Am Ch Misty Moor's Divine Pleasure ROMX - in total they produced a staggering 15 champions! In all she produced 24 champions. 'Deviny' came to Bo-Betts from Jerry Edwards. She was smaller and shorter coupled than most of the dogs around at that time. She was sound and enjoyed a very loving relationship with Carol Parker Harris. It seems that her strength was in producing females, but she also produced Best In Show Specialty Am Ch Bo-Bett's My Friend Ken.

Hamrya

Donna Lynch purchased her first Whippet in 1982, Am Ch Bitterblue's Moon Fire LCM

Am Ch Chelsea Drakkar of Oxford aged two and a half years old.

ROM who was to become her foundation bitch. When mated with Am Ch Plumcreek Walk On Water ROMX they produced five champions, one of which was Am Ch Hamrya's Moon Scape v Tyobi ROM. A litter from Moon Scape by Am Ch MorShor's Majestic Prince produced Am Ch Hamrya's Lucky Charm F Ch ROM and Am Ch Hamrya's Four Leaf Clover. Lucky Charm was a great producer. He sired two National Specialty winners: Am Ch Sporting Fields Chosen One and Am Ch Starlines Claim to Fame. He also sired two top producing males: Am Ch Starlines Reign On ROMX and Am Ch Broadstrider's By George ROM. Four Leaf Clover is the dam of six champions including Am Ch Hamrya's Teacher's Pet. Donna Lynch is a great believer in soundness and the 'form follows function' school of thought.

Chelsea

Lee and Deann Christianson started the Chelsea Whippets in 1983 after buying two Spectre bitches from Donna and David Lukasky. They were Am Ch Spectre White Hot (Am Ch Runners Notorious of Aryal x Am Ch Lycra X-Rated Novel) and Am Ch Spectre Chalcedony (Am Ch MorShor's Appraxin Ariel x Am Ch Spectre Westgate Temptress). Following on from these they have been involved as either breeder or co-breeder of many champions, including multi-Specialty Best In Show Am Ch Chelsea Drakkar of

Am Can Ch Surrey Hill's I'm No Angel F Ch SC ROMX.

Am Ch Starline's Reign On JC ROMX. Photo: R Bergman

Oxford F Ch ROMX. The Christiansons are also keen that their dogs can succeed in the other disciplines and have bred LCM winners, Field Champions and CD Obedience title holders. Whilst their Whippets are firmly family first and show dogs as a bonus, they are keen to continually strive to meet their ideal and to this end will introduce new bloodlines when necessary. Movement is considered to be paramount in their view.

Surrey Hill

The Surrey Hill Whippets are another mother and daughter kennel, Carolyn Bowers and Karen Bowers Lee. The first Whippet Carolyn Bowers had was Whippoorwill Moonstone ROM (Am Ch Misty Moor's Thornwood Dondi x Am Ch Lady Blair of Whippoorwill ROM). Her main interest lay in the Pembroke Welsh Corgi and the Whippet was to be a genial companion. However, yet again through a set of circumstances proving the great character of the breed, Moonstone slipped into a special place in her heart and the seed was sown.

The next purchases were to be the two Surrey Hill foundation dams, Am Ch Whippoorwill Surrey (Am Ch Blue Fox at Whippoorwill x Am Ch Whippoorwill Red Poppy) and Am Ch Baywood's Surrey Hill Heather (Am Can Ch Misty Moor's Chalmondoley ROMX x Am Can Ch Baywood's Misty Morning CD F Ch). Both were successfully mated with Moonstone.

From Surrey came the top producer Am Can Ch Surrey Hill Houston F Ch ROMX. He later sired Specialty Best In Show Am Can Ch Allerei's Ain't Misbehavin' F Ch SC ROMX and Ch Surrey Hill Savannah ROM, dam of Am Can Ch Surrey Hill's I'm No Angel F Ch SC ROMX. The latter was, herself, the dam of ten American champions. From Heather came Am Can Ch Surrey Hill Tiger Lily and her sister Best In Show Am Can Ch Surrey Hill Goldenrod. Goldenrod was the number one ranking Whippet in the United States for two years in the mid-eighties.

The Surrey Hill stock reflects the family background in Herding breeds and in movement are consequently more angulated than most fore and aft. Both these ladies have a desire to perpetuate the older Barn Dance-based lines in the United States and have, unlike their contemporaries, finished and used Whippets with blue dilute coat colour.

Starline

Carey and Lori Lawrence started the Starline kennels in the mid 1980s with the assistance of Mary Dukes. They attribute their success mainly to their foundation bitch Am Ch

Ringmaster's Gold Fever. She had a very successful mating with Am Ch Hamrya's Lucky Charm. There were four champions in the litter including Am Ch Starline's Claim to Fame (Best In Show and National Specialty winner), and Am Ch Starline's Reign On JC ROMX.

Statistics

Many thanks to Barbara Parsons for the interesting statistics on top producers from 1950 to 1996.

Top Five Leading Sires (1950 - 1996):

113 Champions: Am Ch Misty Moor's Chalmondoley ROMX (Am Ch MorShor's Appraxin Ariel x Am Ch Hill's Harvest Moon Dance)

107 Champions: Am Ch Delacreme De La Renta ROMX (Am Ch Saxon Shore Amber Waves x Am Ch Runners Creme Da La Creme)

72 Champions: Am Ch Saxon Shore Amber Waves ROMX (Am Ch Rolling's Viktor x Am Ch Rafina Rhianda of Kamara ROMX)

63 Champions: Am Ch Greenbrae Barn Dance ROMX (Ch Laguna Ligonier x Am Ch Greenbrae Laguna Lucia)

58 Champions: Am Ch Starline's Reign On JC ROMX (Am Ch Hamrya's Lucky Charm x Am Ch Ringmaster's Gold Fever)

Top Five Leading Dams (1950 - 1996):

24 Champions: Ch Misty Moor's Divine Pleasure ROMX (Am Ch April's No Fooling Around x Am Ch Misty Moor's Ravendune Alwyn)

18 Champions: Am Ch Rafina Rhianda of Kamara ROMX (Am Ch Misty Moor's Royal Huntsman x Am Ch Cyranos Ms Demeanor)

15 Champions: Am Ch Stoney Meadows Imp of Satan (Am Ch Stoney Meadows Bold Chance x Am Ch Stoney Meadows Hells Bells)

14 Champions: Am Ch Winterfold Bold Bid (Am Ch Coveydown Greenbrae Wayfarer x Stoney Meadows Bold Queen)

13 Champions: Am Ch Misty Moor's Sure To Tick ROMX (Am Ch Somerset Stop The Clock x Am Ch Misty Moor's Divine Pleasure ROMX)

American and Canadian Titles

ARM Award of Racing Merit title
CD Companion Dog, obedience title
F Ch Field Champion, lure coursing title
JC Junior Courser, lure coursing title
LCM Lure Courser of Merit, lure coursing title
ORC Oval Racing Champion title
ROM Register of Merit title
ROMX Register of Merit Excellent title
SC Senior Courser, lure coursing title
AKC American Kennel Club
AWC American Whippet Club

The top sire is multiple Specialty winning Am Ch Misty Moor's Chalmondoley ROMX, whelped September 9 1971, bred by Jerry Edwards and owned by Roberta Russ. It is interesting to note that the sires listed above all have Chalmondoley in their pedigree. Amber Waves is the sire of De La Renta, who is the grandsire of Reign On.

Carrying the same affix is the top producing dam, Am Ch Misty Moor's Divine Pleasure ROMX. Born on June 12 1981, she was bred by Roberta Russ and Jerry Edwards and owned by Carol Parker Harris. Divine Pleasure's daughter, Sure To Tick, also appears in the top five dams. Am Ch Rafina Rhianda of Kamara ROMX is a Chalmondoley granddaughter.

The End
(almost!)

Oh, what a perfect day.

	1	2	3	4	5	6	7	8	9	10	11	12	13	14	15	16	17	18	19	20	21	22	23	24	25	26	27	28	29	30	31
Mated Jan:	1	2	3	4	5	6	7	8	9	10	11	12	13	14	15	16	17	18	19	20	21	22	23	24	25	26	27	28	29	30	31
Whelp Mar/Apr:	5	6	7	8	9	10	11	12	13	14	15	16	17	18	19	20	21	22	23	24	25	26	27	28	29	30	31	1	2	3	4
Mated Feb:	1	2	3	4	5	6	7	8	9	10	11	12	13	14	15	16	17	18	19	20	21	22	23	24	25	26	27	28	(29)		
Whelp Apr/May:	5	6	7	8	9	10	11	12	13	14	15	16	17	18	19	20	21	22	23	24	25	26	27	28	29	30	1	2	(3)		
Mated Mar:	1	2	3	4	5	6	7	8	9	10	11	12	13	14	15	16	17	18	19	20	21	22	23	24	25	26	27	28	29	30	31
Whelp May/Jun:	3*	4	5	6	7	8	9	10	11	12	13	14	15	16	17	18	19	20	21	22	23	24	25	26	27	28	29	30	31	1	2
Mated Apr:	1	2	3	4	5	6	7	8	9	10	11	12	13	14	15	16	17	18	19	20	21	22	23	24	25	26	27	28	29	30	
Whelp Jun/Jul:	3	4	5	6	7	8	9	10	11	12	13	14	15	16	17	18	19	20	21	22	23	24	25	26	27	28	29	30	1	2	
Mated May:	1	2	3	4	5	6	7	8	9	10	11	12	13	14	15	16	17	18	19	20	21	22	23	24	25	26	27	28	29	30	31
Whelp Jul/Aug:	3	4	5	6	7	8	9	10	11	12	13	14	15	16	17	18	19	20	21	22	23	24	25	26	27	28	29	30	31	1	2
Mated Jun:	1	2	3	4	5	6	7	8	9	10	11	12	13	14	15	16	17	18	19	20	21	22	23	24	25	26	27	28	29	30	
Whelp Aug/Sep:	3	4	5	6	7	8	9	10	11	12	13	14	15	16	17	18	19	20	21	22	23	24	25	26	27	28	29	30	31	1	
Mated Jul:	1	2	3	4	5	6	7	8	9	10	11	12	13	14	15	16	17	18	19	20	21	22	23	24	25	26	27	28	29	30	31
Whelp Sep/Oct:	2	3	4	5	6	7	8	9	10	11	12	13	14	15	16	17	18	19	20	21	22	23	24	25	26	27	28	29	30	1	2
Mated Aug:	1	2	3	4	5	6	7	8	9	10	11	12	13	14	15	16	17	18	19	20	21	22	23	24	25	26	27	28	29	30	31
Whelp Oct/Nov:	3	4	5	6	7	8	9	10	11	12	13	14	15	16	17	18	19	20	21	22	23	24	25	26	27	28	29	30	31	1	2
Mated Sep:	1	2	3	4	5	6	7	8	9	10	11	12	13	14	15	16	17	18	19	20	21	22	23	24	25	26	27	28	29	30	
Whelp Nov/Dec:	3	4	5	6	7	8	9	10	11	12	13	14	15	16	17	18	19	20	21	22	23	24	25	26	27	28	29	30	1	2	
Mated Oct:	1	2	3	4	5	6	7	8	9	10	11	12	13	14	15	16	17	18	19	20	21	22	23	24	25	26	27	28	29	30	31
Whelp Dec/Jan:	3	4	5	6	7	8	9	10	11	12	13	14	15	16	17	18	19	20	21	22	23	24	25	26	27	28	29	30	31	1	2
Mated Nov:	1	2	3	4	5	6	7	8	9	10	11	12	13	14	15	16	17	18	19	20	21	22	23	24	25	26	27	28	29	30	
Whelp Jan/Feb:	3	4	5	6	7	8	9	10	11	12	13	14	15	16	17	18	19	20	21	22	23	24	25	26	27	28	29	30	31	1	
Mated Dec:	1	2	3	4	5	6	7	8	9	10	11	12	13	14	15	16	17	18	19	20	21	22	23	24	25	26	27	28	29	30	31
Whelp Feb/Mar:	2	3	4	5	6	7	8	9	10	11	12	13	14	15	16	17	18	19	20	21	22	23	24	25	26	27	28	1*	2	3	4

• Adjust for leap year.

Whelping Table

Appendix

At the end of a book such as this you would usually find names and addresses for contacts with clubs and other various bodies involved in the world of dogs. I do feel that the only constant reference point can be The Kennel Club. People move on, secretaries and officials change and so the information printed as an aid in books is quite often out of date. The Kennel Club keep up-to-date information on almost anything to do with dogs and will always be able to refer you to a suitable body for whatever information you require. Their address and telephone number are as follows:

The Kennel Club
1 -5 Clarges Street
Piccadilly
London
W1Y 8AB
Tel: 08706 066 750

Humble little house dog? Plleaasse - lights, camera, action, darlings!

Index